Mental health policy and practice

Mental health policy and practice

Second edition

Helen Lester and Jon Glasby

First edition 2006
Reprinted twice
Second edition 2010

Published by
PALGRAVE MACMILLAN

Palgrave Macmillan in the UK is an imprint of Macmillan Publishers Limited, registered in England, company number 785998, of Houndmills, Basingstoke, Hampshire RG21 6XS.

Palgrave Macmillan in the US is a division of St Martin's Press LLC, 175 Fifth Avenue, New York, NY 10010.

Palgrave Macmillan is the global academic imprint of the above companies and has companies and representatives throughout the world.

Palgrave® and Macmillan® are registered trademarks in the United States, the United Kingdom, Europe and other countries.

ISBN 978–0–230–58475–4

This book is printed on paper suitable for recycling and made from fully managed and sustained forest sources. Logging, pulping and manufacturing processes are expected to conform to the environmental regulations of the country of origin.

A catalogue record for this book is available from the British Library.

A catalog record for this book is available from the Library of Congress.

10   9   8   7   6   5   4   3   2   1
19   18   17   16   15   14   13   12   11   10

Printed and bound in Great Britain by
CPI Antony Rowe, Chippenham and Eastbourne

To Huw – for being there in all weathers

To Mary and Matthew – for everything

Contents

List of Boxes, Figures and Tables

Boxes

Figures

Tables

List of Abbreviations

Mental health services use a large number of acronyms and abbreviations. To aid readers new to this language, we have set out the main terms below:

ACT	Assertive Community Treatment
A&E	Accident and Emergency
AIMS	Accreditation for Acute Inpatient Mental Health Services
AO(T)	Assertive Outreach (Team)
ASW	Approved Social Worker
BMA	British Medical Association
BPS	Biopsychosocial
CAIPE	Centre for the Advancement of Interprofessional Education
CBT	Cognitive Behavioural Therapy
CEHR	Commission for Equality and Human Rights
CHD	Coronary Health Disease
CHI	Commission for Health Improvement
CMHT	Community Mental Health Team
CPA	Care Programme Approach
CPN	Community Psychiatric Nurse
CQC	Care Quality Commission
CR	Crisis Resolution
CSIP	Care Services Improvement Partnership
CTO	Community Treatment Order
DALY	Disability Adjusted Life Years
DDA	Disability Discrimination Act
DH/DHSS	Department of Health/of Health and Social Security
DRC	Disability Rights Commission
DSH	Deliberate Self-harm
DSM	Diagnostic and Statistical Manual of Mental Disorders
DSPD	Dangerous Severe Personality Disorder
DUP	Duration of Untreated Psychosis
ECR	Extra-contractual referral
ECT	Electro-convulsive Therapy
EI(S)	Early Intervention (Service)
EU	European Union
FLEAT	Forensic, Liaison, Emergency and Assessment Team
GAD	Generalised Anxiety Disorder

GDP	Gross Domestic Product
(n)GMS	(new) General Medical Services
GP	General Practitioner
GPwSI	GP with a special interest
HIV	Human Immuno-deficiency Virus
HMSO/TSO	Her Majesty's Stationery Office/The Stationery Office
HT	Home Treatment
IAPT	Improving Access to Psychological Therapies
ICD	International Classification of Disease
IPP	Imprisonment for Public Protection
IRTC	In-Reach and Through-Care Service
IT	Information Technology
JCB	Joint Commissioning Board
LINks	Local Involvement Networks
MAPPAs	Multi-agency Protection Arrangements
MCA	*Mental Capacity Act*
MH-PIG	Mental Health Policy Implementation Guidance
MHRT	Mental Health Review Tribunal
NDDP	New Deal for Disabled People
nGMS	new General Medical Services Contract
NHS	National Health Service
NICE	National Institute for Clinical Excellence
NIMBY	Not in my back yard
NIMHE	National Institute of Mental Health in England
NR	Nearest Relative
NSF	National Service Framework
ODPM	Office of the Deputy Prime Minister
OECD	Organisation for Economic Co-operation and Development
ONS	Office for National Statistics
PACT	Programme for Assertive Community Treatment
PALS	Patient Advisory and Liaison Services
PCG/T	Primary Care Group/Trust
PCGMHW	Primary Care Graduate Mental Health Worker
PCO	Primary Care Organisation
PET	Psychiatric Emergency Team
PICU	Psychiatric Intensive Care Unit
PMS	Personal Medical Services
PRiSM	Psychiatric Research in Service Measurement
QNIC	Quality Network for Inpatient Child and Adolescent Mental Health Services
QOF	Quality and Outcomes Framework
RAND	Research and Development Corporation
RCGP	Royal College of General Practitioners
RCT	Randomised Controlled Trial
RMO	Responsible Medical Officer
SDO	Supervised Discharge Order

SCIE	Social Care Institute for Excellence
SCT	Supervised Community Treatment
SSI	Social Services Inspectorate
STR	Support Time and Recovery
SURGE	Service User-Led Research Hub
SWOT	Strengths, Weaknesses, Opportunities and Threats
TAPS	Team for the Assessment of Psychiatric Services
UKAN	United Kingdom Advocacy Network
UPIAS	Union of the Physically Impaired Against Segregation
WHO	World Health Organization
WONCA	World Organization for Family Doctors

Acknowledgements

The authors and publishers are grateful to a number of individuals and health/social care/mental health organisations for giving permission to reproduce diagrams or tables in the main body of this book: The Royal College of General Practitioners (RCGP) for Figure 3.1 from *RCGP Information sheet number 21: the primary health care team* (London: RCGP, 2003); The Sainsbury Centre for Mental Health for Table 6.1 from *Mental Health Care and the Criminal Justice System* (London: Sainsbury Centre for Mental Health, 2002), Edward Peck for Table 3.1 from E. Peck *et al.*, 'Information, consultation or control', *Journal of Mental Health*, 11 (4), 2002; The ....Box 10.9; Paul...from R. Means and R. Smith, *Community Care*, 2nd edn (Basingstoke: Palgrave Macmillan, 1998).

Every effort has been made to content all the copyright holders, but if any have been inadvertently omitted the publishers will be pleased to make the necessary arrangements at the first opportunity.

All internet references were accurate at the time of going to print – but details of individual sites are likely to change over time.

1 Introduction

In this chapter we discuss:

- What we mean by mental health
- The strategic importance of mental health and illness
- Different ways of thinking about mental illness
- The incidence and prevalence of mental illness

This revised and updated book is designed as an introduction to mental health policy and practice in the United Kingdom (UK) for students as well as for qualified practitioners, their managers and policy makers. That a second edition is needed after three years reflects the rate of change in mental health policy and practice. The ten-year plan, the *National service framework for mental health* (Department of Health, 1999a), has now reached the end of its lifespan and there is much to celebrate, including progress on developing new types of mental health teams and a far greater focus on health inequalities across services. However, there are still problem areas, particularly insufficient partnership working across health and social care and, despite an overall increase in funding for mental health services this decade, continued underfunding relative to physical health services. This book suggests that there is much still to do if mental health service users and practitioners are to receive and give the same standards of care as their non-mental health counterparts.

Each chapter in the book continues to follow the same basic style, with key points highlighted at the beginning, and a series of reflective exercises and suggestions for further reading at the end. You might find the exercises useful in helping to consider how the issues raised in the chapter relate to your own geographical area or personal context.

Each chapter has been written to 'stand alone', that is, to make sense and be of use if read in isolation from the rest of the book. Occasionally, this may mean that some chapters briefly summarise material presented in more detail elsewhere, but the book signposts readers to the relevant section so that they can follow this up in greater depth. However, as with most aspects of life (and, indeed, as we argue below with regard to mental health services), the whole is always greater than the sum of its parts, and you will achieve a better understanding of the mental health system if you read each chapter sequentially.

We have not taken a particular political or theoretical stance since this might lead us to offer a less 'balanced' overview of the mental health system. This does not, however, equate to a non-critical approach. As health and social care practitioners as well as researchers and teachers, we have day to day experience of the frustrations and the very real rewards of working with people with mental health problems within the National Health Service (NHS) and social care and have, as you will see, highlighted not only the successes and exemplars of positive working practices but also policy non-sequiturs and disempowering aspects of the system. Above all, this book is an introductory text, written to help you begin to explore this interesting and complex aspect of health and social care. We hope you enjoy the journey and are encouraged to translate some of the ideas from paper to practice.

Throughout this second edition of the book, we attempt to present an updated 'whole systems approach' (that is, trying to see the mental health system from the perspective of somebody using services and viewing individual components as part of a wider spectrum of interdependent services). However, within this 'whole system', we place particular emphasis on those health and social care services that specialise in working people with mental health problems. While we recognise that people with mental health problems are often much more affected by and concerned with the everyday services and supports that are so essential to all of us (for example, housing, employment, income, education, family, neighbourhoods, transport, leisure and community safety), there is nevertheless a range of health and social care services that devote themselves to working with people with mental health problems. Although we acknowledge the importance of wider services whenever possible, it is these specialist mental health services that form the focus of this book.

What do we mean by mental health and illness?

Mental health is more than simply an absence of symptoms of mental illness or distress. Mental health refers to a positive sense of well-being and a belief in our own worth and the worth of others (Health Education Authority, 1997). Everyone has mental health needs, whether or not they have a diagnosis of mental illness. Positive mental health includes the ability to understand and make sense of our surroundings, to be able to cope with change and to communicate effectively with other people. When mentally well, we are aware of and have control over different strands of our life; we have the will to live life to its full potential; things make sense to us. In other people's eyes, a mentally healthy person talks and behaves in a culturally appropriate way; there is an apparent ability to maintain their health and develop a role in society. Mental health is therefore an essential component of our general health.

It is however, even more difficult to define what is meant by 'mental illness'. This is largely because the meaning has changed across time, and is influenced by geography, discipline and personal perspective. A lawyer will have one definition, a psychiatrist another, a service user another still.

The legal definition, at least under the *Mental Health Act 2007*, is 'any disorder or disability of the mind' which is broad enough to be open to a range of interpretations.

The writings of people who have experienced mental illness first hand are invaluable in providing an insight that neither romanticises nor underestimates the meaning, effects and consequences of mental illness. William Styron (2001, pp. 46–7) describes his depression as: 'a storm of murk ... near paralysis, psychic energies throttle back close to zero. Ultimately the body is affected and feels sapped, drained ... I began to conceive that my mind itself was like one of those outmoded small town telephone exchanges, being gradually inundated by flood waters: one by one, the normal circuits began to drown, causing some of the functions of the body and nearly all those of instincts and intellect to slowly disconnect'.

Users' experience and writings can, however, also demonstrate the ways in which people find value even in the most difficult circumstances. David Karp (1996, p. 104) records how one of his interviewees, a female freelance writer, aged 41, described her depression as a gift: 'that if we can befriend it, if we can travel with it, that it is showing us things. Somewhere along the line we have got to integrate it into our lives. All of us are depressed someway, somewhere at sometime. If we don't allow it in, it can be disruptive. If we allow it in, it is a teacher.'

As we discuss in Chapter 2, it is largely through the writings of mental health service users that the notion of recovery has become an increasing part of the discourse of mental illness.

The strategic importance of mental illness

Mental illness now touches most peoples' lives. At a global level, depression will be the second most common cause of 'disability', after ischaemic heart disease, by 2020 (World Health Organisation, 1999). The burden of psychosis is exceeded only by quadriplegia and dementia at a global level, when assessed by people's perception of disease burden (Ustun *et al.*, 1999). Mental and behavioural disorders affect more than 25 per cent of all people at some time during their lives, and are present in about 10 per cent of the population at any one time (World Health Organisation, 2001). Mental health problems account for 20 per cent of disability adjusted life years (DALY) lost, compared to around 17 per cent and 15 per cent for cardiovascular disease and cancer respectively (Friedli and Parsonage, 2007).

Mental illness also contributes to individual as well as national poverty through lost production from people being unable to work, reduced productivity from people who are ill at work, lost production from absenteeism, and loss of the bread winner of a dependant family (see Chapter 3 for more detail). This cycle can sometimes be perpetuated to future generations through untreated illness in a parent leading to childhood educational failure, future unemployment and perhaps illness in adult life.

The prevalence of mental illness also impacts on the emotional well-being of a nation and, as Jenkins *et al.* (1998) argue in Box 1.1, on the social capital of society (see also Wilkinson, 1996).

Box 1.1	The effects of common mental health problems

'It is no longer tenable to argue that the burden of common mental disorders can be ignored – the costs of doing so are immense in terms of repeated GP consultations, sickness absence, labour turnover, reduced productivity, impact on families and children. In addition, there is the more difficult to quantify but nonetheless important concept of the emotional well being of the country and nation which undoubtedly influences its future.'

(Jenkins *et al.*, 1998, p. 138)

Mental health expenditure

There are a number of different estimates of what mental illness costs the economy, depending on what is included and how it is calculated. The Sainsbury Centre for Mental Health (2003) estimated the total costs of mental illness to the UK economy were around £77 billion; £12.5 billion on health and social care; output losses of £23.1 billion; and £41.8 billion in human costs. More recently, Friedli and Parsonage (2007) estimated the overall cost of mental health problems in the UK to be over £110 billion. According to the former Care Services Improvement Partnership (CSIP) (2008), in 2006–7 the NHS spent £8.4 billion on mental health services (excluding substance misuse) for all age groups. This was the highest spend on any individual area of health care (12 per cent of the NHS budget), over £1.5 billion more than on coronary heart disease and almost twice as much as on cancer. Planned investment in mental health services has also increased yearly since 2003 in real terms. However there are also large variations in the amount of mental health spend per head of population each year, ranging from £174–207 in London to £128 in Greater Manchester (Appleby, 2006). It is also important to recognise that, compared to the rest of the European Union, England and Wales spend the highest proportion of the health budget on mental health. Albania, Portugal and Bulgaria, for example, spend only 3 per cent of their health budget on mental health (World Health Organisation, 2008).

This increase in spending has had a positive impact in a number of different ways (see Box 1.2). However, so far, increases in mental health have not matched increases in the rest of the health service. Indeed expenditure on mental health services from 2001/2 to 2004/5 was about 1.3 per cent behind the rest of the health services (Oxford Economics, 2007). As a result, mental health still lags behind physical health provision. For example, mental health premises are dirtier than physical health care facilities (Healthcare Commission,

2005a) and 28 per cent of safety issues reported to the former Healthcare Commission come from mental health trusts and a further 43 per cent from mental health and learning disability trusts (Healthcare Commission, 2006). Expenditure on mental health also needs to increase because the number of people with mental health problems will increase from 8.65 million in 2007 to 9.88 million by 2026. This has been predicted to lead to an increase in service costs and lost employment costs from £48.6 billion in 2007 to £88.45 billion (McCrone *et al.*, 2008).

Box 1.2	The positive effects of additional expenditure on mental illness in England

- Services have improved at a local level, with 49 per cent of carers saying that standards of mental health care in their local area have improved for service users during the past three years (Rethink, 2003b).
- There have been significant increases in frontline staffing levels and an associated increase in patient satisfaction levels. 64 per cent of people said they had sufficient time with their psychiatrist in 2006, up from 63 per cent in 2005 and 60 per cent in 2003 (Healthcare Commission, 2006).
- Service provision and expenditure has moved from a focus on inpatient care to the community, with the emergence of early intervention and crisis services (Department of Health, 2004a).

International perspectives

At a global level, at least two-thirds of people with a mental health problem will receive inadequate or no treatment. Mental health problems have received little priority in the developing world, despite the fact that 85 per cent of the world's population live in these countries. Patel *et al.* (2007) have argued that low- and middle-income countries are still in need of the resources, manpower and infrastructure for an adequate mental health service. Indeed, many of these low- and middle-income countries lack even basic mental health legislation; a third of the World Health Organization's 191 member countries have no mental health laws.

Within the European Union, there is huge variability in access to services and psychiatrists and in modes of treatment. On average there are 8.9 psychiatrists per 100,000 population in Europe, but access to them varies hugely, with 30 per 100,000 in Switzerland, thirteen in the UK and one in Turkey. Access to mental health nursing is also mixed. There are 51.9 mental health nurses per 100,000 population in the UK (the average in Europe is 18.7), but many countries have at least twice as many – 163 in Finland and 122 in the Netherlands. To some extent, of course, these figures also reflect the emphasis each individual nation places on primary care mental health services and inpatient versus community mental health services (World Health Organization, 2008).

The changing constructions of mental illness

As Coppock and Hopton (2000) have suggested, there is a tendency for mental health professionals to opt for one particular approach to understanding mental illness, often allied to their training and professional background (see Box 1.3). We firmly believe, however, that no one approach has all the answers and that the origin of mental illness must inevitably represent a confluence of different factors. This implies that we need to be reflexive in our thinking rather than holding fast to one particular conceptual model. As Tyrer and Steinberg suggest, 'those who imprison themselves within the confines of one model only have the perspective of the keyhole' (2003, p. 138).

Box 1.3	**Difficulties in conceptualising mental illness**

'Despite over a hundred years of scientific research into the causation and treatment of mental distress, we are still unable to provide any incontrovertible evidence of either what causes mental distress or how it can be treated effectively. There is though a considerable body of circumstantial evidence, which suggests that mental distress is the product of the interplay between various psychological, social, political, environmental and biological factors. Regrettably few mental health professionals are willing to take account of all of these factors. Instead many adopt one theoretical perspective and therapeutic approach as their own and disregard any new research findings, which might challenge their belief. While such identity politics and celebration of difference are in keeping with the post modernist zeitgeist of the time [*sic*], it will not necessarily lead to us furthering our understanding of what causes mental distress, how to prevent it and how to respond to it.'

(Coppock and Hopton, 2000, p. 10)

We have therefore deliberately chosen to discuss a range of perspectives on the nature and cause of mental illness, some of which are frankly contradictory, and hope this will allow you to understand something of the age-old debates in this area and why your own views will not always be readily accepted by the people you are talking to. Our discussion, however, aims to give you a flavour rather than a detailed exploration of the area and we make suggestions for further reading to enable you to follow up these and other models in greater depth at the end of the chapter.

Whatever your belief about the origins of mental illness, the notion of 'madness' is indisputably ancient and ubiquitous. There is probably no society past or present that has failed to acknowledge its existence. Madness became associated with health and sickness through the writings of the early Greeks, particularly Hippocrates (470–410 BC). Hippocratic medicine explained health and illness in terms of the rhythms and shifting balances of humours (juices or fluids). Within this belief system, 'humoral balance' of vital fluids was essential for good health, and illness was the result of an increase or decrease in the humours. In terms of mental illness, excess blood and yellow bile were thought to lead to mania and surplus black bile to melancholy or depression.

Perhaps the next great leap in thinking, at least in terms of rationalising madness, came from the work of René Descartes (1596–1650), who moved away from the more mystical elements of the Hippocratic tradition, towards a theory of particles of matter obeying mathematical laws. Descartes proposed that there are two types of material in the world: the mental or mind, and the physical or body. He equated the mind with the soul and stated that the mind docked with the body at the pineal gland. He also proposed that the mind and body were therefore separate entities (sometimes talked about as 'Cartesian dualism'). This had significant consequences for thinking about madness since, in effect, it implied that mental and physical health are separate entities.

That madness was the result of a disease process and a bodily malfunction became the dominant paradigm of the Enlightenment. In Britain, Thomas Willis (1621–1675) coined the term 'neurology', and, as an avid dissector, tried to localise mental functions to particular regions of the brain. In Philadelphia, Benjamin Rush (1745–1813), the physician officially acknowledged by the American Psychiatric Association as 'the father of American psychiatry', believed that 'madness' was an arterial disease for which the logical remedy was, therefore, blood letting.

By the late nineteenth century, the main priority for the growing number of psychiatrists was to legitimise their discipline as a hard biomedical science alongside neurology and pathology. Creating a credible knowledge base for psychiatry helped to underpin psychiatrists' claims for their medical authority over 'madness'. Scull (1979) cites an editorial from the *Journal of Mental Science* (the former title of the *British Journal of Psychiatry*) in 1858 that captures this early biomedical professional justification: 'Insanity is purely a disease of the brain. The physician is now the responsible guardian of the lunatic and must remain so.'

A key figure in this movement was Emil Kraepelin (1856–1926), a German psychiatrist who assumed that there were a discrete and discoverable number of psychiatric disorders and argued that each disorder had a typical symptom picture. He also believed that each disorder was associated with a different brain pathology and different aetiology (that is, cause and origin). As Bentall (2003, p. 13) suggests, 'on Kraepelin's analysis, therefore the correct classification of mental illness according to symptoms would provide a kind of Rosetta stone, which would point directly to the biological origins of madness'. Kraepelin also highlighted the importance of long-term outcomes and of illness trajectories by suggesting that the natural history of psychiatric illness was a better clue to its nature than the symptoms a patient showed at one particular point in time. Kraepelin was therefore responsible for a significant innovation in the conceptualisation and classification of illness, encouraging psychiatrists to describe and taxonomise mental disorders and informing and shaping the dominant disease model in twenty-first-century psychiatry (see Box 1.4).

Box 1.4	Central tenets of the disease model

- Mental pathology is accompanied by physical pathology
- Mental illness can be classified as different disorders which each have characteristic common features
- Mental illness is biologically disadvantageous
- The causes of physical and mental pathology in psychiatric illness are all explicable in terms of physical illness

(Summarised from Tyrer and Steinberg, 2003, p. 10)

The persistence of Kraepelinian ideology is also demonstrated by the influence of the ever-expanding World Health Organization (WHO) produced International Classification of Disease (ICD) and the Diagnostic and Statistical Manual of Mental Disorders (DSM) published by the American Psychiatric Association (see Box 1.5).

Box 1.5	The growth of the Diagnostic and Statistical Manual of Mental Disorders

- In 1917, the American Psychiatric Association recognised 59 psychiatric disorders
- With the introduction of the Diagnostic and Statistical Manual (DSM) in 1952, this rose to 128
- The second edition, DSM 2 (1968), had 159 categories
- DSM 3 (1980) had 227 and the revised DSM 3R (1987) had 253 categories
- DSM 4 (2000), the current system, has 374 categories
- The DSM 5 is scheduled for mid-2012. With tongue firmly in cheek, the American psychologist Roger Blashfield (1996) has suggested that, based on the escalation of categories to date, DSM 5 will be over 1200 pages long and contain over 1800 diagnostic criteria

The notion of mental illness as a biomedical entity was challenged in the 1960s by a number of disparate individuals and groups, including UK anti-psychiatrists such as Ronny (R.D.) Laing and the American psychiatrist Thomas Szasz. Laing, in classic texts such as *The Divided Self* (1960) and *The Self and Others* (1961), claimed that psychotic symptoms are meaningful in themselves and therefore cannot be understood as medical phenomena. Szasz (who vehemently denied any association with the anti-psychiatry movement), claimed that the concept of mental illness is incoherent and that mental illness is not a disease, but a myth fabricated by psychiatrists for reasons of professional advancement and endorsed by a society looking for easy solutions for problem people (1960). Szasz (1970, p. 23) stated that:

> The expression mental illness is a metaphor which we have come
> to mistake for a fact. We call people physically ill when their body
> functioning violates certain anatomical and physiological norms;
> similarly we call people mentally ill when their personal conduct
> violates certain ethical, political and social norms. This explains
> why many historical figures from Jesus to Castro and from Job to Hitler,
> have been diagnosed as suffering from this or that psychiatric malady.

Although intellectually influential, Szasz's views have not been widely
accepted. However, as we shall see in Chapter 2, they resonate with UK
debates about treatment orders in the community and the preventive detention of people with Dangerous Severe Personality Disorder (DSPD).

Michael Foucault, a French historian, argued that mental illness is a cultural
construct, sustained by a grid of administrative and medico-psychiatric practices (1961). The history of madness is therefore less an account of disease
and treatment than of freedom and control, of knowledge and power.
The American sociologist Irving Zola similarly argued that:

> Medicine is becoming a major institution of social control, nudging
> aside, if not incorporating, the more traditional institutions of
> religion and law ... this is not occurring through the political power
> physicians hold or can influence, but is largely an insidious and often
> un-dramatic phenomenon accomplished by 'medicalising' much of daily
> living, by making medicine and the labels healthy and ill relevant to an
> ever increasing part of human existence. (Kosa and Zola, 1975, p. 170)

This social construction of mental illness sees the primary function of mental
health policy as the regulation of behaviour, with the process of categorising
and labelling people a way of pathologising rule-breaking behaviour that is
unacceptable to wider society.

The social causation model of mental illness has become an increasingly important model, and argues that social forces are the most important
influence in the aetiology of mental illness (see Box 1.6).

Box 1.6	Central tenets of the social causation model

- Mental disorder is often triggered by life events that appear to be independent
- Social forces linked to class, occupational status and social role are the precipitants of mental disorder
- People with mental disorder often become and remain disordered because of societal influences

(Summarised from Tyrer and Steinberg, 2003, p. 87)

Key figures in this movement include Emile Durkheim (1897) who, in his classic work on suicide, argued that social factors, especially isolation and loss of social bonds, were important in predicting and even causing suicide. More recently, Brown and Harris (1978) found that depressed women living in a London borough were more likely to have more young children at home, less part-time or full-time employment and fewer confidantes with whom they could discuss their worries than non-depressed women. This increasing evidence base has led many people working in mental health to recognise the influence of social factors and the environment on developing mental illness and to focus treatment on helping individuals find an acceptable social role and addressing underlying social issues rather than on treating presumed biochemical imbalances.

Closely allied to the social causation model is the biopsychosocial (BPS) model of illness. The BPS model refers to a position spelt out perhaps most clearly by George Engel (1980), who argued that, for psychiatry to generate a fully scientific and inclusive account of mental disorder, biomedical accounts needed to be superseded by ones that incorporated ideas from general systems theory. In contrast to the biomedical model, this approach recognises that psychological and social factors influence patients' perceptions and actions and therefore the experience of what it feels like to be ill. Pilgrim (2002) suggests that the BPS model does not object to diagnosis in principle, but that it privileges the patient and their longitudinal context over the medical categories applied to them and that the model's inclusive approach creates the possibility of thinking about mental health problems on both scientific and humanistic terms. Certainly the BPS model appears to have achieved recognition and popularity in many branches of medicine, but Pilgrim also warns that in mental health its popularity may reflect service-level pragmatism and a form of mutual tolerance within increasingly multidisciplinary teams rather than its acceptance as a stable theoretical orthodoxy.

Writing from a somewhat provocative psychological perspective, Bentall (2003) has challenged the entire Kraepelinian foundation of psychiatric practice, suggesting that psychosis in particular should be seen as just part and parcel of human variation, rather than as an illness. He cites studies showing that up to 11–13 per cent of people have experienced hallucinations at some point in their lives (Tien, 1991) and the work of Marius Romme and Sandra Escher (1989) in the Netherlands suggesting that many people hear voices, but have little difficulty coping with them and indeed have never sought psychiatric treatment for them. Bentall argues that the boundaries of madness are fluid and that many experiences that might be attributed, on DSM criteria, to a psychotic illness, are not necessarily pathological. His 'Post-Kraepelinian' position is that:

> We should abandon psychiatric diagnoses altogether and instead try
> to explain and understand the actual experiences and behaviours of
> psychotic people ... Once these complaints have been explained,
> there is no ghostly disease remaining that also requires an explanation.
> Complaints are all there is ... an advantage of this approach is that it

does not require us to draw a clear dividing line between madness and sanity. (2003, pp. 141–2)

At the turn of the twenty-first century, it could be argued that the biomedical disease model of mental illness is enjoying a resurgence, driven by the development of new physical treatments, of brain scans assessing differences in brain size and composition between people with and without mental illness, and the success and publicity accorded to the human genome project. It is interesting, however, to note that those that service users and community mental health workers might perceive as dominant within the world of mental health, themselves feel threatened by the rise of the evidence base of psychological and social interventions (Craddock *et al.*, 2008). However the fact that medically trained psychiatrists (described by Pilgrim as 'chemotherapists with a prescription pad'; 2002, p. 591) and GPs remain influential professionals within the diagnostic and treatment process affects the emphasis accorded to different viewpoints of the causation and construction of mental illness. This biomedical approach, with its strong links to 'mind-body dualism' where the body and mind are seen as separate and unconnected entities, is also, as we shall see throughout this book, reflected in the separate services for people with physical and mental health problems. As Wade and Halligan (2004, pp. 1398–9) suggest:

Health commissioners, budgetary systems, health care professionals and the public all act as if there is some clear, inescapable separation between physical and mental health problems, ignoring evidence that the person's emotional state always affects their function and presentation of physical symptoms.

How many people have mental health problems?

From a pragmatic point of view, this book talks about mental illness as being either a 'serious mental illness' or a 'common mental health problem'. We are mindful, however, that people can have both a serious and a common mental health problem sequentially or at the same time, and some common mental health problems such as obsessive compulsive disorder can be just as disabling in terms of activities of daily living as the more 'serious' problems such as schizophrenia and bipolar affective disorder.

It is difficult to quote gold-standard statistics for the incidence and prevalence of mental illness (prevalence refers to the number of people with a particular illness at a point in time in the population, whereas incidence refers to new cases). A definition based on service contact only captures people who become patients and not the real number of people within society who have mental illness. Previous community surveys (Goldberg and Huxley, 1992; Hannay, 1979) suggest that many more people experience symptoms than are diagnosed with a specific illness. Results of prevalence studies also vary greatly both between and within countries due to differences in diagnostic practices and to social and environmental factors (Warner, 1985).

The Office National Statistics (ONS) suggests that an estimated one in two hundred people have experienced a psychotic disorder in the past year (Singleton *et al.*, 2001), although this survey is likely to underestimate the true prevalence as it only reflects people living in private households, not those living in institutions or who are homeless. People with serious mental illness are also less likely to respond to surveys than the general public, once again leading to an underestimate of the real figure. Using available data, however, it appears that up to 16 per cent of people have common mental health problems at any one time, a figure that has been stable for approximately the last ten years (Fryers *et al.*, 2002; Singleton *et al.*, 2001).

The prevalence of mental illness is affected by a number of different factors including ethnicity, age, gender, occupation, education and family responsibilities (see Box 1.7).

Box 1.7	**Factors affecting prevalence rates of mental illness**

Ethnicity and gender. See Chapter 9 for further detail on the over-representation of some minority ethnic communities and of women in some sections of the mental health system.

Age: The highest rates of suicide are in young men aged 25–34, 1,300 young men died by suicide in 2001, and suicide accounts for one in five deaths of young people (Department of Health, 1998a, 2001a). Common mental health problems peak for men aged 45–9 years and for women from 50–4 years (Singleton *et al.*, 2001).

Occupation: People working in certain jobs can be at particular risk of mental health problems, with those working in the medical and farming professions being at the greatest risk of suicide.

Education: Having less education, and being unemployed or economically inactive are the most consistent risk factors associated with common mental health problems (Fryers *et al.*, 2002).

Family responsibilities: An estimated 28 per cent of lone parents have common mental health problems (Melzer *et al.,* 2002). Approximately 1.26 million people in the UK care for someone with a mental health problem (National Schizophrenia Fellowship, n.d.), including between 6,000 and 17,000 young carers (Aldridge and Becker, 2003). Carers are twice as likely to have mental health problems themselves if they provide substantial care (Singleton *et al.,* 2002) (see also Chapters 9 and 10 for further detail on anti-discriminatory practice and carers' perspectives).

Key themes in each chapter

Mental health policy and practice has eleven chapters in total, spanning the mental health system from professional, user and carer perspectives. An initial policy overview is followed by chapters on four specific service areas: primary care, community mental health, acute care and forensic mental health services. Chapters seven to ten address broader issues of partnership working, user involvement, anti-discriminatory practice and carers' perspectives. The final chapter draws together key themes and suggests underlying reasons for the rhetoric/reality gap between policy and practice.

Traditionally, mental health services have tended to see themselves as different from the rest of health and social care because of the unique challenges they face. However, as we demonstrate throughout this book, mental health is also influenced by broader policy changes in health and social care and in social policy more generally. As a result, it is important for mental health students, workers and managers to understand how the issues and pressures they face fit into wider debates about welfare and service provision.

As you read through this book, you may notice recurring themes of a lack of real voice and choice for services users and carers, the rhetoric/reality gaps between policy prose and implementation in practice and the constant call by health and social care professionals and users and carers for a 'whole systems approach' to mental health. There are also a series of critical but uncomfortable issues that individuals and teams face around the culture of their organisation and the underlying attitudes and values of staff, managers and policy makers towards people with mental health problems. This book will, we hope, enable you to explore these issues, understand historical and current strengths and weaknesses of services and, above all, discover what we might be able to do to work towards more inclusive, integrated, user-focused services that make sense both to those providing and receiving them.

In Chapter 2, we provide an overview of mental health policy, which is key to understanding many aspects of the subsequent chapters. The chapter begins with a discussion of the meaning of the term 'policy' and influences on how policy is made, and concludes with some of the reasons why policies are not always implemented in practice. It also presents a detailed chronological history of mental health policy, contextualised, from the 1970s onwards, through discussions of wider policy issues in generic health and social care. While the detail relates to English law, the underlying principles and wider service implications are applicable throughout the UK. We suggest that although there is growing evidence that mental health has moved up the political agenda, particularly during the last decade, chronic long-term underfunding means that many aspects of the mental health system are starting from a low baseline relative to services within the wider NHS. There are also a series of unresolved tensions particularly between the wider modernisation agenda of partnership working and patient choice, and mental health policy that appears increasingly coercive and controlling. In addition to summarising key policy initiatives, this chapter also presents some key theoretical frameworks for explaining current policy tensions and dilemmas.

Chapter 3 describes the complex world of primary care, which is perhaps the most rapidly changing part of the NHS. Primary care is a key partner in providing and increasingly commissioning good quality mental health services since most people with mental heath issues, including serious mental illness, are seen and treated within this setting. After describing the history and current state of primary care in the UK, particularly the advent of pay for performance in primary care and of practice-based commissioning, we focus on the potential benefits offered by workforce developments such as the extended role of practice nurses, primary care graduate mental health workers (PCGMHWs) and GPs with a special clinical interest (GPwSI). We also explore the recent developments improving access to psychological therapies for people with mental health problems. The chapter concludes with a discussion of integrated models of working in primary care mental health.

Community mental health services are a complex and controversial area of practice that has received increasing attention in the last decade, within the context of wider deinstitutionalisation debates. Against this background, Chapter 4 discusses the uncertain origins of community mental health care, the development and roles of generic community mental health teams (CMHTs), the advent and impact of more specialised functionalised teams and alternative ways of providing community-based services. We also discuss the multiple and reinforcing ways that people with mental illness are excluded from wider society, and examples of positive practice in community inclusion. We suggest that to provide good quality care for people with mental health problems, community mental health, assertive outreach (AO), home treatment/crisis resolution (HT/CR) and early intervention (EI) teams need to work together with clear lines of communication, an understanding of each others' roles and responsibilities and with additional rather than redistributed funding streams. Health and social care workers also have a part to play in encouraging wider community acceptance of people with mental illness, so that community care becomes more than simply a geographical concept.

Hospital services still play a key role in the UK health care system and mental health inpatient care costs approximately £800 million per year, representing nearly 25 per cent of the total health and social care budget for mental health. However, largely as a result of the current emphasis on community care, acute mental health services have tended to be neglected by policy makers and researchers. In Chapter 5, we discuss trends in acute psychiatric care, highlighting key concerns about pressures on acute beds, changes in admissions thresholds, the effects of high bed occupancy on standards of care and the poor quality of some service users' experiences of hospital services. We also discuss grounds for optimism, including national guidance to improve the physical environment of acute wards, and initiatives to develop a generalisable model of care that users experience as both safe and therapeutic, and where staff strengthen their skills and experience.

Forensic mental health services are both extremely complex and high profile. They involve working with a wide range of partners and with people with potentially challenging behaviour and very different needs. There are also a large number of people with unmet mental health needs in prison and a significant number of people inappropriately placed in secure settings.

In Chapter 6, we discuss these issues in more depth and suggest that placing and moving people through the system in an appropriate manner could free up capacity to help with current unmet needs in other parts of the system, including prisons. Successful forensic mental health care therefore requires a spectrum of services and more effective partnership working between key agencies. We also discuss the 'mad v bad' debate, and, in particular, stereotypes and misunderstandings about the alleged link between mental illness and crime/violence, and the difficulties inherent in assuming that risk assessment is a precise science rather than a subjective art.

Partnership working between different agencies is crucial if users are to receive co-ordinated services that meet all of their needs. Chapter 7 discusses how the UK welfare state has tended to be relatively fragmented, the consequences of failure to work together (for example, the death of Victoria Climbié or the care of Christopher Clunis) and the recent impetus to partnership working following New Labour's commitment to 'joined-up solutions to joined-up problems'. Different models of partnership working are discussed, along with key barriers and success factors. We conclude that partnership working remains a complex task and that there are few quick fixes. The way forward may lie in an incremental approach, with individual partners making use of whatever avenue they think may be beneficial and locally appropriate.

Until very recently, mental health service users have been almost universally perceived as passive recipients of care. However, over the past 20 years, users' views on service provision have become more accepted as a valuable part of health and social care. Chapter 8 charts the many, varied and overlapping meanings of the term 'mental health service user' and the history of user involvement both within the wider NHS context and mental health services. We discuss the importance of user involvement in developing mental health services, barriers to user involvement and examples of positive practice. Tensions between notions of partnership and coercion of mental health service users, and evidence of professional ambivalence towards greater user involvement are also highlighted. We conclude that meaningful user involvement cannot be a one-off intervention or a discrete programme of work, but a much broader and more empowering way of working which affects every aspect of mental health provision.

Discrimination exists at many different levels, both within mental health services and wider society. Chapter 9 discusses the concept of discrimination and anti-discriminatory practice, the current policy context and relevant legislation. Discrimination in mental health services and in particular the experience of women, people from minority ethnic communities, people with physical impairments, people with learning difficulties, older people and gay men, lesbian and bisexual people are highlighted. We suggest that discrimination, like social exclusion, cannot be tackled simply by changing the way individuals behave. Instead, attempts to root out discrimination in mental health services need to be accompanied by similar efforts within wider society at a personal, cultural and structural level.

The majority of community care is provided not by statutory services, but by carers – often family, friends and neighbours supporting others on a voluntary basis. While caring can be a positive experience, it can also bring a series of negative consequences, both for the carer and for the person being cared for. Despite much greater recent recognition of the needs of carers in a range of policies, many carers continue to feel unsupported. In Chapter 10, we discuss the complex definition and importance of carers, the policy context (including the relative neglect of carers of people with mental health problems) and carers' own needs. We suggest that a way forward may lie in providing a range of support from accessible information and practical advice to specialist and crisis support. However, we also highlight the importance of the value base and interpersonal skills of individual workers, with a need for human skills such as empathy and the ability to listen, and a much greater willingness to acknowledge the expertise of carers and value them as people with a key contribution to make.

Suggestions for further reading

1. Key statistics on mental health and illness can be found in: Singleton *et al.* (2001) *Psychiatric morbidity among adults living in private households. 2000*. London, TSO

2. Pilgrim, D. and Rogers, A. (2005) *A sociology of mental health and illness*. Buckingham, Open University Press

   This classic text (now in its third edition) has a useful overview of perspectives on mental health and illness from both within and beyond sociology, including sections on labelling theory, critical theory and social constructivism.

3. Rosenhan, D.L. (1973) On being sane in insane places, *Science*, 179, 250–8

   For readers interested in social construction, Rosenhan's (1973) classic paper on what happens when 'normal' people feign mental health symptoms to gain admission to a psychiatric hospital, and are then treated as an inpatient with a presumed diagnosis of schizophrenia, is essential reading.

4. Bentall, R. (2003) *Madness explained: psychosis and human nature*. London, Allen Lane

   This doorstop-sized tome is an interesting and deliberately provocative read that draws on a wide range of evidence from psychology, psychiatry, anthropology and the neurosciences, arguing that there is no discrete dividing line between mental health and illness. Bentall suggests that we can explain and understand many psychotic symptoms as part and parcel (or at least at the extreme end) of normal psychological processes.

2 Mental Health Policy

In this chapter we discuss:

- The meaning of the term 'policy' and influences on how policy is made
- The theoretical frameworks that help to understand key policy dilemmas and debates
- A chronological history of mental health policy within the broader context of generic NHS and social care policy
- The influence of the modernisation agenda on mental health policy and practice
- The reasons why policies are not always implemented in practice

In trying to unravel the complexities of mental health policy and practice, the most useful organising principle is probably a chronological (historical) perspective (Porter, 1987). Comparing mental health policy over time enables us to see how successive governments have built on or responded to previous policy and to the social, political and economic climate of the time (see Appendix for a full policy chronology). Although we concentrate on mental health, we have also sought to contextualise more recent debates in mental health policy and practice through discussions of wider policy issues in generic health and social care. This approach enables us to see the origins of current policy and to appreciate that many current key debates have been rehearsed for decades. This, of itself, raises a number of interesting questions about the barriers and facilitators to implementation and the differences between policy rhetoric and the practical realities of delivering mental health services on the ground. The end result is, unsurprisingly, less a neat signposted pathway of incremental, evidence-based change than a messy trek with missed turns, sudden deviations from the highway and, at times, a sense of muddling through. Before setting out on the journey, however, it is worthwhile reflecting briefly on what we mean by the term 'policy' and on how policy is made. It is also important to have a grasp of some of the basic concepts that recur throughout this book to see how they help us understand why policy is formulated in certain ways and also why it sometimes fails to deliver services in ways that make sense at an individual and community level. We will therefore also discuss three useful underlying theoretical frameworks that can help to illuminate some of the tensions and dilemmas in current policy and practice.

What do we mean by 'policy'?

The concept of 'policy' is both highly contested and difficult to encapsulate. Ham (2009) suggests that the notion of policy is complex, involving a series of related decisions and a number of different people, many of whom are responsible only for the policy making rather than the implementation phase.

In terms of mental health policy, Rogers and Pilgrim (2001, p. 226) suggest, 'The term mental health policy at the turn of the 21st century refers to legal arrangements, policy directives and service investments in relation to the aggregate picture which have accumulated over the past 100 years. It is partly about the control of behaviour, partly about promoting well-being, partly about ameliorating distress and partly about responding to dysfunction.' With such a broad remit, it is perhaps unsurprising that the mental health policy narrative is a complex and at times paradoxical story.

How is policy formed?

One of the consequences, Ham (2009) suggests, of the diverse interests in the policy community is that the history of the development of health and social care is characterised by long periods of incremental change and only occasional episodes of radical reform. Indeed, as we shall see, the move towards emptying asylums and providing care in the community is a story of slow, gradual change. Kingdon (1995) suggests that a 'step change' in policy is only likely to occur under two circumstances: a major event like war or an economic crisis that forces politicians to go beyond the accepted realms of possibilities (indeed, the NHS itself was established under such circumstances), and as a response to events that cast doubt on the credibility of insider groups such as the British Medical Association (BMA). This happened to some extent in the late 1990s when plans to regulate the medical profession (including compulsory revalidation and appraisal procedures) were introduced in many ways as a response to scandals involving poor outcomes for children undergoing heart surgery in Bristol and the discovery that a GP, Dr Harold Shipman, had been able to murder some of his patients without detection over a period of years.

Sometimes policy has been made as a result of a bargain struck with key stakeholders. The concessions made to hospital doctors in terms of options for private practice and access to pay beds in NHS hospitals, for example, helped pave the way for the birth of the NHS in 1948. However, at other times, policy has been made and implemented despite opposition from the field. For example, the NHS and Community Care Act 1990, which introduced the controversial idea of the purchaser/provider split, was bitterly opposed by many in the medical profession. However, it was championed by a Conservative government sure of its majority and not afraid of taking on significant pressure groups.

Policy is also not always fully thought through at the time it becomes law. For example, a number of aspects of the *NHS and Community Care Act* 1990 were delayed in terms of implementation and modified and adapted as policy makers and practitioners realised that they needed to sort out how the new system was going to work, with the full Act not coming into force until 1993.

Is policy evidence based?

From the discussion above, it is perhaps not surprising to learn that policy is not always evidence based. White Papers do not automatically carry annexes with detailed analysis of policy evaluations; ministerial speeches are not published with a list of references.

However, since the mid-1990s, government circles and the health and social care professions have actively moved from a system based on expert knowledge to one founded more on principles of evidence-based practice. At a national level, official health and social care research and development programmes are now in place and actively commissioning research to provide an underpinning evidence base for policy and practice (Parker, 2002). Recent policy documents including *The national service framework for mental health* (NSF) (Department of Health, 1999a), *The national service framework for mental health – five years on* (Department of Health, 2004a) and the *Quality and outcomes framework* in the new GP contract (British Medical Association/ NHS Confederation, 2009) are, at least in part, evidence based.

Indeed, 6 (2002) argues that policy makers are, in fact, frequently faced with excessive rather than insufficient evidence about what works. The major difficulty for policy makers is then to reconcile the interests of multiple partners and to ensure that policy reflects government pledges and financial flows. As Marmot (2004, p. 906) suggests, 'a simple prescription would be to review the scientific evidence of what would make a difference, formulate policies and implement them – evidence based policy making. Unfortunately, this simple prescription, applied to real life, is simplistic. The relationship between science and policy is more complicated. Scientific findings do not fall on blank minds that get made up as a result. Science engages with busy minds that have strong views about how things are and ought to be.'

It could, of course, be argued that basing policy only on research evidence might also be detrimental to health and social care. Research tends to focus on selected patient populations and so cannot tell clinicians what to do with specific individuals. There is also often an unacceptably long delay in publishing research findings, with a definite publication bias for studies that have positive findings (Higgitt and Fonagy, 2002). There are also debates over what we mean by 'evidence.' Often traditional research hierarchies favour more quantitative approaches such as systematic reviews and randomised controlled trials (often known as 'type I' or 'type II' evidence). However, small-scale qualitative work can provide a collectively powerful evidence base.

For example, the collation of individual patient views (including 65,000 telephone calls, 124,000 website hits and 1374 emails) over the antidepressant medication Paroxetine in response to the television programme *Panorama* in 2001 helped to influence National Institute for Clinical Excellence (NICE) guidelines on depression (NICE, 2004a) and was a key factor in prompting subsequent calls for an investigation into the regulation of the pharmaceutical industry (Medawar *et al.*, 2002).

Useful theoretical frameworks

There are a number of theoretical frameworks that are helpful in making sense of the way in which policy is both formulated and implemented. We highlight three frameworks that we have used throughout this book to illuminate the way in which recent mental health policy has developed and influenced practice to greater and lesser extents.

The social model of disability

In the UK in the mid–1970s, the concept of disability began to be challenged by a number of different groups including the Union of Physically Impaired Against Segregation (UPIAS, 1976) and disability was recast in a socio-political light. Oliver (1983) identified 'the social model of disability' in order to reflect the growing demand by disabled people and their allies for:

> nothing more fundamental than a switch away from focusing on the physical limitations of particular individuals to the way in which the physical and social environments impose limitations on certain groups or categories of people. (Oliver, 1983, p. 23)

The social model of disability is based on the principle that disability is a denial of civil rights caused by exclusionary practices in all sectors of society. It recognises that people have impairments but argues that it is society which disables them. The social model has arguably provided the basis for a transformed approach to disability among disabled people, and informed the politics of the Disability Movement (Oliver, 1990, 1996). This has led to major changes in the UK and internationally in disability legislation, policy, practice and thinking including the passage of the *Disability Discrimination Act* (DDA) (1995), direct payments legislation (1996) and the establishment of the former Disability Rights Commission (DRC) (2000).

The place of impairment within the social model of disability has been hotly disputed. At times it has been excluded from analysis with Oliver (1996) and Barnes (1998), key thinkers in the disability movement, both arguing that the personal experience of dealing with impairment is not the concern of disability studies and instead that intellectual and political energies should be concentrated on understanding and tackling the wider social causes of disability. In contrast, the importance of attention to impairment has been emphasised on a number of different grounds. Feminist writers in particular have argued that impairment does restrict activities in important ways. French (1993), for example, argues that her visual impairment imposes some social restrictions such as an inability to recognise people and read non-verbal clues in social interactions that cannot be resolved by the application of the principles of the social model. Lee (2002) suggests it is politically dangerous to accept that adapting the environment is a sufficient response to the issues of disability since it minimises, and indeed potentially trivialises, the social care and accommodation needs that many disabled people have.

Initially, the social model of disability focused almost exclusively on physical impairment (Campbell and Oliver, 1996), which may perhaps reflect the relative invisibility of conditions that primarily affect the way someone feels rather than the more 'discrediting' stigma associated with congenital or acquired physical impairments. More recently, work around 'embodied irrationality', that is, the impact of having and living with a mental illness, has helped to focus thinking on aspects of mental illness as impairment and the ways in which impairment interacts with disability (Lester and Tritter, 2005; Mulvany, 2000). Beresford also argues that there are at least three key reasons why people with mental illness should recognise and indeed use the social model of disability:

> Survivors are now also among those experiencing the sticks and carrots of government welfare to work policy as disabled people. Thus *regardless of what survivors themselves may think*, they are frequently officially included as disabled. Secondly, there are significant overlaps between the two populations. Some survivors also have impairments, sometimes related to the damaging effects of the chemical and other treatments they have received, or to impoverishment ... Thirdly, disabled people and psychiatric system survivors are both subject to discrimination and oppression. While the forms these take may vary and restriction of rights is an explicit commitment of policy for psychiatric system survivors, the denial of their human and civil rights is a shared experience of disabled people and survivors. (2000, pp. 169–70)

Political action is therefore as important as talking or pharmaceutical treatments. This model can, however, alienate some mental health service users who do not necessarily identify themselves with the notion of being disabled (see also Chapters 8 and 9).

The recovery model

Deinstitutionalisation, the emergence of community care and of psychosocial rehabilitation, the growth of the user movement, the rise of consumerism in general and the publication of a small number of longitudinal studies of people with serious mental illness that suggested that significant numbers of patients had positive outcomes (Harding and Zahniser, 1994; Harrison *et al.*, 2001) all paved the way for the emergence of the discourse of recovery.

Recovery itself, however, is something of a contested concept. There is neither a single agreed-upon definition of recovery nor a single way to measure it. Indeed, Pilgrim (2008) suggests that there are at least three different ways in which the notion of recovery could be conceptualised (see Box 2.1)

Box 2.1	Concepts of recovery

- From a biomedical perspective, patients are seen as recovered if they are symptom-free as a result of usually pharmacological treatment. Those who fail to recover despite treatment or who avoid treatment become 'treatment-resistant'.
- The second approach to recovery is associated with community-orientated social psychiatry and emphasises supportive and personally tailored skills training to enable patients to stay out of hospital and be rehabilitated in terms of social functioning.
- The third approach is based on a more explicit social model and demands freedom from coercive services and the aspiration to be self-determining. There is an emphasis on experts by experience and of surviving the system where mental health professionals are often seen as part of the problem.

Pilgrim also suggests that the boundaries between the three positions are, at times, blurred. Hopper (2007) has proposed an amalgam conception of recovery as:

- Renewing a sense of possibility
- Regaining competencies
- Reconnection and finding a place in society
- Rebuilding self-confidence and individual agency

Recovery from mental illness, according to mental health service users' writings (Pilgrim's third perspective), involves much more than recovery from the symptoms themselves but also recovering from the stigma people experience and internalise, from the side effects of treatments and treatment settings, and from the negative effects of social exclusion such as unemployment and reduced social networks. Service users describe recovery as a process, as a personal journey, of making sense of what has happened to them, reconstructing a positive identity, accepting, living with and growing beyond the limits of their mental health problem. It incorporates notions of hope for the future, of taking the least amount of medication necessary, of being involved in treatment planning in a partnership with professionals, of taking control over your life, of tapping into multiple sources of support and of learning about the illness to have better control over it. Anthony (1993) suggests that recovery can occur without professional intervention and even though symptoms are present. It is also not a linear process. Thus, periods of insight or growth can happen unexpectedly while at other times there may be no change for months on end.

Recovery was formally recognised in UK policy documents in 2001 when the *The journey to recovery* (Department of Health, 2001b) emphasised the need to replace hopelessness and pessimism in mental health services with a more positive and optimistic approach. It is also worth noting that, during the last decade, attempts to reduce barriers to recovery have extended beyond the realms of health and social care into, for example, the spheres of housing and particularly employment (see Chapter 3). However, we would also argue that despite the official emphasis on choice, patient centredness and user involvement, recent policy developments such as the sanctioning of community treatment orders within the 2007 Mental Health Act suggest tensions between different elements of the current mental health policy framework.

Communitarianism

The term 'communitarianism' was first used in 1841 by Barmby, who founded the Universal Communitarian Association. In this and other nineteenth-century usage, communitarian meant 'a member of a community formed to put into practice communistic or socialist theories'. The more common and contemporary usage of 'pertaining to or characteristic of a community' first appeared in Webster's dictionary in 1909. Etzioni (1995), perhaps the most well-known current thinker in this field, suggests that communities are webs of social relations that encompass shared meanings and shared values. He suggests that families may qualify as mini communities, as do some neighbourhoods and cities. Well-integrated national societies may also be said to have communitarian elements. Specifically Etzioni (1995, p. 25) suggests that:

> A communitarian perspective recognises both individual human dignity and the social dimension of human existence. A communitarian perspective recognises that the preservation of individual liberty depends on the act of maintenance of the institutions of civil society where citizens learn respect for others as well as self respect ... a communitarian perspective recognises that communities and policies too have obligations – including the duty to be responsive to their members and to foster participation and deliberation in social and political life.

Etzioni also suggests that a communitarian social movement has an important role in 'asserting moral voices that should be heeded in a society that increasingly threatens to become normless, self centred and driven by greed' (1995, p. 26) and that the best place to start in terms of building a communitarian platform is where each generation acquires its moral anchoring; in the family.

The communitarians have had a direct influence on New Labour thinking, representing a 'call to restore civic virtues ... and to shore up the moral foundations of society' (Etzioni, 1995, p. 31) and in the emphasis on the responsibilities of individuals to each other as members of communities of people living in proximity to each other.

However, communitarianism has a number of associated problems. If they become too strong, communities can breed identity politics and therefore have a potential for social division or even disintegration rather than cohesion. Barnes (1997) suggests that community can mean much more than geographical locality and that notions of communities of interests and of identity are becoming increasingly important yet are largely ignored in communitarian theory. The normative assumptions on which communitarianism is based, for example the acceptance of traditional gender subordination and the emphasis on family and geographical communities, can therefore exclude people whose identities and affiliations come from a different type of collective. Communitarianism from the standpoint of people with mental health problems, black people or gay and lesbian people can therefore potentially be a source of oppression and social exclusion.

A 'brief history' of mental health policy

Locking up the mad: the rise of the asylum

On the whole, throughout history and across civilisations, madness has usually been seen as a domestic responsibility, something that friends and families deal with (see Chapter 10 for a discussion of the role of carers). Indeed, it was not until the end of the Middle Ages that separation from society was used as a management strategy, with, for example, the religious house of St Mary of Bethlehem, known as Bethlem (Bedlam), set up to care for 'distracted' patients in London in 1377. Treatment was rudimentary, with patients chained to the wall in leg irons and whipped or ducked in water. From the early 1600s, visitors were allowed in to view the patients for a penny. A trip to Bedlam became a great treat for Londoners, with over 100,000 people a year paying to see the patients, who were placed in cages on the hospital's galleries.

The practice of private madhouses in England began in 1670, with some degree of licensing imposed a century later through the 1774 *Madhouses Act*. Some of these early private madhouses like Ticehurst House in Sussex allowed patients to bring their own personal servants and even to follow the hounds (Porter, 2002).

By 1800, there were approximately 5000 people housed in a mixed economy of private asylums, far less salubrious state-run county asylums and workhouses. However, during the nineteenth century, the number of asylums and inmates increased dramatically. The underlying reasons for the rise in asylum care are complex (see Box 2.2).

The 1845 *Lunatics Act* required the building of a network of publicly owned county asylums and formally established the Lunacy Commission, which inspected, licensed and reported (indeed performance managed) the progress of the new institutions. However, the new state asylums largely failed to live up to early expectations, particularly of the early philanthropists and

| Box 2.2 | The rise of the asylum in Victorian England |

- The most popular theory at the time was that there had been a rise in the rate of mental illness, particularly schizophrenia
- It has been suggested that the sheer force of human misery in an increasingly industrialised and urbanised nation pricked a new social conscience, sparking off philanthropic gestures including developing charitable institutions in which 'insanity might be healed by a gentle system of rewards and punishments, amusements, occupation and kind but firm discipline' (Murphy, 1991, p. 34) rather than leaving vulnerable mentally ill people open to exploitation in workhouses
- Scull (1993, p. 3) suggests that the increase in institutionalisation was 'embedded in far more complex ways in broader transformations of the English political and social structure' as the asylum became a convenient dumping ground for a wide range of individuals who could not cope in the community and hence could not contribute to the political economy of early Victorian England
- Pilgrim and Rogers (2005) suggest the change reflects the general move towards increased state intervention in social problems including the *Poor Law Act* of 1834, the *Factory Acts* of 1833 and 1844, the *Mines Act* of 1842 and the *Public Health Act* of 1848

proponents of moral therapy and non-restraint. For most people in Victorian England, as the number of inpatients increased, asylums became effectively warehouses for the unwanted.

To some extent, psychiatrists and policy makers were also victims of their own propaganda. The proclamation by Lord Ashley during debates around the 1845 *Lunatics Act* that asylum treatment would 'effect a cure in seventy cases out of every hundred' (Hansard 6.6, 1845, column 193) was, to say the least, overly ambitious. Older people with dementia, people with general paralysis of the insane and epilepsy were increasingly admitted to asylums yet were never realistically going to recover and leave. By 1890, Gibbons (1988, p. 161) describes a situation where 'there were 66 county and borough Asylums in England and Wales with an average 802 inmates and 86,067 officially certified cases of insanity – more than four times as many as 45 years earlier'. The 1890 *Lunacy Act* was also the first time that mental health legislation prioritised and protected the civil rights of individuals outside the asylum, rehearsing current debates around the 2007 *Mental Health Act*.

The influence of the First World War

A major change in government policy and public attitudes occurred quite swiftly during and immediately after the First World War in response to the recognition and treatment of soldiers with shell shock. Until then, asylum doctors had emphasised the inherited vulnerability of mental illness and argued that a tainted gene pool accounted for most forms of madness, criminality, alcoholism, epilepsy, physical disability, prostitution and idiocy (Marshall, 1990), a eugenic view that was common across Europe and North America at that time. However, during the First World War, between 4 and 7 per cent of volunteer soldiers were deemed to be suffering from shell shock (now commonly known as Post Traumatic Stress Disorder), including officers and gentlemen thought of as England's 'finest blood'. In some sense, this made the eugenic view of mental illness both illogical and, indeed, a form of near treason (Stone, 1985).

Prior to 1914, there had also been only a handful of British doctors using psychological methods of treatment, but by the end of the First World War this had also changed dramatically. There was a relative boom in outpatient facilities in an attempt to deal with the thousands of ex-soldiers suffering from the effects of shell shock, and an accompanying emphasis on using new psychological techniques (Coppock and Hopton, 2000).

The 1930 *Mental Treatment Act* gave full legislative support to the introduction of voluntary treatment and to local authorities spending money on outpatient facilities at a time when only 7 per cent of all admissions were voluntary (Leff, 1997). However there was no central money allocated to implement many of the changes in the Act, a recurring theme in the story of mental health and community care throughout the twentieth century.

The birth of the NHS

The 1911 *National Insurance Act* enabled working men to access free health care and was, in part, responsible for enabling debates on the benefits of a free NHS. However, it was William Beveridge's well-received 1942 report on the development of a cradle to grave welfare state (Beveridge, 1942), followed by the success of the wartime Emergency Medical Service, that created a political climate where a huge step change in health and welfare policy could be both conceived and implemented. The NHS was born on the 5th July 1948, after negotiations with the medical community that Aneurin Bevan, the Health Minister, rather euphemistically described as 'not ... altogether trouble free' (Bevan, 1948).

A central tenet of the vision for the new NHS was that it would be free at the point of use. The first page of the explanatory leaflet distributed to all homes at the outset of the new service proudly declared: 'It will provide you with all medical, dental and nursing care. Everyone – rich or poor, man, woman or child – can use it or any part of it. There are no charges except for a few special items. There are no insurance qualifications. But it is not a charity. You are all paying for it, mainly as tax payers, and it will relieve your money worries in time of illness' (cited in Webster, 2002, p. 24).

The NHS assumed responsibility for mental health which, up to that point, had been under the jurisdiction of the county councils and boroughs, a move that could potentially have led to equality of care between mental health and non-mental health services. However, by the 1950s, Mental Health Hospitals (the terminology introduced in the 1930 *Mental Treatment*

Act) and Mental Deficiency Hospitals (for people with learning disabilities) were still overcrowded and underfunded. They contained 40 per cent of the NHS inpatient beds but received only 20 per cent of the hospital budget (Goodwin, 1997). The average cost of treating a mental health inpatient was 3 pound 15 shillings and 11 pence in 1951 compared with 4 pound 13 shillings and 11 pence in 1959/60 (at 1950/1 prices). However, during the same period, the cost of inpatient maternity care rose from 6 pound 9 shillings and 5 pence to 16 pound 11 shillings and 3 pence. Goodwin suggests 'these figures clearly underline why the mental health services have earned the tag of a Cinderella service' (1990, p. 67). As we saw in Chapter 1, despite extra funding for services across the NHS in the last decade, mental health services still lag behind physical health services in terms of expenditure.

Community care policy imperatives

By the late 1950s, there had certainly been some progress towards community care as the number of outpatient clinic attendances increased from virtually none in 1930 to 144,000 in 1959. However, mental health was still dominated by a hospital-based approach. The need to move towards a more community-based system of care and treatment was again highlighted by the Royal Commission on Mental Illness and Mental Deficiency (1954–7) (the Percy Commission). The report suggested 'in relation to almost all forms of mental disorder, there is increasing medical emphasis on forms of treatment and training and social services which can be given without bringing patients into hospitals as inpatients or which make it possible to discharge them from hospital sooner than in the past' (Percy Commission, 1957, p. 207). It endorsed the development of a complex infrastructure of local authority community services such as hostels, day care, social work support and sheltered employment schemes that would support a policy of deinstitutionalisation and encourage greater use of treatments in a community setting. However, in a pattern repeated across the decades, the aspirations of the Percy Commission were never fully supported in legislation since the *Mental Health Act* of 1959 simply invited local authorities rather than required them to produce community care plans and no additional money was made available (Goodwin, 1990).

In 1961, Enoch Powell's now infamous 'water tower speech' once again heralded government policy intentions to shift the focus of mental health practice from the institution to the community (see Box 2.3 for a quotation from the speech).

A hospital plan for England and Wales (1962) proposed the development of small-scale psychiatric units in District General Hospitals and envisaged that local authorities would provide a full range of domiciliary services to support patients in their own homes. However, despite the recognition of what needed to be done, financial pressures continued to undermine community care policy.

Box 2.3	The water tower speech

'I have intimated to the hospital authorities who will be producing the constituent elements of the national Hospital Plan that in 15 years time there may well be needed not more than half as many places in hospitals for mental illness as there are today. Expressed in numerical terms, this would represent a redundancy of no fewer than 75,000 hospital beds ... Now look and see what are the implications of these bold words. They imply nothing less than the elimination of by far the greater part of this country's mental hospitals as they exist today. This is a colossal undertaking, not so much in the new physical provision which it involves, as in the sheer inertia of mind and matter which it requires to overcome. There they stand, isolated, majestic, imperious, brooded over by the gigantic water tower and chimney combined, rising unmistakable and daunting out of the countryside – the asylums which our forefathers built with such immense solidity to express the notions of their day. Do not for a moment underestimate their powers of resistance to our assault.'

(Powell, 1961)

It is also interesting to note that even at that stage, a time long before community care was a significant reality, concerns were beginning to be expressed about both the real meaning of the word and, allied to this, the rhetoric/reality gap of an underfunded and understaffed community service. As Richard Titmuss, Professor of Social Administration at the London School of Economics, suggested:

> We pontificate about the philosophy of community care; we may feel righteous because we have a civilised mental health act on the statute books; but unless we are prepared to examine it ... at the level of concrete reality, what we mean by community care is simply indulging in wishful thinking ... at present we are drifting into a situation in which, by shifting the emphasis from the institution to the community – a trend which, in principle and with qualifications, we all applaud – we are transferring the care of the mentally ill from trained staff to untrained or ill equipped staff or no staff at all. (1968, pp. 106–7)

By 1974, there were 100,000 people in UK mental hospitals (60,000 fewer residents than there had been in 1954), but very few extra services to support the people who had been discharged into the community, prompting notions of a 'careless community' (Harrison, 1973). Indeed, it is more than a little ironic that the push for deinstitutionalisation was in part a result of concerns about conditions experienced by long-term residents in the old mental hospitals yet, as Grove (1994, p. 433) claims 'it is clear that this group who were supposed to benefit most from the closure of the institutions have in many cases fared worse'. While subsequent research has highlighted the usually positive outcomes of discharging people from hospitals into the community, this was not the case for everyone (Leff, 1997; see Chapters 4 and 5 for further discussion).

Causes of deinstitutionalisation

There are a number of competing theories on the causes of de-institutionalisation. Goodwin (1997) proposes the following ideas (see Box 2.4 for a summary).

Box 2.4	Deinstitutionalisation

1. *The development of new treatments*
   The development of anti-psychotic medication in the late 1950s is the most frequently cited factor for the shift from institutional to community-based services. However, there is little evidence to suggest a strong causal link since the coincidence of the introduction of psychotropic drugs and peaks of mental health inpatient populations are largely confined to the UK and the United States (US), not to other western countries.
2. *The development of social psychiatry*
   The association between the move towards community care and progressive social psychiatrists (that is, people interested in the effects of social conditions on behaviour and the relationship between psychiatric disorders and the social environment) is also inadequate since some professionals' livelihoods depended on the continued existence of the asylums.
3. *The emergence of anti-psychiatry and the civil rights movement*
   The views of the anti-psychiatrists (that is a group of psychiatrists who by and large felt that mental illness was a myth and a societal construct) and civil rights activists in the 1960s provided an academic impetus for arguing for greater equality and better provision of community health care for people with mental illness. However, the influence of these groups was relatively limited in policy circles.
4. *The poor conditions in the old asylums*
   By the late 1950s, many of the old asylums were overcrowded and increasingly dilapidated. However, this of itself was insufficient to provide a direct impetus for deinstitutionalisation.
5. *Increased community tolerance*
   In the 1950s, a number of policy statements suggested a substantial change in the general climate of public opinion so that people were more ready to tolerate mental illness in the community. However, the supporting evidence base for this is slim.
6. *Constitutional structures*
   Differences in constitutional structures between countries with similar onsets of deinstitutionalisation suggest that structures per se do not have a clear relationship with the development of community care.
7. *Funding systems*
   There is some evidence that insurance-based funding systems tended to hinder policy change in the direction of community care. However, this is still only a

> | Box 2.4 | **Deinstitutionalisation** *(continued)* |
>
> relatively marginal influence concerned with the rate of policy change rather than its instigation or implementation.
>
> 8. *Fiscal pressure*
>   Scull (1977) argues that, after the Second World War, the government increasingly struggled to contain the fiscal pressures of the welfare state and community care was seen as a cheaper option. However, analysis of the relative costs and effectiveness suggests that adequate community care is no cheaper than inadequate hospital care.
>
> 9. *The changing nature of mental illness*
>   Goodwin (1997, p. 111) suggests that 'the shift in the second half of the twentieth century from an institutional to a community based system of mental health service provision represents little more than the administrative façade for the more substantial aspects of this process: an increase in accessibility of treatment facilities in order to address the newly defined and expanded range of mental health problems'. This is supported by the rapid increase in the number of conditions, particularly more common mental health problems, classified as a mental illness throughout the twentieth century. Community care may therefore represent a policy response to the changing nature and expansion of mental health problems in the twentieth century.
>
> In summary, the causes of de-institutionalisation are multiple and often interlinked and it is over simplistic to suggest that a single theory is sufficient to explain this complex transition within mental health policy and practice.

Better services for the mentally ill?

In 1975, the White Paper *Better services for the mentally ill*, as the 1930 *Mental Treatment Act*, the *Mental Health Act* of 1959 and the *Hospital plan* in 1962 had before it, explicitly stated that developing community care would be encouraged and would need significant financial investment (see Box 2.5 for a quote which summarises the government's argument). It also stated that 'joint planning of health and local authority services is essential' (p. 86) given that it is 'not easy to draw an exact line between the functions of day centres ... [managed by local authority Social Services Departments] ... and those of day hospitals ... [managed by the NHS]' (p. 34) (see Chapter 7 for further discussion of partnership working between health and social care).

However, by the mid-1970s, the Labour government, struggling with debt problems amplified by the oil crisis in 1973, approached the International Monetary Fund for a loan. A condition of the loan was that public spending had to be brought under control, precipitating a series of welfare cuts. As Webster points out (2002, p. 74):

> The oil crisis precipitated an economic collapse throughout the western world. The economic growth rate which had been maintained

Box 2.5	*Better services for the mentally ill*

'Mental illness is ... perhaps the major health problem of our time. It is also a major social problem ... What we have to do is get to grips with shifting the emphasis to community care. The problems are many. Social services facilities have to be built up ... Staff to run them have to be recruited and trained ... Psychiatric services have to be developed locally, in general and community hospitals and in health centres. We have to recognise, moreover, that the pace at which community based care can be introduced depends not only on resources but on the pace of response of the community itself ... Local services mean more day hospital treatment, more day care, more treatment and support in the home itself and less in-patient treatment ... The policy can only be achieved if there is substantial capital investment in new facilities and if there is a significant shift in the balance of services between health and the local authority.'

(Department of Health and Social Security (DHSS), 1975, pp. 2–3)

since 1960 at an average of about 5% in the OECD [Organisation for Economic Co-operation and Development] area slumped to nothing. From 1975 onwards the entire OECD area shared the UK's experience of low growth, high inflation, high unemployment and an adverse balance of trade ... gloomy voices declared that 1975 represented the death knell of the welfare state.

Lack of funds to fully implement community care policies in the face of hospital closures has been, as we have seen, a recurring theme throughout the history of mental health services but, set within this particular economic context, it is perhaps less surprising that few of the proposals and principles enshrined in *Better services for the mentally ill* were implemented in practice.

The NHS: under new management?

When the Conservative government came to power under Margaret Thatcher in 1979, the main focus of welfare policy was how to make it more business-like in the face of increasing demands from an ageing population, rising patient expectations and advances in medical technology (Bloor and Maynard, 1994). The first defining NHS policy report associated with the Thatcher era was the *NHS management inquiry* report (DHSS, 1983), produced by a team led by Roy Griffiths, who was then Managing Director of the Sainsbury supermarket chain. The report identified the absence of a clearly defined general management function as the main weakness of the NHS and recommended that consensus management should be replaced by a system of general management at all levels (see Box 2.6 for a quote which summarises some of the key themes of the review).

Box 2.6	The Griffiths Report (1983)

'The absence of this general management support means that there is no driving force seeking and accepting direct and personal responsibility for developing management plans, securing their implementation, and monitoring actual achievement. It means that the process of devolution of responsibility, including discharging responsibility to the units, is far too slow ... If Florence Nightingale were carrying her lamps through the corridors of the NHS today, she would almost certainly be searching for the people in charge.'

(DHSS, 1983, paras 5 and 12)

Part of the government's overall efficiency drive also included a programme of privatisation of state-owned enterprises, reductions in some forms of taxation and tighter controls over public spending. This tight fiscal background had a direct effect on the NHS. By 1988, the cumulative shortfall in hospital and community health service funding since 1981–2 amounted to 1.8 billion. For 1987–8 alone, expenditure was almost £400 million below the government's own estimated target funding level (King's Fund Institute, 1988).

In the face of a developing NHS funding crisis, highlighted by growing medical disquiet and perennial winter bed-shortage crises, the BMA called for additional resources to help meet the financial shortfall. The immediate government response included an additional £101 million funding in December 1987 and a Ministerial Review on the future of the NHS. There was little desire in the Review for a major change in how the NHS was financed since experience from other countries suggested that the funding mechanism per se was not the key to running an efficient health service. The Review instead focused on how resources could be used more efficiently through changes in how health services were delivered. A key proposal, based on the ideas of an American economist Alain Enthoven (1985), was that responsibility for purchasing care and providing services should be separated (the purchaser/provider split) to create the conditions for a competitive internal market within the NHS. In essence, services would be provided by hospitals and community units as self-governing Trusts, and these services would be bought by the Health Authorities and also by fund-holding practices (practices with a budget to purchase a limited range of services for their patients by negotiating contracts with NHS Trusts). This meant, in effect, that providers would compete with each other to sell their services, creating a quasi-market, that would, in theory, encourage more cost-effective services and make the NHS more efficient.

At the same time, the pressures for reform of community care were also beginning to build up again, with growing criticism of a lack of joined-up working between health and social care (Audit Commission, 1986). In social services in particular, this was linked to concerns about the rapidly rising cost of care home placements for older people and a desire to bring this budget back under control (see Means *et al.*, 2008, for an overview). At the same time, there were also growing concerns about the essentially unpaid and significant contribution that informal, often family, carers were increasingly being expected to provide, harking back to the pre-Victorian, pre-asylum era of mental health care (see Chapter 10 for further discussion of carers).

In 1988, the government commissioned Roy Griffiths (again) to review the funding and organisation of community care. His report *Community care: an agenda for action* (1988) reaffirmed criticisms of inadequate resources and the apparent abdication of responsibility by central government: 'community care, everyone's distant relative but no-body's baby' (Griffiths, 1988, p. iv). Griffiths recommended that in order to reduce the confusion between agencies, local authority social services department should be given the lead role in the provision of community care and suggested an increased role for the private and voluntary sectors. Many of these proposals were later enshrined in the White Paper *Caring for people* (Department of Health, 1989a) and the *NHS and Community Care Act* (1990) (see below).

Within the NHS, ideas from the Ministerial Review and the 1988 Griffiths Report were drawn together in the White Paper *Working for patients* (Department of Health, 1989b). These proposals were described by Margaret Thatcher as 'the most far-reaching reform of the National Health Service in its forty year history' (Foreword to *Working for patients* (Department of Health, 1989b)). The paper, however, provoked a storm of protest and opposition from the medical profession and others, and was further complicated by the difficult negotiations taking place with the BMA at the same time over a new contract for GPs. In spite of opposition, the timetable for implementation set out in *Working for patients* was largely achieved and the *NHS and Community Care Act* (1990) became law in 1990 with many of its recommendations effective from April 1991 and full implementation by 1993 (see Box 2.7).

However, a number of difficulties soon became apparent in terms of implementing the provisions of the Act. Inefficient interagency collaboration (particularly where different parts of the system – NHS, Social Services, voluntary and private sectors – had different ideologies and priorities), inadequate mechanisms for enabling the shift of finance from hospitals to community care and professional attachment to traditional working practices meant that problems soon developed. Partnership working was, in effect, part of government rhetoric rather than a practical reality (Bean and Mounser, 1993) (see also Chapter 7).

In the specific context of mental health, the BMA (1992, p. 30) indicated that 'there is concern that most local authorities lack the skills and expertise to take on the responsibility for supporting mentally ill people in the community' (an accusation that some in local government would probably also level at the medical profession). As Coppock and Hopton suggest, moreover, 'while the rhetoric of government ministers focused on a commitment to giving people who use mental health services more of a say, the reality highlighted a system plagued by gross under funding and role confusion' (2000, p. 43) (see Box 2.8).

Box 2.7	*The NHS and Community Care Act 1990*

The Act, which brought in some of the biggest changes in the welfare state since the Second World War, represented the first occasion on which community care per se had provided the central focus for welfare legislation and aimed to enable people to live an independent and dignified life at home or elsewhere within the community for as long as they were able and wished to do so. It also recommended that service providers made practical support to carers a high priority. Significantly, it also set out the role of health services as well as local authority social services in the provision of community care. Specific provisions included:

- Giving local authority social services departments lead responsibility for community care
- The introduction of market principles into the provision of publicly funded health and welfare services, including purchasing from private and voluntary agencies. Further impetus for this policy also came when it was announced that 85 per cent of the funding for social services' new responsibilities would have to be spent in the independent sector. From the early 1990s onwards, this meant that social care practitioners gained considerable experience of working with a 'mixed economy of care' (that is, with the public, private and voluntary sector)
- Health Authorities assuming responsibility for purchasing health care, with NHS trusts taking the responsibility for providing services. GP fund holders were able to purchase care for their patients as well as provide primary health care to individuals and families
- A requirement for local authorities to produce and publish community care plans
- Recognition of the importance of carers' roles and their need for practical support

Of course, not all the evidence on co-operation between sectors was as bleak, and there were examples throughout the 1990s of excellent dialogue between health and social services as a result of the community care reforms, especially where boundaries were co-terminous (Means *et al.*, 2008). However, as we shall see, high profile cases of poor joint working also led to significant shifts in community mental health policy and practice.

Box 2.8	**Role confusion over the continuity of care**

A good example of role confusion is the dual development of the health-led Care Programme Approach (CPA) for people under the care of specialist mental health services, and the social services-led care management approach (Department of Health, 1990a). As Hannigan suggests, 'confusingly, both care management and CPA were introduced as mechanisms through which multidisciplinary and multi-agency continuity of care could be organised and delivered. In many areas the lack of integration between the two methods resulted in duplication of effort, excessive bureaucracy and construction of a barrier to effective joint working' (2003, p. 32).

Increasing resistance to community care

The difficulties inherent in joint working, duplication of effort and indeed the potential for no one taking ultimate responsibility were highlighted by the Ritchie Report (1994), which, with the benefit of hindsight, was a watershed in the history of mental health in the last decade. The Ritchie Report was the culmination of the inquiry into the killing of Jonathan Zito by Christopher Clunis at a London underground station on 2 December 1992 (before the full implementation of the *Community Care Act*). Although there were other high profile cases of people with mental health problems harming themselves or others, this particular event helped to shift the emphasis from talking about greater care in the community to fear about the risk posed by a small number of people with mental health problems to the community. The Ritchie Report did not, on the whole, blame individuals or suggest that the policy of community care should be reversed (and indeed noted that Christopher Clunis was in some sense a victim of the system since he had spent over five years moving between different sectors of the health and welfare service, between hospital, hostels and prison, with no overall plan for his care). However, the Report did state that 'the serious harm that may be inflicted by severely mentally ill people to themselves and others is a cost of care in the community which no society should tolerate' (para. 47, point 0.1).

Despite this, the notion of dangerousness implied by the Report is not evidence based. This is discussed in much more detail in Chapter 6, with more recent research suggesting that the proportion of homicides committed by people with a mental health problem is not only very small, but has also fallen. Nevertheless, the intensity of the media coverage of Christopher Clunis and

---

Box 2.9	Care in the community?

- In April 1994, supervision registers were introduced to identify and provide information on service users 'who are and are liable to be at risk of committing serious violence or suicide or serious self neglect' (NHS Executive, 1994, p. 1)
- In 1995, Supervised Discharge Orders (SDOs) allowed clinicians to specify where patients should live, to require them to attend for treatment and to require that they allow access to members of a clinical team for the purpose of assessment
- In 1995, the government produced good practice guidance (Department of Health, 1995) that stressed that the CPA and care management were based on the same principles and so should be capable of being fully integrated

It is interesting, however, to note that supervision registers were used inconsistently between Trusts (Bindman *et al.*, 2000) and that revised guidance (Department of Health, 1999b) removed the requirement to maintain a supervision register if a simplified two-tier CPA is in place. Evidence also suggests that SDOs are rarely used and are of limited effectiveness (Pinfold *et al.*, 2001). Perhaps this suggests that policies based primarily on public safety are actually very difficult to enforce?

a small number of other cases in the 1990s (including the 1996 murders of Lin and Megan Russell by Michael Stone, diagnosed as having an untreatable personality disorder) created considerable public unease and a series of government policies focused on notions of public safety (see Box 2.9). As we shall see later in this chapter, these arguments were later rehearsed at the time of the implementation of Community Treatment Orders in 2008.

New Labour

In May 1997, New Labour swept into government vowing to save and rebuild the NHS. However, within months, the political rhetoric began to change, with an announcement that there would be a continuation of Conservative spending plans (Department of Health, 1997a). This lack of immediate change was also, to some extent, a reflection that from 1991 onwards, the tone of successive Conservative Health Ministers had slowly changed, with partnership rather than competition increasingly emphasised. This position was most clearly expressed in the 1996 White Paper, *The National Health Service: a service with ambitions*, which outlined a future in which priority would be given to information technology, professional development and managing quality rather than to further developing the market economy in public services (Department of Health, 1996a).

New Labour's big policy ideas across all sectors of government were largely focused on the notion of modernisation (see Box 2.10 for a summary of key principles), reflected in key policy documents including *Modernising social services* (Department of Health, 1998d), *Modernising local government* (Department of Employment, Transport and Regions, 1998) and *Modernising government* (Cabinet Office, 1999).

Box 2.10	Principles of modernisation

- A focus on outcomes to enable working across organisational structures
- The promotion of partnership between different areas of government and with the voluntary and private sectors
- Greater use of evidence
- Consultation with service users
- The use of targets and performance monitoring to secure quality and continuous improvement in public services
- Additional investment to be conditional on improved results
- A greater valuing of public services by developing skills and rewarding results
- The development of information technology (IT) throughout government

(Summarised from Cabinet Office, 1999)

The Labour government's first substantive NHS proposals were published towards the end of the first year in office in the White Paper *The new NHS: modern, dependable* (1997a). It stressed the modernisation principles of partnership working and the importance of a 'third way' in running the NHS:

> The Government is committed to building on what has worked
> but discarding what has failed. There will be no return to the old
> centralised command and control of the 1970s … but nor will there be
> a continuation of the divisive internal market system of the 1990s …
> Instead there will be a third way of running the NHS – a system based
> on partnership and driven by performance. (Department of Health,
> 1997a, p. 10)

The concept of the 'third way' took on particular meaning at this time as it became associated not only with the politics of the Labour Party in the UK but also with the New Democrats led by Bill Clinton in the US. Tony Giddens (1998, 2000), a professor at the London School of Economics who has written extensively about this topic, suggested the third way proposed to construct a new social contract based on the idea of:

> no rights without responsibilities. Those who profit from social goods
> should both use them responsibly and give something back to the
> wider social community in return. Seen as the feature of citizenship
> no rights without responsibilities has to apply to politicians as well
> as citizens, to the rich as well as the poor, to business corporations as
> much as the private individual. A left of centre government should be
> prepared to act upon it in all these areas. (1998, p. 52)

Third way politics also emphasise the need for active government intervention to respond to social exclusion with a transition from passive to active welfare policies.

The New NHS also included a clear commitment to abolish the internal market but retain the Conservatives' provider/purchaser split. The main change was that commissioning would be in the hands of Primary Care Groups (PCGs) (subsequently replaced by PCTs) rather than Health Authorities and GP fund holders, and that competition would be replaced by collaboration and partnership between commissioners and providers. This structural decentralisation also enabled the integration, at least in theory, of primary care and community services, and, by linking provision with commissioning powers, could theoretically address longstanding issues of fragmentation within the NHS. However, modernisation also encompassed a greater use of targets and performance monitoring to make sure that any new funding provided was spent in different ways in the future to improve services (see Box 2.11).

In 2004, *The NHS improvement plan* (Department of Health, 2004b), signalled three big shifts in policy focus:

1. A desire to put patients first through more personalised care
2. A focus on health and well-being rather than simply sickness
3. A further devolution of decision making (see Chapter 3)

Box 2.11	Monitoring performance in health and social care

Key mechanisms included:

- The introduction of National Service Frameworks (the first of which, in 1999, addressed mental health)
- Star rating systems to assess the performance of health and of social care – replaced by the Annual Health Check performance rating system for all PCTs and Trusts in 2007
- The creation of NICE (a special health authority that develops and publishes cost benefit analysis for specific technologies and pharmaceuticals) and the Social Care Institute for Excellence (SCIE) (to identify and disseminate 'what works' in social care)
- The creation of the Commission for Health Improvement (CHI) (subsequently known as The Healthcare Commission) and the Commission for Social Care Inspection
- From 1 April 2009, a new organisation called the Care Quality Commission (CQC) became responsible for regulating health care and social care in England and took over the roles of the three organisations that were previously responsible for this regulatory work: The Healthcare Commission, The Commission for Social Care Inspection and The Mental Health Act Commission

This direction of travel was reinforced the following year with the publication of *Commissioning a patient-led NHS: delivering the NHS improvement plan* (Department of Health, 2005a) within health, and *Independence, well-being and choice* (Department of Health, 2005b) in social care. In 2006, the White Paper, *Our health, our care, our say* (Department of Health, 2006a) reiterated similar themes, including:

- More personalised care driven by better access and more funding following the patient
- Services brought closer to home and away from centralised hospitals
- Better co-ordination between local councils and the NHS
- Increased choice
- A greater emphasis on prevention of illness

The most influential policy document of recent years, however, looks set to be *High quality care for all: NHS next stage review* (Department of Health, 2008a). This review of the English NHS, carried out by a London-based surgeon, Lord Darzi, was published in the 60th year of the NHS. Its core themes of improving quality, ensuring patient safety and improving the effectiveness of care are underpinned by previous policy directives on health and well-being, personalised care and patient choice (see Box 2.12 for a summary of some of the main recommendations).

<table>
<tr><td>Box
2.12</td><td>NHS next stage review recommendations</td></tr>
</table>

Creating an NHS that helps people to stay healthy

- Every PCT will commission comprehensive well-being and prevention services in partnership with local authorities, with services personalised to meet the specific needs of their local populations
- Everyone with a long-term condition will have a personalised care plan
- Personal health budgets will be piloted (see also Chapter 4)
- Integrated fit for work services will be introduced to help people that want to return to work but are struggling with ill health

Quality at the heart of the NHS

- Information about the quality of care will be systematically measured and published. This will include patients' own views on the success of their treatment and the quality of their experiences
- All registered health care providers working for or on behalf of the NHS will be required by law to publish Quality Accounts of their care
- Practice accreditation in primary care will be supported

Working in partnership with staff

- Staff will be enabled and encouraged to set up social enterprises to deliver services

The first NHS constitution

- An NHS constitution will set out patient rights and responsibilities in relation to the NHS

It is also notable that during the past decade, there has been a much stronger focus on the role of the independent sector within the NHS. Government policy now actively encourages its 'important contribution to increasing capacity, patient choice and service innovation ... We expect commissioners to recognise and make appropriate use of independent sector providers to optimise patient care across all sectors' (Department of Health, 2007a, p. 32).

Modernising mental health services

As we have suggested throughout this chapter, there has been much to modernise in mental health. *The journey to recovery* (Department of Health, 2001b) admitted that mental heath was a poor relation among services with 'shabby and depressing wards that would never have been tolerated in medicine or surgery' and care in the community that 'too often became a bleak and neglected environment' (p. 4). However, by the end of the 1990s, a number of seemingly separate but ultimately interlinking factors such as the adverse publicity of a small number of high profile cases including violence and people with serious mental illness and an increasingly vocal mental health services user movement (see Chapter 8) meant that mental health began to become more of a political priority.

The mental health modernisation agenda was heralded and implemented through two key policy documents: *Modernising mental health services: safe, sound and supportive* (Department of Health, 1998a) (see Box 2.13) and the *National service framework for mental health* (Department of Health, 1999a). *Modernising mental health services* was, in effect, the first comprehensive government statement about the future direction of mental health policy since *Better services for the mentally ill* in 1975 and, unlike that White Paper, was underpinned by £700 million of new investment over three years.

Box 2.13	*Modernising mental health services*

The key recommendations in the 1998 White Paper were to:

- Strengthen comprehensive care (with particular emphasis on services for people with severe mental illness, including acute beds, 24 hour nursed care secure beds, assertive outreach teams and crisis intervention teams)
- Provide 24 hour access to services
- Develop, train and recruit staff with the skills and motivation to deliver modern services
- Improve the planning and commissioning of services
- Develop partnership
- Develop mental health promotion
- Improve the use of information technology

The supportive element of the White Paper, working with patients and services users, families and carers to build healthier communities, reflected the increasingly overt communitarian approach adopted by New Labour.

However, it is also interesting to note that the major emphasis was on public safety rather than support for service users (an issue we return to later in this chapter). Frank Dobson, the Health Secretary at the time, echoed the rhetoric of the Ritchie Report in his introduction to the White Paper (Department of Health, 1998b) stating that:

> Care in the community has failed because while it improved the treatment of many people who were mentally ill, it left far too many walking the streets, often at risk to themselves and a nuisance to others ... Discharging people from institutions has brought benefits to some, but it has left many vulnerable patients trying to cope on their own ... A small but significant minority have become a danger to the public as well as themselves ... We are going to ensure that patients who might otherwise be a danger to themselves and others are no longer able to refuse to comply with the treatment they need.

The following year, the *National service framework for mental health* (Department of Health, 1999a), set out a ten-year plan for the development and delivery of mental health services for adults of working age (see Box 2.14).

Box 2.14	*National service framework for mental health*

The framework included seven standards in five areas of care:

1. *Mental health promotion* – to ensure health and social services promote mental health and reduce discrimination and social exclusion associated with mental health problems
2. *Primary care and access to services* – to deliver better primary mental health care, and to ensure consistent advice and help for people with mental health needs, including primary care services for individuals with severe mental illness
3. *Effective services for people with severe mental illness* – to ensure that each person with severe mental illness receives the range of mental health services they need; that crises are anticipated or prevented where possible; to ensure prompt and effective help if a crisis does occur, and timely access to an appropriate and safe mental health place or hospital bed, as close to home as possible
4. *Caring about carers* – to ensure health and social services assess the needs of carers who provide regular and substantial care for those with severe mental illness and provide care to meet their needs
5. *Preventing suicide* – to ensure that health and social services play their full part in reducing the suicide rate by at least one fifth by 2010

The *National service framework* or NSF (Department of Health, 1999a) had a number of key strengths, including the fact that it was the first document in mental health to set a common agenda for local agencies. It was comprehensive in scope and focused as much on health promotion and common mental illness within primary care as it did on serious mental illness. As *Modernising mental health services* had done, the NSF also reflected a communitarian philosophy of promoting access to the mainstream for people with mental illness through social inclusion involving the wider community as well as through developing health and social care services. It was also partially evidence based, which, as we suggested at the beginning of this chapter, is relatively rare in a policy report. However, as the Sainsbury Centre for Mental Health at the time (1999) and the Wanless Report since have recognised (Wanless, 2002), it was not a fully resourced document. There were also basic inequities in a framework devoting a standard to carers but not service users. Indeed, users were depicted largely as recipients of services and, once again, as potential sources of risk to the community.

A half term report review of the NSF concluded: 'We are now five years into a 10 year programme of reform. No one would claim that the problems that have affected mental health care for decades have been solved or that we have yet the services nationally that services users deserve or that staff can feel proud of' (Department of Health, 2004a, p. 74). However, ten years on, we can, perhaps, more objectively judge progress. On the positive side of the balance sheet, the promised assertive outreach and crisis resolution/home treatment teams are now in place (CSIP, 2008). In one survey of inpatient care, the numbers of beds per ward ranged from five to 32, and the majority were operating with a bed occupancy of less than 100 per cent (mean = 93 per cent) (Royal College of Psychiatrists/Healthcare Commission, 2007). Successive censuses of inpatients have also shown a decline in numbers (see Chapter 5 for further discussion).

Less promisingly, the former Healthcare Commission (2008a) found that 16 per cent of care records in inpatient care indicated that service users had not had a one to one session with nursing staff on any day during their first week in hospital and one survey of people who use mental health services reported that 40 per cent said that their relatives or carers had not had enough support from health and social services (see Chapter 10).

Recent generic health policy directives have created a series of other tensions for mental health service users. The 'personalisation' agenda aims (at least in principle) to give greater choice and control to individual service users, viewing them more as citizens with a right to support than as passive recipients of traditional services (see Chapter 4 for greater detail). Although this has led to some exciting developments in community services, this way of working has found it harder to infiltrate adult mental health – perhaps at least in part because of the strong emphasis on risk, protection and compulsion. Quite how the system seeks to balance individual choice and control with public protection seems a classic example of the tensions that can emerge within the policy process between rhetoric and reality. The emphasis on addressing social inclusion through work-related initiatives is also potentially problematic for mental health service users where perhaps more attention should be paid to users' aspirations for education, relationships and other chosen routes to recovery (Spandler, 2007).

The costs of modernisation

By 2000, despite the plethora of policy reforms, a desire to stick within the previous administration's spending limits meant that 'Ministers were deluded by their own rhetoric into thinking that Labour's programme of modernisation possessed some kind of magic that permitted miracles to be wrought without the application of resources' (Webster, 2002, p. 215). In 1998, UK total health care expenditure was 6.8 per cent of Gross Domestic Product (GDP) compared with an income-weighted average of 8.4 per cent in European Union countries. The UK's total health care spending per capita was then about 25–30 per cent lower than in Australia, France and the Netherlands, around 35 per cent lower than in Canada and Germany (OECD, 2001) and comparable to that of the Czech Republic, Poland and South Korea. The OECD statistics show that the UK spent £863 per person on health in 1999, while Norway spent £1484 on each person (Wanless, 2002).

Public disquiet over long waiting lists and variable treatment experiences, negative publicity and public criticism of the government's record on the NHS by respected experts put pressure on the government to consider changes in NHS funding. The Prime Minister announced that the government would, over a period of five years, increase the level of health spending to the European average (Tony Blair, interviewed by David Frost, BBC TV, 16th January 2000). The budget that year gave sufficient money to the NHS to allow it to grow in real terms by 6.1 per cent, nearly twice the historic average.

In July 2000, *The NHS plan* (Department of Health, 2000a) represented, in many senses, a relaunch of Labour's now more robustly funded NHS policy. New investment in staff and IT systems and new NHS structures including Care Trusts (new integrated health and social care bodies; see Chapter 7) were announced. Three clinical priority areas were highlighted: cancer, coronary heart disease and mental health. From a mental health perspective, *The NHS Plan* promised an extra annual investment of over £300 million by 2003/4 to fast forward the NSF but was also, true to the principles of modernisation, fundamentally concerned with what had to be delivered in return for the money (see Box 2.15).

Box 2.15	**Mental health policy and *The NHS plan***

- 1000 new graduate mental health staff to work in primary care
- An extra 500 community mental health team workers
- 50 early intervention teams to provide treatment and support to young people with psychosis
- 335 crisis resolution teams
- An increase to 220 assertive outreach teams
- Provision of women-only day services
- 700 extra staff to work with carers
- More suitable accommodation for up to 400 people currently in high security hospitals
- Better services for prisoners with mental illness
- Additional placements and staff for people with severe personality disorders

---

Unfortunately, despite pledges on primary and community care, there was relatively little emphasis on acute services (see Chapter 5) or mental health promotion. Indeed, it could be argued that the overall mental health emphasis was on compulsion and perhaps even reinstitutionalisation, with funding being directed towards forensic beds, involuntary hospital admissions and places in supported housing to provide proactive care for people traditionally seen as difficult to engage in the community (Priebe *et al.*, 2005). *The NHS plan* also relied heavily on a flourishing, well-trained and motivated workforce for implementation, which in terms of mental health, as in many other areas of the NHS, has not necessarily materialised.

In addition, *The NHS plan* also assumed that the NHS had a management structure that could embrace and lead change. Although the 1983 Griffiths Report arguably laid the foundations for such significant changes by creating a group of staff receptive to management ideas and policies, *The NHS plan* was introduced at a time in NHS history when significant change was occurring at all levels of the service (Department of Health, 2001c, 2002a) which led to a dilution of management expertise. New PCTs were given specific responsibility for commissioning services including mental health services, and, in April 2002, Health Authorities in England were replaced by 28 larger Strategic Health Authorities with a performance management brief, which were in turn reduced to ten in 2006. The organisation of mental health services also changed rapidly with the creation in England of specialist Mental Health Trusts and the increasing integration of health and social care provision.

To help resolve uncertainty about future NHS finances, the Treasury asked Derek Wanless, the former chief executive of the National Westminster Bank, to produce a report on future NHS funding. In 2002, the Wanless Report concluded that 'to deliver the high quality service envisaged, the review projects that NHS costs will rise to between 154 billion and 184 billion by 2022–23 (in 2002/03 prices). Across the 20-year period, this implies total NHS spending increasing at an average rate of between 4.2 and 5.1 per cent a year in real terms' (Wanless, 2002, Introduction). In response, the April 2002 budget announced significant new investment in the NHS from 2003–8, financed in part by an extra 1 per cent on National Insurance.

Although expenditure on the NHS did indeed increase, particularly between 1999 and 2006, the Comprehensive Spending Review 2008/9 to 2010/11 (HM Treasury, 2007) increased spending on the NHS by only 4 per cent per year in real terms, taking its budget from £90 billion in 2007/8 to £110 billion by 2010/11. Parsonage (2009) has also confirmed earlier fears that there will be a 20 per cent shortfall in the funding level required to deliver the *NSF for mental health* (Department of Health, 1999a) in full. Perhaps more worryingly for mental health services, McCrone *et al.* (2008) have projected needs and costs of mental health to 2026 and current service costs are estimated to increase by 45 per cent to £32.6 billion in 2026 (at 2007 prices). While some of this is due to estimated service costs for people with dementia, it nevertheless highlights the continued need to keep mental health and mental health services firmly on the political agenda. At the time of writing, the future funding of both health and social care is under significant pressure following a global recession.

The continuing debate about community care

By the late 1990s, patient choice and partnership working were becoming buzz words within the wider health and social care community, and were, to a lesser extent, also beginning to impact on mental health services (see Chapters 7 and 8). Issues of social inclusion, represented perhaps most starkly by the unacceptably high unemployment rates for people with mental illness, were also beginning to be addressed by a series of policy initiatives (see Box 2.16).

> **Box 2.16** **Mental illness and the wider social inclusion agenda**
>
> - The *Disability Discrimination Act* (1995) was the first attempt by a British government to legislate against the discrimination faced by disabled people, including people with mental illness. The number of disabled people with mental health problems in Britain covered by the DDA definition is estimated to be 580,783, just over 10 per cent of the total DDA disabled population of working age (ONS, 2003)
> - There is, however, an inherent tension within the Welfare to Work programme between the very low rates of employment for people with mental health problems, the resulting poverty and additional social exclusion that this can lead to, and also the recognition that, for some people, full-time paid work may never be possible. There is, however, still a need for people to engage in meaningful activity that keeps them well in the community with the open-ended possibility of recovery (Rankin, 2005)

It was, paradoxically, against this emerging more inclusive policy background that service users and professionals clashed with a government that seemed determined to prioritise media-spun notions of public safety over the evidence base on community care. Frank Dobson's statement in the House of Commons on 29 July 1998 that care in the community had 'failed' heralded a series of papers and consultation documents on the revision of the 1983 *Mental Health Act*, including a report from an expert committee chaired by Genevra Richardson and a Green Paper, *Reform of the Mental Health Act 1983: proposals for consultation* (Department of Health, 1999c, 1999d). In particular, Richardson argued that issues of capacity, reciprocity (that is safeguarding patients' rights and providing appropriate services), a statutory right to early advocacy and the inclusion of advanced statements needed to be recognised in future legislation.

The Green Paper, however, ignored these recommendations and instead emphasised questions of risk in a traditional paternalistic sense, referring to community treatment orders (CTOs) for those posing a risk to self or others. The subsequent White Paper, *Reforming the Mental Health Act* (Department of Health, 2001d, 2001e) attracted a great deal of attention, largely because of its over-riding emphasis on public safety (Grounds, 2001). The first *Draft Mental Health Bill*, published on 25 July 2002, contained safeguards of rights of appeal and access to advocacy services and safeguards for certain patients treated informally who are not capable of consenting, but also included a number of issues that create considerable concerns for health and social care professionals, services users and for wider society, particularly in terms of increased powers of compulsion. An umbrella organisation, the Mental Health Alliance, consisting of over 60 mental health organisations was established in response to the Bill and was vociferous in its opposition. The second (revised) Draft Bill was published on 8 September 2004. Although there were some improvements, critics still argued that services provided to an individual would be largely determined by the risk they posed to society rather than, as the

Richardson report proposed, the level of their mental capacity (Mooney, 2004). The Report of the Joint Scrutiny Committee of the House of Commons

Box 2.17	Summary of the Amendments in the 2007 *Mental Health Act*

Definition of mental disorder: it changes the way the 1983 Act defines mental disorder, so that a single definition applies throughout the Act, and abolishes references to categories of disorder. The single category is 'any disorder or disability of the mind'. It now includes people with a personality disorder and autism.

Criteria for detention: it introduces a new 'appropriate medical treatment' test which will apply to all the longer-term powers of detention. As a result, it will not be possible for patients to be compulsorily detained or their detention continued unless medical treatment which is appropriate to the patient's mental disorder and all other circumstances of the case is available to that patient. At the same time, the 'treatability test' will be abolished.

Professional roles: it is broadening the groups of practitioners who can take on the functions currently performed by the approved social worker (ASW) and responsible medical officer (RMO). The approved social worker role will be replaced by the approved mental health professional which will be open not only to social workers but also to first-level nurses whose field of practice is mental health or learning disability, occupational therapists and chartered psychologists. The responsible medical officer role will be replaced by the responsible clinician role which is open to other senior appropriately trained professionals as well as doctors (NIMHE, 2008).

Nearest relative (NR): it gives to patients the right to make an application to displace their NR and enables County Courts to displace an NR where there are reasonable grounds for doing so. The provisions for determining the NR will be amended to include civil partners among the list of relatives.

Supervised community treatment (SCT): it introduces SCT for patients following a period of detention in hospital. It is expected that this will allow a small number of patients with a mental disorder to live in the community while subject to certain conditions, to ensure they continue with the medical treatment that they need. Supervised discharge has been abolished.

Mental Health Review Tribunal (MHRT): it introduces an order-making power to reduce the time before a case has to be referred to the MHRT by hospital managers. It also introduces a single Tribunal for England.

Age-appropriate services: it requires hospital managers to ensure that patients aged under eighteen admitted to hospital for mental disorder are accommodated in an environment that is suitable for their age (subject to their needs).

Advocacy: it places a duty on the appropriate national authority to make arrangements for help to be provided by independent mental health advocates.

Electro-convulsive therapy (ECT): it introduces new safeguards for patients (for example, an advance decision covering use cannot be over-ridden). However, ECT can still be used for all in emergencies where necessary to save life or prevent serious deterioration.

and the House of Lords on the 2004 Bill was also highly critical (House of Commons and the House of Lords, 2005). Faced with opposition from key players, the Government decided not to proceed with the Bill but instead to introduce amendments to the Mental Health Act 1983.

The new Mental Health Act 2007 for England and Wales finally came into force on 3rd November 2008. Technically, the Act amends the Mental Health Act (1983) with a series of key changes (see Box 2.17).

One of the most controversial changes is the introduction of the responsible clinician role. This role is now open not only to doctors but also to social workers, nurses whose field of practice is mental health or learning disability, occupational therapists and chartered psychologists. All responsible clinicians will need to demonstrate prerequisite competencies not only around assessment and treatment but also leadership and communication skills. Although the new arrangements have the potential to enhance multidisciplinary ways of working, there are some concerns that they may lead to conflict between professions and possibly undermine the role of the psychiatrist (Hall and Ali, 2009).

A further particularly contentious aspect of the changes is the replacement of supervised aftercare powers with new supervised community treatment powers. Under supervised community treatment, patients compulsorily detained in hospital for treatment may, on discharge, be placed on a community treatment order which will require them to comply with certain conditions, such as attending outpatients. Community treatment orders will also enable individuals to have their treatment supervised and be recalled swiftly to hospital without the need for formal recertification to occur. They are intended to enable people with a chronic mental health problem to live safely in the community, increase opportunities for community inclusion and reduce the number of 'revolving door' admissions. However, Lawton-Smith et al. (2008) suggest there are at least four reasons why they should be challenged:

1. The international evidence base for the effect of community treatment orders on key outcomes such as hospital readmission, length of hospital stay and improved medication adherence is, at best, equivocal (Churchill, 2007).
2. Community treatment orders will almost inevitably increase overall use of compulsion in England and Wales. The Department of Health estimates that, on average, patients will stay under community treatment orders for nine months, which is significantly longer than the length of time the average patient is treated in hospital (around 3.5 months) (Department of Health, 2006b).
3. Community treatment orders pit patient autonomy against professional paternalism, raising serious ethical concerns. Given that the majority of psychiatric inpatients have the capacity to make treatment decisions, community treatment orders will commonly be imposed on people who have capacity (Okai et al., 2007).
4. A system that allows for the regular use of community treatment orders may distract services from finding voluntary solutions to manage hard to engage patients and focus scarce resources on the few rather than the many.

Overall, it is difficult to see how the new Act fits with the agenda of partnership working, personalisation, access and patient choice. Instead, a more effective way of improving the safety of the public and the care of people with mental health problems is surely to devise mental health services that genuinely engage users, where users have information and are truly consulted and given control over aspects of their care (see Chapter 8). As Laurance suggests (2003, p. xxi):

> The most effective way to improve the safety of the public and the care of those who are mentally ill is to devise services that genuinely engage users and meet their desire for greater control so that they are encouraged to seek treatment and lead stable, risk-free lives. If instead, politicians pander to public prejudice and adopt a heavy handed, coercive approach, they will drive people away from services.

The other recent legal change with implications for mental health care and practice is the *Mental Capacity Act* (MCA) 2005, which came into force in 2007. This provides a legal framework for how to act and make decisions on behalf of people who lack capacity to make specific decisions for themselves (Department for Constitutional Affairs, 2007). It generally applies to people aged sixteen or over, includes people with mental health problems and covers major decisions about health care and treatment.

People can make advance decisions to refuse treatment should they lose capacity in future. The *Mental Health Act* can overrule any advance decisions made about psychiatric treatment. But since November 2008, it has not been able to overrule an advance decision refusing ECT (except in an emergency). Since April 2009, the *Mental Health Act* has changed the MCA to address the 'Bournewood' problem: that is, to protect people who are detained in hospital but lack capacity to consent or refuse admission by introducing the Deprivation of Liberty Safeguards.

The Act is underpinned by a set of five key principles:

- A presumption of capacity – every adult has the right to make his or her own decisions and must be assumed to have capacity to do so unless it is proved otherwise
- The right for individuals to be supported to make their own decisions – people must be given all appropriate help before anyone concludes that they cannot make their own decisions
- That individuals must retain the right to make what might be seen as eccentric or unwise decisions
- Best interests – anything done for or on behalf of people without capacity must be in their best interests
- Least restrictive intervention – anything done for or on behalf of people without capacity should be the least restrictive of their basic rights and freedoms

Implementation

Despite the policy focus and extra funding, mental health services, like many other generic aspects of the NHS, are still getting 'mixed reviews', particularly in terms of implementation. An interesting question, and one that could have been asked at almost any point in the last 150 years, is therefore why central policy imperatives are not consistently implemented on the ground? There appear to be at least five key issues that affect implementation:

1. Implementation is more likely to occur if different organisations have clear roles and responsibilities. However, in terms of mental health, there is significant overlap between different programmes and organisations. Suicide prevention, for example, is tackled not only as Standard 7 of the *NSF*, but specifically within the *National Confidential Inquiry into Suicide and Homicide*, *The NHS plan*, *Adult acute in-patient care provision* guidance and the *National suicide prevention strategy* (Department of Health, 1999a, 2000a, 2001a, 2002a, 2002b).
2. The culture of an organisation is also important in implementing change. In a study exploring the relationship between organisational culture and performance in the NHS, Mannion *et al.* (2003) identified a range of cultural characteristics that appeared to be linked to positive organisational performance including:

   ■ Strong leadership
   ■ A culture of clear and explicit performance objectives
   ■ Clear lines of upward accountability
   ■ A proactive approach to managing the local health community
   ■ A considerable emphasis on developing and harnessing staff potential

   Despite this, the evidence base on the nature of organisational culture in the NHS, its role in performance and quality, and the extent to which policies have succeeded in securing change is still relatively sparse (Leatherman and Sutherland, 2003) and more work is needed to understand this link in the context of the NHS.
3. It is also difficult to implement new working practices within a system that is in a constant state of change. It is interesting that the shape and size of PCTs have undergone major change twice this decade at precisely the point in their history when they require space to work on implementing current policy initiatives, build relations with local health care communities and secure much-needed clinical engagement and improvements in service (Walshe *et al.*, 2004).
4. There are also problems associated with a state of near hyper-active policy making. As Means *et al.* suggest, there is: 'the impression of a modernisation muddle in which managers and field level staff are struggling to keep pace with the demand for policy change and the ever increasing flood of directives, guidelines and indicators' (2008, p. 214). Successful implementation requires a break from new policy and time and space to understand and implement existing directives.

5. Perhaps the key barrier to implementation is the age-old tension between central policy edicts and local flexibility, with implementation deficits due either to top-down or bottom-up problems (Hill and Hupe, 2002). In a seminal book on this issue, Pressman and Wildavsky (1973) argue that relatively small failures of co-operation between different organisations can easily multiply to create a major implementation deficit. Major policy change is especially likely to create this situation because of the complexity it both requires and engenders. As the government attempts to enforce change through a top-down approach, it is likely to provoke resistance from vested interests and also generate a mass of unintended consequences. In practice, policy directives from the Department of Health have to be filtered down through Strategic Health Authorities, PCTs and Acute Trusts before they can have an impact on services. All of these bodies are semi-autonomous organisations and can influence if and how central policy is implemented. In addition, social care is overseen by local councillors, and services are therefore accountable to locally elected representatives rather than nationally.

Structural decentralisation in the NHS, through the creation of PCTs and Strategic Health Authorities to performance manage their local health system, suggests that local control and autonomy at the coalface are becoming increasingly common. The creation and promotion of Foundation Trusts also demonstrates the government's desire to delegate autonomy to the field through the *Community Health and Standards Act* (2003) since Foundation Trusts can opt out of central government control and have greater flexibility over their financial position. However, the modernisation agenda with its organisations, frameworks and widespread central quality controls has exerted and continues to exert a powerful centralising influence within health and social care. The clash of top-down and bottom-up approaches creates tensions within the system and means that policies may not necessarily be implemented in practice.

Conclusion

Aneurin Bevan said: 'we ought to take a pride in the fact that despite our financial and economic anxieties, we are still able to do the most civilised thing in the world – put the welfare of the sick in front of every other consideration' (House of Commons, 1948). However, as this chapter has suggested, over the intervening six decades, the NHS has slipped from being the number one government priority, and indeed has been, at times, both poorly managed and financially neglected.

There is, however, definite evidence of a change in the political priority accorded to the NHS since 2000, underpinned by extra funding. Quite where social care fits in with this agenda is harder to gauge – sometimes included in policies that focus primarily on health care, sometimes receiving additional funding (but less than the NHS) and sometimes receiving relatively little attention at all.

Is Cinderella finally going to the ball?

Mental health has also been seen as an increasing political priority since 1998, the subject of the first NSF in 1999, a key area within *The NHS plan* (Department of Health, 2000a) and one of the three highlighted clinical areas in the *Priorities and planning framework* for 2003–2006 (Department of Health, 2002c). However, its prominence has diminished somewhat in recent years. It has not featured as one of the key areas in the NHS Operating Frameworks since 2006, although 'improving access to psychological therapies' and a 'continued focus on implementing early intervention services' do still feature in the list of PCT local priorities (Department of Health, 2008b).

Sufficient financial investment is, of course, crucial in improving mental health services, but, as we have seen, there was a shortfall in implementing the *NSF for mental health* (Department of Health, 1999a) and predictions of considerable future funding requirements at a time of global recession.

There is also still a central paradox at the heart of mental health policy and practice. While there are legal structures that encourage partnership working, better acute and community mental health provision and policy directives that seem to be taking user involvement more seriously, compulsory mental health treatment in the community and ongoing social exclusion suggest an underlying culture of coercion. In a health and social care system that increasingly values patient and user choice, mental health now poses a particular paradox for policy makers and presents a series of challenges to practitioners and users to shape mental health services in a way that truly reflects what users want, what the country can afford and what the workforce is able to deliver.

Suggestions for further reading

For those wishing to explore the policy context in more detail, the following books offer critical and well-written appraisals of the history and politics of the NHS and social care:

1. Coppock, V. and Hopton, J. (2000) *Critical perspectives on mental health.* London, Routledge

   This book explores the social, political and intellectual developments that have shaped mental health practice over the last four decades, using as a guiding framework the ideas of the anti-psychiatry, anti-racism and radical feminism movements.

2. Rogers, A. and Pilgrim, D. (2001) *Mental health policy in Britain* (2nd edn). Basingstoke, Palgrave

   This key text offers a critical analysis of mental health policy, including a discussion of the mental health users' movement and the influence of users' views on policy formation.

3. Webster, C. (2002) *The National Health Service: a political history.* Oxford, Oxford University Press

   This book provides an overview of the key issues that have shaped the NHS during the past 50 years. Although mental health does not feature prominently within the text, the political and economic influences on generic NHS policy are helpful in contextualising the position of mental health.

4. Laurance, J. (2003) *Pure madness: how fear drives the mental health system.* London, Routledge

   Pure madness is an impressionistic, anecdotal, but nevertheless powerful account of the state of mental health care in Britain today, written by the health editor of *The Independent.* Laurance examines issues of care or control in the community and explores alternatives to inpatient treatment.

5. For anyone interested in the history of madness, there is no better source than the unique and always fascinating Roy Porter. Try:

   - Porter, R. (2002) *Madness: a brief history.* Oxford, Oxford University; or
   - Porter R. (1999) *A social history of madness: stories of the insane.* London, Phoenix

6. Means, R., Richards, S. and Smith, R. (2008) *Community care: policy and practice* (4th edn). Basingstoke, Palgrave Macmillan

   For a general overview of community care services for older people, people with learning difficulties and people with mental health problems, Means *et al.* offer a detailed but accessible account that helps to place many of the issues discussed in this chapter in a wider social policy context.

7. Brooker, C. and Repper.J. (eds) (2009) *Mental health: from policy to practice.* Edinburgh, Elsevier

   This clearly written edited book provides a series of critical overviews of the success and failures of the *National service framework for mental health.*

8. Details of government policy documents are available on: www.official-documents.co.uk. Relevant statutes can be found on: www.hmso.gov.uk/

3 Primary Care and Mental Health

The structure and workload of primary care in the UK

GPs, practice nurses, dentists, pharmacists and opticians form the primary care level of the NHS and, as such, are the 'front line' of the health service. On the whole, patients cannot consult a doctor in secondary care such as a hospital consultant or member of a community mental health team unless they are referred by a GP. This filtering process has led to GPs being described as the 'gate keepers' of the NHS.

The core group of staff working in a practice is known as the 'primary health care team' (see Figure 3.1). The actual composition of any primary health care team differs between practices but the Royal College of General Practitioners (RCGP, 2002) have identified a core team as consisting of:

- GPs
- Practice nurses
- District nurses
- Health visitors
- Practice managers
- Administrative staff

In some surgeries, midwives, physiotherapists, counsellors and psychiatric nurses are also members of the team.

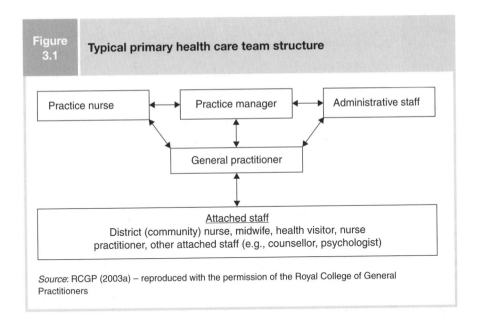

Figure 3.1 Typical primary health care team structure

Source: RCGP (2003a) – reproduced with the permission of the Royal College of General Practitioners

Ninety seven per cent of the population are registered with one of the approximately 36,000 GPs in the UK (RCGP, 2003b). GPs in England carried out over 299 million consultations and saw patients an average of 5.4 times in 2007 compared to 3.9 times in 1995 (Information Centre, 2008a). Eighty-three per cent of these were conducted on surgery premises, 11 per cent on the phone, 4 per cent were home visits and 3 per cent were conducted at other locations.

The exceptional potential of primary care?

Primary care in the UK has a number of unique strengths (see Box 3.1). It offers rapid access for routine and crisis care in a low-stigma setting. It occupies an important space at the interface of users, families, communities and professional worlds and is able to address mental, physical and social aspects of care. It has, until very recently, also been able to guarantee a cradle to grave doctor–patient relationship, with informational, longitudinal and interpersonal continuity of care (Saultz, 2003).

Primary care is also a place of great complexity. As Heath suggests (1999, p. 565): 'uncertainty, contradiction and complexity are the stuff of general practice and the measure of much of its fascination for us'. Each day, people arrive to see their GP or other members of the primary care team with coughs and colds and cancer and depression and have on average just ten minutes to explain their problems and negotiate a solution. This compares to 20–30 minutes in a hospital setting, where a referral letter has set the agenda and the doctor is an acknowledged specialist in that clinical area.

> ### Box 3.1   The strengths of primary care
>
> - Offers a low-stigma and accessible setting
> - Enables a holistic approach to problems
> - Can provide informational, longitudinal and interpersonal continuity of care
> - Sees individuals in the context of their past, their social networks and the wider community
> - Is able to deal with both the general and the particular

Primary care is, by way of contrast, delivered by specialists in generalism (Willis, 1995), by people taking an interest in whatever is of interest to the patient. As a result, primary care has developed sophisticated ways of working with the uncertainty and complexity of its environment (Wilson and Holt, 2001). Decisions, for example, may be based more on intuition, experience and knowledge of the patient's previous history than slavish adherence to medical algorithms. General practitioners are also able, although not all are necessarily willing, to act not only as an individual's advocate within the wider system, but to combine this role with a wider social and political responsibility to speak out on behalf of the most needy and least heard within our society. As Tudor Hart suggests (1988, p. 332): 'if social factors influence the behaviour of disease on a community-wide scale, GPs and other primary care workers must concern themselves with them as a normal and central part of their work, not a fringe option to be added by some doctors and ignored by others'.

Primary care practitioners are also uniquely placed to understand both the general and the particular, an ability that Heath (1999) has termed the 'oscillating gaze'. Thus, when a practitioner focuses on the individual, they see the patient as a single human being (perhaps a tearful young woman with a new baby and sleep problems), and when they focus on the group, they see that young woman as part of a broader group within social life (that is, as a person with possible postnatal depression):

> The categorisation of people devalues individual experience and can leave individuals feeling unrecognised and the reality of their symptoms unheard .... the general practitioner while actively using the generalisation for biomedical science, has a constant responsibility to refocus on the individual, the detail of their experience and the meaning they attach to that experience. We cannot see the particular patient and the generalisation simultaneously. At a given instance we have to choose one way of seeing or the other. If we are to maximise our understanding, if we are not to become stranded and impotent at one pole of the dualism, we must learn to oscillate our gaze. (Heath, 1999, p. 652)

The history of primary care

The structure of primary care in the UK has its roots in the nineteenth century when medical care was provided by three groups of people – apothecaries, physicians and surgeons. The latter two had superior qualifications and status. During the early nineteenth century, the term GP came to be applied to a growing number of apothecaries who took the membership examination of the Royal College of Surgeons of England. However, at that stage there was still considerable freedom to move between the branches of the profession.

The practice of GPs referring patients to specialists began at the end of the nineteenth century and was well established by the time of the 1911 *National Insurance Act*, which ensured free state primary care provision for a proportion of the population (working men).

The birth of the NHS as we might begin to recognise it today was in 1948. From the beginning there were complex negotiations. Ultimately, GPs agreed to register all patients and provide 24-hour care for them, establishing universal access to family doctors for the first time in the UK, but were allowed to retain their 'independent contractor status' so that they, in effect, remained their own bosses. Hospital consultants still had the option of private practice and access to pay beds in NHS hospitals and negotiated a system of financially advantageous 'merit awards' (now known as 'clinical excellence' awards) leading Bevan to admit he had 'stuffed their mouths with gold' (Abel-Smith, 1964, p. 480) to achieve agreement.

Ham (2009) has argued that an important outcome of the negotiations was to effectively divide the medical profession in two, winning the support of hospital consultants with generous financial payments and isolating and further reducing the power and status of GPs, reinforcing the notion of second-class citizenship created by the subordinate position of the apothecaries. Calnan and Gabe (1991) have argued that between 1948 and the negotiation of the next new contract in 1966, this lower status was demonstrated by GPs seeking to emulate hospital medical practice, for example, by undertaking sessional clinical attachments in local hospitals.

However, from the mid-1960s onwards, GPs became swept up by a series of changes which transformed their practices and brought them into the mainstream of the health service. The contract introduced in 1966 encouraged a move from single-handed to group practices through the introduction of the 'group practice allowance' (funding specifically for multi-doctor practices). GPs were able to claim 70 per cent reimbursement of salary costs for up to two staff per full-time GP partner, encouraging the employment of ancillary staff such as receptionists and practice nurses. A new terminology appeared, with uni-professional general practice being replaced with the notion of a multi-professional primary health care team working from a health centre.

These changes were underpinned by changes in vocational training. The Royal Commission on Medical Education (the Todd Report) made a series of recommendations designed to achieve parity between general practitioners and other specialities in terms of undergraduate education, postgraduate training, continuing education and a higher profile academic role in medical schools (Todd, 1968).

The work of GPs was also changing out of all recognition, largely due to the decline of infectious diseases, the ageing population and a recognition of the central importance of proactive as well as reactive care (see Box 3.2 for key quotes which summarise these changes). Reactive care (fire fighting), with a limited number of drugs, was replaced by a growing emphasis on holistic care and on health promotion and illness prevention as well as addressing acute and ongoing health complaints (Stott and Davis, 1979). These changes required a new workforce and new approach to work in primary care.

Box 3.2	The changing workload of primary care

'The old emergencies, lobar pneumonia, empyema, mastoids, have disappeared: doctors are being cast whether they like it or not in a new role as interested in and responsible for all the human frailties.'

(Butterfield, 1964, Foreword)

'The primary physician has an unequalled opportunity to balance long-term health needs against short-term clinical pressures. He can practise from a broad clinical base by integrating the psycho-social and biological components of each illness. He can implement applied continuity of care to defined population by learning to use the skills and aids which are required to achieve this. He can also make maximum use of the opportunities for health promotion and thereby begin to discover the need to modify the traditional clinical approach. Finally, he can permit his knowledge and skills in the modification of help-seeking behaviour to influence his clinical decisions, his practice organisation and his relationship with his patients. The larger number of patients coming to primary care, the nature of their problems, and the relationship they may have with their doctor – all reinforced these opportunities in a way not usually possible for other specialities.'

(Stott and Davis, 1979, pp. 204–5)

Primary care in the UK

During the last twenty years, primary care has become increasingly central to the development and delivery of health services, an emphasis that is a global phenomenon (Rogers and Pilgrim, 2003). The political and fiscal context of the 1980s are described in detail in Chapter 2, but, essentially, changes in terms of tighter public spending controls and the dominant political ideology focused on the importance of market forces led to a series of reviews of NHS funding mechanisms and organisation that culminated in the late 1980s, in the White Paper *Working for patients* (Department of Health, 1989b).

This included radical ideas about the delivery of health services, creating competition through the separation of purchaser and provider responsibilities and the establishment of self-governing NHS Trusts and GP fund holding (where practices were given a budget to purchase a limited range of services for their patients by negotiating contracts with NHS Trusts).

At the same time, the new 1990 GP Contract included provision for health checks for new patients, three-yearly checks for patients not otherwise seen by a GP and annual checks for patients aged 75 or over. Targets were also set for vaccinations, immunisation and cervical cancer screening and financial encouragement was given for the development of health promotion clinics. The Contract monies attached to health promotion were a significant stimulus to employing practice nurses. A survey at the time found that 51 per cent of GPs had created new practice nurse posts because of the Contract (Robinson *et al.*, 1993). Overall, the proportion of GP income that derived from capitation payments (where money was attached to each individual registered patient regardless of their health status or use of the health service) was increased from 46 per cent to 60 per cent, which could of course be seen as an incentive to increase list sizes rather than improve quality of care.

During the 1990s, the proposals in *Working for patients* were implemented, but in a progressively modified form. For example, the rules on GP fund holding changed on a number of occasions. Initially, only practices with 11,000 or more patients could apply to become a GP fund holder, but this limit was subsequently reduced to 7000, 5000 and eventually 3000 patients. In the process, various options were offered to GPs, ranging from a limited version of the scheme known as 'community fund holding' through 'standard fund holding' to 'total purchasing'. Fund holding was voluntary but by 1997 nearly half the GPs in the UK had become fund holders of some description.

The election of a Labour government in 1997 theoretically offered the prospect of quieter times for the NHS, although, as we have seen in Chapter 2, in fact the Blair and Brown governments developed policies for the modernisation of the NHS that were in many ways as radical as those contained in *Working for patients*. Within months of coming into office, the publication of *The New NHS: modern, dependable* (Department of Health, 1997a) announced the demise of GP fund holding and the internal market. Instead, it placed an emphasis on equity of access and provision and the need to ensure quality through clinical governance and accountability to local communities. However, *The New NHS* conceded that fund holding had demonstrated the value of GP commissioning of services although it took a further seven years before this policy was developed more fully as 'practice-based commissioning' (Department of Health, 2004b).

The introduction of Primary Care Groups/Trusts

The major structural change introduced to deliver these policy goals was the formation of PCGs, with the expectations that they would mature to PCTs (that is, fully autonomous bodies commissioning a much broader range of services).

In April 1999, 481 PCGs were established throughout England. Seventeen of these formed the first wave of PCTs a year later. When PCGs were formed, their Board was constituted to have a majority of GPs. However, as PCGs developed into PCTs, the focus changed to one of stronger managerial leadership and greater accountability. The number of GPs on the PCT Board was reduced and the post of chairman of the PCT board became an independent lay appointment. The professional voice was still influential through PCT Professional Executive Committees, although their overall influence was reduced.

Shifting the balance of power (Department of Health, 2001c) dramatically accelerated the timeframe for maturation from PCGs to PCTs and acknowledged them as the leading NHS organisation. In *Shifting the balance of power – the next steps* (Department of Health, 2002d), PCTs were specifically given responsibility for commissioning all mental health services. The strength of PCTs was also increased by giving them complete control over the new personal medical services (PMS) schemes, an initiative developed under the 1997 *Primary Care Act* that encouraged new ways of working in primary care, particularly in deprived areas. The 303 PCTs controlled and indeed continue to control 80 per cent of the NHS budget. They in effect became substitute Health Authorities for their geographical areas, but operating from primary care rather than acute care platforms. There has also been significant financial investment in primary care with an additional £1.9 billion in the three years to 2005/6, an average increase of 11 per cent per year in cash terms (Department of Health, 2002e).

Concentrating power at the PCT level exercised a domino effect on the rest of the system. Health Authorities lost their main function, replaced by a smaller number of Strategic Health Authorities, and the balance between the hospital and primary care sector has tipped further in favour of primary care. However, the rate and pace of change was almost certainly too great for some PCTs. Surveys suggested problems with management capacity and expertise in commissioning services including mental health (Sainsbury Centre for Mental Health, 2001; Audit Commission, 2004). The experience of forerunners to PCT commissioning, such as the total purchasing pilots and GP commissioning schemes, also found difficulty in achieving effective involvement of grass roots GPs, and noted the demands on lead GPs and the importance of good management in enabling improvements in services (Mays *et al.*, 1998; Regen *et al.*, 1999). Some PCTs also inherited debts from the old Health Authorities, making it more difficult to plan and provide new services.

Primary care went through yet another major structural reform in 2006, heralded in *Commissioning a patient-led NHS* (Department of Health, 2005a). The number of PCTs was almost halved to 152 and greater co-ordination was created between PCTs and local authority social service boundaries, with approximately 70 per cent of the new PCTs mirroring Local Authority boundaries. At the same time, the number of Strategic Health Authorities was reduced from 28 to ten. One of the consequences of these changes was yet more instability at PCT level, with managers reapplying for their own jobs and inevitable loss of organisational memory.

The impact of recent primary care policy reforms

The emphasis during the last few years in primary care (and indeed within the wider NHS) has been on encouraging competition, including enabling the entry of private providers into the market through Alternative Provider Medical Services contracts, improving access and patient choice more generally and quality improvement (Department of Health, 2007b, 2008a). Perhaps the most far reaching of these reforms are those that focus on the introduction of pay for performance into primary care and on the potential and threats posed by primary care-based commissioning.

Primary care underwent a fundamental revolution with the acceptance in June 2003 of a new General Medical Services Contract (nGMS), effective from April 2004 (BMA/NHS Confederation, 2003). Although, as in 1948, 1966 and 1990, there was something of a bitter and bloody battle between health professionals and the government, seven out of ten GPs voted on the Contract with just under 80 per cent in favour of acceptance.

Under the 1948 Contract, GPs remained independent practitioners, in effect rather like a small business, paid on the basis of the number of patients registered with the practice and also receiving payments for specific activities such as out of hours visits and maternity care. The 1966 Contract saw, as we've described, the rise of the extended primary care team and the fall of uni-professional general practice. The 1990 Contract led to a renewed emphasis on capitation, perhaps at the expense at times of quality of care, although it also included financial encouragement for proactive work such as health promotion and health prevention and was an important catalyst in creating the multi-professional primary care team. The nGMS Contract, which directly affects the 36,000 GPs in the UK and their patients, is a practice-based contract between the primary care organisation (PCO) and the practice, as opposed to a contract with each GP. It breaks the formal link between a named doctor and a named patient and substitutes a contract between organisations. The contract also enabled GPs to relinquish 24-hour responsibility for their patients, passing their role to a variety of different out of hours services and other professions, including nurse-led schemes. Organisational and informational continuity were therefore immediately challenged. A further consequence of the contract, particularly the extra workload and associated financial rewards of the pay for performance scheme (see below), was a sudden increase in the number of salaried GPs, from 1712 in 2003 to 5400 full-time equivalents in 2008, while the number of GP profit-sharing principals remained largely stable at 28,000 (Information Centre, 2007). This expansion of a largely part-time, salaried, female work-force also has consequences for interpersonal continuity at a practice level.

A key part of the 2003 contract was the introduction of a pay for performance system, the Quality and Outcomes Framework (QOF). This consists of over 130 evidence-based indicators, each with payment attached, in clinical, organisational, additional services and patient experience domains of primary care. Seventy per cent of the associated points, and therefore the payments, are focused on clinical areas. The original aims of the framework were both to improve the quality of care delivered in general practice and reward practices for the delivery of existing high quality care. Paul Shekelle (2004, p. 458), in the US-based Research and Development Corporation (RAND), called QOF: 'The boldest such proposal on this scale ever attempted anywhere in the world … with one mighty leap, the NHS vaults over anything being attempted in the United States, the previous leader in quality improvement initiatives.' One of the most striking features of the QOF has been the high level of practice achievement. The average number of points scored in the first year was 959 points (91.3 per cent of total available). This increased to 96.8 per cent in 2006/7 (Information Centre, 2008b).

There have been many positive intended consequences of QOF and some not so positive unintended ones. QOF has, first and foremost, provided a mechanism for an ongoing programme of quality improvement in primary care. This is unique among health care systems in developed countries, and the UK is now regarded as a world leader in quality improvement initiatives. QOF also appears to have contributed to an improvement in both the process of care and intermediate health outcomes for patients with a range of clinical conditions, although the size of the contribution is uncertain (Campbell *et al.*, 2007). Low-scoring practices in deprived areas are also seemingly just as able to improve the quality of their care, as measured by QOF, as low-scoring practices in more affluent ones (Doran *et al.*, 2008). This offers the tantalising prospect of QOF as a truly equitable public health intervention. Others, however, have criticised QOF as encouraging and rewarding a reductionist 'tick box' approach to medicine (Heath *et al.*, 2007). The development of QOF is now be led by NICE, which suggests that it has become part of the fabric of primary care.

There are nine indicators relevant to people with mental health problems (see Table 3.1). Those for depression focus on case finding in people with a physical condition where depression is more prevalent, for example after a heart attack (Lesperance *et al.*, 2002), and on assessing the severity of symptoms. Kendrick *et al.* (2005) found that likelihood of being prescribed an antidepressant increased significantly with severity on a validated depression measure and was associated with improved targeting of antidepressant treatment when compared to a study carried out in the same area prior to the introduction of the measure. The most recently introduced indicator has incentivised active follow-up of people diagnosed with depression, recognising that despite an evidence base that demonstrates early cessation of treatment is associated with a greater risk of relapse, treatment is often episodic and short-lived (Kates and Mach, 2007). Indicators for people with a diagnosis of schizophrenia or bipolar disorder are largely focused on providing an evidence-based annual physical health check, recognising the morbidity and mortality associated with the diagnosis and treatment of serious mental illness (DRC, 2006).

The achievement on these indicators is around 90 per cent compared to about 99 per cent for coronary heart disease, perhaps echoing the physicians'

Table 3.1	QOF indicators for mental health problems

Records	Points	thresholds
MH 8. The practice can produce a register of people with schizophrenia, bipolar disorder and other psychoses	4	
Ongoing management		
MH 9. The percentage of patients with schizophrenia, bipolar affective disorder and other psychoses with a review recorded in the preceding fifteen months. In the review there should be evidence that the patient has been offered routine health promotion and prevention advice appropriate to their age, gender and health status	23	(40–90 per cent)
MH 4. The percentage of patients on lithium therapy with a record of serum creatinine and thyroid stimulating hormone blood test in the preceding fifteen months	1	(40–90 per cent)
MH 5. The percentage of patients on lithium therapy with a record of lithium levels in the therapeutic range within the previous six months	2	(40–90 per cent)
MH 6: The percentage of patients on the register who have a comprehensive care plan documented in the records agreed between individuals, their family and/or carers as appropriate	6	(25–50 per cent)
MH 7: The percentage of patients with schizophrenia, bipolar affective disorder and other psychoses who do not attend the practice for their annual review who are identified and followed up by the practice team within fourteen days of non-attendance	3	(40–90 per cent)
Diagnosis and initial management		
DEP 1: The percentage of patients on the diabetes register and/or the CHD register for whom case finding for depression has been undertaken on one occasion during the previous fifteen months using two standard screening questions	8	(40–90 per cent)
DEP 2: In those patients with a new diagnosis of depression, recorded between the preceding 1 April to 31 March, the percentage of patients who have had an assessment of severity at the outset of treatment using an assessment tool validated for use in primary care	25	(40–90 per cent)
DEP 3: In those patients with a new diagnosis of depression and assessment of severity recorded between the preceding 1 April to 31 March, the percentage of patients who have had a further assessment of severity five to twelve weeks (inclusive) after the initial recording of the assessment of severity	20	(40–90 per cent)

Note: For full details, see BMA/NHS Employers (2009)

'disease prestige hierarchy' (their views of the relative status of medical conditions and specialities) where heart disease is also top and mental illness close to the bottom (Album and Westin, 2008). However, the lower achievement in the depression indicators may also reflect the resistance expressed by some GPs to using a structured questionnaire to assess depression rather than listening to a story and asking appropriate questions.

The advent of practice-based commissioning

The idea that PCTs would extend indicative budgets to individual practices to commission a full range of services was initially raised in 1997 (Department of Health, 1997a). However it was brought firmly into the centre of the political arena in June 2004 when *The NHS improvement plan* (Department of Health, 2004b) indicated that, from April 2005, groups of GP practices that wished to do so would be given indicative commissioning budgets by their PCT (who would continue to be legally responsible for money and its administration), accompanied by data about the cost and volume of services patients from their practice were using in the local NHS. Unlike fund holding, the costs of services do not vary but are fixed according to a national tariff set as part of Payment by Results (Department of Health, 2006c). Practices are thus now able to retain a proportion of money saved by any new activity.

Practice-based commissioning was described as a key enabler for the policy of patient choice (Department of Health, 2004c), by helping GPs to identify a variety of different providers for their patients and in the longer term to add to the choices on offer by directly providing and commissioning new services themselves. It was also seen as important in achieving another key Government objective of providing care 'closer to home' (Department of Health, 2006a). Practice-based commissioning was, in addition, seen as a mechanism to secure longer-term savings by incentivising better delivery of preventive care and as a way of reducing GP hospital referrals (Curry and Thorlby, 2007). These are, of course, not necessarily compatible objectives.

Practice-based commissioning achieved 'universal coverage' in the sense that all PCTs had structures in place to implement it by December 2006 (Department of Health, 2007c). However, there is some evidence that 'buy-in' from GPs, and therefore implementation, is patchy. The 2008 Autumn GP practice survey, which includes practices from every PCT in England, found that 62 per cent supported practice-based commissioning, but a further 20 per cent were neutral (and the inference is that 18 per cent are less positive), and only just over half (56 per cent) had commissioned new services through it (Department of Health, 2008c). The quality and timeliness of information supplied to GPs has also been queried, as has the degree to which it is possible to transform the behaviour of yet to be engaged GPs (Lewis *et al.*, 2007). Many of these issues, of course, also reflect the problems created by constant structural reorganisation at PCT level.

There are particular concerns from mental health specialists that, unlike many other areas of the NHS, it is difficult to attach a price tag to mental health services and, indeed, mental health services are excluded from the Payment by Results scheme until at least 2010/11. Practice-based commissioning also requires consistent quality of service delivery and good quality information about services to be able to offer patients a meaningful choice. Neither of these is as far advanced in mental health services as in other parts of the NHS (Sainsbury Centre for Mental Health, 2004a). However with the exception of tertiary services, such as eating disorder services and forensic mental health services, all other services considered to be secondary care services are capable of being commissioned by practices with their indicative budgets, including, for example, CMHT, talking therapies and assertive outreach teams.

Primary care and mental health

As far back as the 1960s, when GPs in the UK were beginning to work in group practices, Michael Shepherd suggested 'the cardinal requirement for improvement of mental health services … is not a large expansion of and proliferation of psychiatric agencies, but rather a strengthening of the family doctor in his/her therapeutic role' (1966, p.176). The World Health Organization echoed this belief in 1978 (WHO, 1978) stating that the primary medical care team was the cornerstone of 'community psychiatry'. Throughout the next two decades, the emphasis both in international research and policy, was in documenting the extent of morbidity of mental health problems in primary care and the quality of care provided by primary care workers. A key theme was the need to increase the recognition and treatment of depression in the community through, for example, the development of guidelines for depression and numerous 'initiatives' on depression such as the Defeat Depression Campaign in the UK (Wright, 1995), the DART programme (Depression Awareness, Recognition and Treatment) (Regier et al., 1988) in the US and the Beyond Blue project in Australia. More recently, the focus has been on how to configure and deliver evidence- based mental health care in the community and how to develop the interface between primary and specialist care (WHO/WONCA, 2008).

In the UK, the majority of people with serious mental illness and with common mental health problems are now registered with a GP and we know that only approximately 10 per cent of people with a mental health problem (including up to 70 per cent of people with severe mental illness), are ever seen by secondary care mental health specialists (Kendrick et al., 2000; Kingsland and Williams, 1997; see also Table 3.2).

Mental health issues are the second most common reason for consultations in primary care (McCormick et al., 1995) and are the sole reason for seeing the doctor in 20–5 per cent of consultations (Goldberg and Huxley, 1992). A survey by the Mental Health After Care Association (1999) of nearly 2000 GPs in England found that they spent on average approximately 30 per cent of their time on mental health problems.

Table 3.2	Numbers of individuals with mental health problems per 1000 in different settings
10/1000	People admitted to an inpatient unit such as a hospital ward
20–30/1000	People referred to Outpatients/CMHT for further care
130/1000	People identified by the GP as having a mental health problem
230/1000	People in the GP waiting room with a mental health problem
250/1000	Community as a whole

Source: Summarised from Goldberg and Huxley (1992)

Mental health and physical health problems also frequently co–exist. People with chronic or recurring physical health problems, traditionally seen as the core work of primary care, often have higher rates of mental health problems than the general population. There is also a significant group of patients with medically unexplained symptoms, classically low back pain, who consult frequently and who often have significant mental health problems such as depression (Waxman *et al.*, 1999).

Box 3.3	Service users' views of the value of primary care

- In Faulkner and Layzell's (2000) study, a user-administered semi-structured questionnaire with 76 mental health service users in six geographical areas across the UK emphasised that satisfaction is increased by longer consultations, and by a GP perceived as caring and who demonstrated respect for the patient's viewpoint. Access and continuity of care were also centrally important to service users
- Kai and Crosland's study (2001) involving in-depth interviews with 34 service users with enduring mental illness found that participants valued an empathetic and continuing therapeutic relationship with professionals in primary care
- Lester *et al.*'s study (2003) with 45 users with serious mental illness in Birmingham found that longitudinal and interpersonal continuity of care, relative ease of access and option of a home visit were valued features of primary care. This was often contrasted with the difficulty of seeing a constant stream of new faces in secondary care mental health services, with painful life stories told and retold for staff rather than patient benefit
- Gask *et al.*'s study of the quality of care for service users with depression (2003) found that the ability to offer structured care and proactive follow-up was important, since non-attendance may signal deterioration rather than recovery and the illness itself may preclude the assertiveness sometimes required to negotiate access
- Lester *et al.*'s focus group study of 45 patients with serious mental illness, 39 GPs and eight practice nurses (2005) found that where health professionals perceived serious mental illness as a life-long condition, patients emphasised the importance of therapeutic optimism and hope for recovery in consultations

Primary care is frequently criticised for the standard of mental health care delivered (Docherty, 1997; Tiemans *et al.*, 1996). However, as described above, primary care is a complex environment – a messy swamp of experiences and interpretations that rarely conform to textbook definitions (Schon, 1983). Many GPs also have little formal training in mental health. One survey found that only one third of GPs had had mental health training in the last five years, while 10 per cent expressed concerns about their training or skills needs in mental health (Mental Health After Care Association, 1999). Detection and diagnosis can also be affected by the way patients present their problems. Some people are reluctant to talk about their mental health symptoms and, even within the lower-stigma setting of primary care, are worried about the effects of divulging symptoms of mental illness.

There is, relatively speaking, little published about the views of service users with mental health problems on primary care, although a number of features, particularly access and interpersonal and longitudinal continuity of care, appear to be particularly valued (Freeman *et al.*, 2002) (see Box 3.3).

Improving access to psychological therapies

Each week 1 million people report sick. Of these, 3000 are still off work six months later, and 80 per cent of those 3000 are still off work five years later. The evidence shows that if a person is off work for twelve months, they are unlikely to return to work for another seven years. If they have been off work for two years, the chances of returning to work decline even further, to the point that they are more likely to retire rather than ever return to work (Sainsbury Centre for Mental Health, 2007a, 2007b; Waddell and Burton, 2006). Forty per cent of the 2.7 million claimants of Incapacity Benefit (now Employment and Support Allowance) have a mental health problem (Oxford Economics, 2007). However, anxiety and depression (and indeed many other common mental health problems) can be treated successfully in primary care.

NICE guidelines on depression (NICE, 2009) recommended that cognitive behavioural therapy (CBT) be provided as the treatment of choice for patients who had mild depression and also in combination with antidepressants in more severe cases. The 2004 NICE guidelines on anxiety disorders recommend CBT for panic disorder and for generalised anxiety disorder (GAD), as the intervention for which there is evidence of the longest duration of effect (NICE, 2004b). Two years after the NICE guidance was published, Lord Layard, a health economist at the London School of Economics, published an influential report on the costs of not treating anxiety and depression (Centre for Economic Performance's Mental Health Policy Group, 2006). The report stated that around 2.75 million people in England visit GP surgeries each year with mental health problems amenable to psychological therapies. Of these, around 4 per cent (11,000 people) receive non-directive counselling, 3 per cent (8000) other 'psychotherapy' and only around 1 per cent (2500) receive CBT. The Layard Report recommended that the number of people referred for CBT each year should rise to around 800,000 in England. One of the central tenets of his argument was an economic one, based on the number of people on Incapacity Benefit for mental health problems. Layard argued that: 'someone on Incapacity Benefit costs £750 a month in extra benefit and lost taxes. If the person works just a month more as a result of the treatment (which is £750), the treatment pays for itself' (Centre for Economic Performance's Mental Health Policy Group, 2006, p. 2).

One of the positive responses to this situation has been the implementation of the Improving Access to Psychological Therapies (IAPT) programme. In October 2007 the Secretary of State for Health announced funding of £33 million in 2008/9, £7 million in 2009/10 and a further £70 million in 2010/11 to train 3600 new therapists at various skill levels who will be able to offer a limited number of sessions of psychological treatment to around 900,000 people. This is a rolling programme currently available in about 32 PCTs across England but becoming England-wide, enabling GPs to offer people with anxiety and depression a range of different treatment options. There is a parallel expansion of computer-delivered CBT as part of the same programme (Department of Health, 2007d). There is, however, a certain naivety in expecting a CBT-based technical fix to significantly reduce the number of people on Incapacity Benefit and the fiscal reasoning behind government support for IAPT is perhaps at odds with the other main driver of promoting social inclusion through a return to work.

The role of practice nurses in primary care and mental health

As described earlier in this chapter, the concept of a primary care team did not really become established until the 1970s. Indeed, the number of directly employed primary care-based practice nurses remained very low until the mid-1980s. However, between 1982 and 1992, the numbers rose more than six-fold from 1515 to 9640 (NHS Executive, 1996), aided by incentives in the 1990 GP Contract. By 1995 there were 18,000 practice nurses in England, equivalent to almost 10,000 full-time equivalent staff; by 2001 this had risen to 11,163 (RCGP, 2002) and in 2007 there were 14,554 full-time equivalent practice nurses in England (Information Centre, 2008c).

Mental health issues are a significant part of the workload of many practice nurses. Between 13 and 43 per cent of nurses feel that early identification of anxiety and depression is a routine part of their role (Thomas and Corney, 1993) and most spend more time responding to psychological problems than managing diabetes or asthma. Practice nurses also work with people with chronic physical illnesses who are often at particularly high risk of developing mental illness. Many practice nurses are also increasingly involved with people with serious mental illness (Kendrick et al., 1998). A national survey of practice nurse involvement in mental health interventions found that 51 per cent were administering depots (injections of anti-psychotic drugs) at least once a month, 33 per cent were involved in ensuring compliance with anti-psychotic medication and 30 per cent with monitoring side effects of medication. Up to 56 per cent of practice nurses were also involved in counselling people with depression (Gray et al., 1999).

Despite this, few practice nurses have had specific training in mental health issues. Only 2 per cent of practice nurses have had dedicated mental health training and, in a survey published in 1999, up to 70 per cent of practice nurses reported receiving no mental health training at all in the previous five years (Gray *et al.*, 1999). It is therefore perhaps unsurprising that many practice nurses report a lack of confidence in their ability to talk to and treat people with mental health problems (Armstrong, 1997; Crosland and Kai, 1998) and that a randomised controlled trial found that practice nurses only detected 16 per cent of patients who probably had mental health problems when screened using a tool called the GHQ-12 (Plummer *et al.*, 2000).

However, practice nurses do have considerable transferable experience, for example, in running specialist clinics for patients with chronic physical health problems that incorporate systematic assessment of symptoms, treatment

---

Box 3.4	Evidence-based roles for practice nurses in primary care mental health

Problem solving: practice nurses trained to deliver six sessions of problem solving in primary care for patients with depression showed significant improvements on patient depression rating scales at twelve weeks (Mynors-Wallis *et al.*, 2000).

Telehealth initiatives: a randomised controlled trial involving practice nurse-based telephone follow-up for patients starting antidepressant medication was found to improve symptom resolution and increase user satisfaction with care (Hunkeler *et al.*, 2000).

Medication adherence: a randomised controlled trial evaluating two different methods of improving adherence with antidepressant medication found that, for people with major depression, practice nurse counselling significantly improved adherence to medication from 50–66 per cent at twelve weeks with the expected clinical benefits (Peveler *et al.*, 1999).

Self-help treatments: practice nurses may have a role to play facilitating skill acquisition for patient self-help for anxiety (Kupshik and Fisher, 1999).

Screening for co-morbidity: psychological morbidity in patients with chronic physical illness is more prevalent than in the general population. Practice nurses often know these patients very well and are ideally placed to make mental health assessments and offer psychological support to their patients, for example, as part of asthma (Rimington *et al.*, 2001) and cardiovascular clinics (Sorohan *et al.*, 2002).

Practice nurse-led walk-in depression clinics: a clinic in primary care was well received by patients and had good medication adherence rates and follow-up rates at four and six months (Symons *et al.*, 2002).

Collaborative care: The Pathways Study (Katon *et al.*, 2004) in the US targeted people with both diabetes and depression or dysthymia and evaluated a collaborative care model. This featured stepped treatment delivered by a specially trained nurse in collaboration with the primary care physician. The Pathways collaborative care model improved depression care and outcomes in patients with co-morbid major depression and/or dysthymia and diabetes.

effects and side effects, the use of protocols for modifying management and proactive follow-up of non-attendees. There is also an evidence base demonstrating the value and effectiveness of practice nurse-led or nurse-run interventions where nurses have been trained to manage mental health problems, particularly where this is part of a larger multifaceted programme (see Box 3.4).

The role of nurses in general and practice nurses in particular is currently undergoing a rapid re-evaluation and expansion. From being seen as the doctor's hand maiden, largely employed to undertake health promotion and prevention duties, practice nurses have opportunities, under the nGMS Contract, to become partners in a practice and to take on more advanced and specialised roles (Department of Health, 2003a; NHS Confederation, 2003). They can extend their interests from the clinical to the business aspects involved in a practice and, with appropriate training, become sub- or specialist providers of services such as mental health. This advanced role mirrors the general direction of change within the wider NHS, with traditional professional hierarchies challenged by a changing workforce, greater emphasis on continuing professional development and a clinical governance agenda that values quality and performance as much as qualification.

The new primary care mental health workforce

The NHS plan (Department of Health, 2000a) heralded the development of a number of new roles to help develop and deliver better quality mental health services. A key component was the commitment that:

> One thousand new graduate primary care mental health workers, trained in brief therapy techniques of proven effectiveness, will be employed to help GPs manage and treat common mental health problems in all age groups, including children. (Department of Health, 2000a, p. 119)

This role has since been developed through further guidance (Department of Health, 2001f, 2003b), with workers usually based in a primary care setting, employed by the PCT and supervised by secondary care specialists.

Although the exact nature of their role may depend on their professional background, the content of their training and local needs, many primary care graduate mental health workers (PCGMHWs) focus on face-to-face client work, including provision of CBT, and on developing the infrastructure of primary mental health care. Some also have a liaison role with both the voluntary sector and secondary care mental health professionals (see Box 3.5).

Recent research has suggested that PCGMHWs are valued by patients, increase satisfaction with care and are cost neutral (England and Lester, 2007; Lester *et al.*, 2007). However, the lack of clarity about the different roles, and the implied differing degrees of autonomy and job complexity have raised concerns among some health professionals. Bower *et al.* (2004)

Box 3.5	Roles and responsibilities of primary care graduate mental health workers

Client work: brief evidence-based interventions such as anxiety management and CBT for people with common mental health problems. Information, assessment, screening and onward referral in partnership with the primary care team. Support for self-help, and mental health promotion.

Practice team work: to provide support for audit, development of a mental illness register, routine measures of outcomes, and for integration of service users and carers into mental health service systems.

Work in the wider community: liasing with primary care team members and statutory (housing, welfare and benefits) and non-statutory sector services (charitable and voluntary sector), as well as specialised services to provide effective services to patients including those with serious mental illness, who are managed in primary care.

found disagreement and ambiguity among some respondents around the relationship with the work undertaken by other mental health professionals such as counsellors, psychologists and nurses. Barriers to successful implementation included the need to address variation in the level and quality of supervision and in payment and terms of service of workers (Fletcher *et al.*, 2008). These issues may help to explain why the five-year review of the NSF in 2004/5 found only 600 PCGMHWs in place (Department of Health, 2004a). However, more hopefully, an audit of higher education programmes offering the postgraduate certificate programme for this role identified 735 individuals entering training between January 2004 and August 2006 (Baguley *et al.*, 2006). The evidence to date, therefore, suggests that, if utilised and implemented effectively, PCGMHWs will be a useful adjunct to the primary care mental health team.

General Practitioners with Special Interests

The RCGP has defined General Practitioners with Special Interests (GPwSIs) as GPs with additional training and experience in a specific clinical area who take referrals for the assessment/treatment of patients that may otherwise have been referred directly to a secondary care consultant; or who provide an enhanced service for particular conditions or patient groups (RCGP, 2006). GPwSIs were originally heralded in *The NHS plan* (Department of Health, 2000a) which stated that by 2004 'up to 1,000 specialist GPs will be taking referrals from fellow GPs for conditions in specialties such as ophthalmology, orthopaedics, dermatology and ear nose and throat surgery. They will also be able to undertake diagnostic procedures such as endoscopy' (ch. 12, para.7). The GPwSI initiative is part of the broader government drive to keep care as close to home as possible, and the role should find a natural place within a system of practice-based commissioning and nationally and locally enhanced services.

The emerging evidence base (in the context of dermatology) suggests that GPwSIs are more costly than hospital outpatient care, are more accessible, are preferred by patients and achieve similar clinical results (Coast *et al.*, 2005; Salisbury *et al.*, 2005). According to national guidance, GPwSIs in mental health will have a clinical role in 'providing assessment, advice, information and treatment on behalf of primary care colleagues for patients with common mental health problems ... in most cases working alongside other mental health providers ... and supporting the development of care pathways across the primary–secondary–community interface' (Department of Health, 2003c, p. 2). At the moment, fewer than 5 per cent of PCTs are able to identify a GP with this role although over 25 per cent state they plan to do so (Pinnock *et al.*, 2005). From April 2009, GPwSIs in a clinical area have to be accredited in line with new competency frameworks (see www.rcgp. org. uk).

Creating a new model of primary mental health care

Primary care, as we have seen, now employs a mental health workforce of its own and is in a position to commission and run services. All these changes have meant adjustments in the way in which primary care now conceptualises itself and how other parts of the health and social care sector respond. This has provided a number of opportunities to re-examine how mental health services could be constructed and organised in primary care.

There are currently four main working models of mental health care at the interface of primary/secondary care, all translocated from secondary care services (Gask *et al.*, 1997) (see Box 3.6). Although it could be argued that these models are part of a continuum that patients can access to meet varying needs at different stages in their illness, in practice, the variation in availability of locality-based resources means that primary care practitioners are often only able to access one or at best two of the models described in Box 3.6 at a single point in time.

Box 3.6	Traditional models of mental health care at the primary/secondary interface

1. Community mental health teams that provide increased liaison and crisis intervention.
2. Shifted outpatient clinics where psychiatrists operate clinics within health centres.
3. Attached mental health workers, usually community psychiatric nurses (CPNs), designated to work with those with mental health problems in a primary care setting.
4. The consultation liaison model where primary care teams are provided with advice and skills from specialist mental health services.

Each of these models has particular strengths and weaknesses, yet none fully recognise primary care's central role in delivering good quality mental health care. For example:

1. The creation of community mental health teams often brings about a major increase in the rate of new patients referred, but the new clientele consists largely of patients with common mental health problems who might otherwise have been managed by their GP. There are also problems with non-attendance at community mental health team appointments (Killaspy *et al.*, 2000a) and the issue of 'inappropriate' referrals, where patients are seen on one occasion in secondary care and assessed as requiring a different type of response. Communication across the primary/secondary care interface can also be slow or incomplete, with missing information in referral letters and delayed clinic letters adversely affecting patient care (Killaspy *et al.*, 1999).
2. The shifted outpatient model attracts similar referrals and has similar significant non-attendance rates as traditional outpatient appointments in a hospital setting (Murray, 1998). It also appears that both the community mental health team and shifted outpatient models lead to little improvement in GP mental health skills (Warner *et al.*, 1993).
3. The impact of attached mental health professionals on referral patterns is still unclear. A Cochrane Review of the effect of on-site mental health workers in primary care found that the effect on consultation rates is inconsistent (Bower and Sibbald, 2003). Referral to a mental health professional reduces the likelihood of a patient receiving a prescription for psychotropic drugs or being referred to specialist care, but the effects are restricted to patients directly under the care of the mental health professional. Roles and responsibilities are also unclear with consequently less efficient working patterns (Corney, 1999).
4. The Cochrane Review (Bower and Sibbald, 2003) also concluded that consultation liaison interventions may cause short-term changes in psychotropic prescribing, but these are usually limited to patients under the direct care of the mental health worker.

The aspiration to achieve closer integration between primary care and community services should now enable the development of more integrated approaches to delivering primary mental health care. This direction of travel towards more integrated working reflects the growing emphasis on a partnership approach throughout health and social care. The extended role of the practice nurse and creation of GPwSIs (Gerada *et al.*, 2002) and PCGMHWs, the GMS guidance on care for people with severe long-term mental health problems, the prominence given to the new workforce in primary care in *The national service framework for mental health – five years on* (Department of Health, 2004a) and the opportunities offered through practice-based commissioning also provide opportunities for developing a more integrated approach to primary care mental health.

What does an 'integrated approach' to primary care mental health look like?

An integrated approach is not one particular model of care but rather a way of working that acknowledges the importance of creating seamless patient pathways through the health system and which avoids the dichotomy of either physical or mental health when defining and treating a patient's problems. From a structural perspective, integrated care goes one step beyond collaboration to co-ordination and often co-location of care. Recent work on the model of 'collaborative' care which developed in the US (Katon and Unutzer, 2006) and builds on earlier work on redesign of delivery systems for people with chronic health problems such as diabetes, is now generating a great deal of interest in terms of developing more integrated approaches to delivering primary care mental health services. Recent guidelines for the care of depression in the UK (NICE, 2009) have also highlighted the concept of 'stepped care' in service delivery, with differing levels of intensity of care from primary to specialist care provided seamlessly with decision-making about 'stepping up' or 'stepping down' according to severity, progress and patient choice. Models of integrated working based on collaborative care both in depression and for people with serious mental illness are currently being trialled in the UK.

To be sustainable, any integrated approach needs to be underpinned by opportunities for health professionals from different backgrounds to train and learn together. It depends on good communication across the interface, particularly around criteria for referral and discharge (NICE, 2003; WHO, 2004). Work, largely from the US, suggests that a more integrated approach to care has a number of benefits compared to usual practice (see Box 3.7).

Box 3.7	The benefits of integrated primary mental health care

- It can improve adherence to medication and satisfaction with care. A US initiative, involving collaborative management by the primary care physician and psychiatrist, improved adherence to antidepressant regimens in patients with persistent depression (Katon et al., 1999)
- It is the best way of improving the skills of primary care providers in dealing with the psycho-social aspects of care, with training through teamwork and a significant transfer of expertise between team members (Mauksch and Leahy, 1993)
- Integrated approaches appear to break even or be cost saving in the longer term (Blount, 1998)

Barriers to partnership working

The emergence of a primary care agenda for the integration of mental health service delivery has sometimes been seen as more of a problem than an opportunity. Change, particularly if it impacts on professional roles and boundaries, can be perceived as threatening the power base of that individual or team and needs to be discussed in an open and non-confrontational way. The success of a more integrated approach to care will therefore depend on a number of factors (see Box 3.8).

Box 3.8 — **Factors affecting the success of integrated working**

- New services are often championed by 'hero innovators' who are likely to move on and seek fresh challenges once a service is up and running (Georgiades and Phillimore, 1975). To be truly sustainable, new approaches to working need to be team owned, and not dependent on single individuals
- Change in working practices requires a commitment from primary care health professionals and PCTs to the issue. There is, however, evidence to suggest that the *NSF for mental mealth* was being marginalised in some PCT agendas, unable to compete on an equal footing with other clinical priorities (Rogers *et al.*, 2002)
- New ways of working rely on secondary mental health workers being comfortable and valued within a primary care working environment (Katon *et al.*, 1996; Peck and Greatley, 1999). Secondary care skills and knowledge in key areas such as triage, risk assessment and delivery of specific psychological therapies need to be acknowledged and valued when new integrated approaches to care are debated

---

Conclusion

During the last twenty years, primary care has become increasingly central to the development and delivery of good quality NHS care. The emergence of PCTs has resulted in primary care exerting a significant influence over the shape and provision of services and has had a domino effect on the rest of the NHS.

This quiet primary care revolution has seen the end of the monopoly over provision of independently contracted GPs, changes to access and continuity, the implementation of an innovative pay for performance scheme and, latterly, a renewed interest in primary care-based commissioning. Primary care is set for even more change in the next few years, with reforms that will inevitably lead to in an expansion of market forces in primary health care (Pollock *et al.*, 2007). Change can, of course, create opportunities, but may also lead to uncertainties for the primary care workforce which impact on patient care.

While mental health has always been a core part of primary care, this central role has only recently been recognised through policy imperatives around the new mental health workforce and opportunities to re-examine how mental health services could be constructed and organised in primary care (Department of Health, 2004a). However, in the rush for the new, it is important to remember that a key strength of UK primary care is the open access, cradle to grave approach, where the patient is seen as part of a complex network of family, friends, work and social life. As David Widgery, who was a socialist GP in the East End of London and political writer and activist, wrote prophetically in 1991 (p. 32):

> It is a process of decivilisation in which what doctors prided as a personal relationship between themselves and the patient, is now reshaped by the commodity process. Prevention for populations, service according to need, the family doctors' very idea of themselves as people who had time to grieve with their patients, to share the joy of childbirth, the crisis of illness and the time of day in the corner shop, are swept away.

Reflection exercises

1. Setting up a clinic for people with serious mental illness

Exercise for practice nurses, GPwSIs, PCGMHWs, CPNs

The nGMS GP Contract suggests the provision of structured care for people with schizophrenia and bipolar disorder should include the creation of a practice-based register and an annual health review. As a group, discuss the strengths and weaknesses of a more structured approach including:

■ The value of reviewing people when they are well and the effect this may have on the health professional/patient relationship
■ What that review should ideally contain and why (and then check your views against the latest QOF guidance in this area, available on both the BMA and DH websites)
■ How primary care and secondary can work together to ensure the best outcomes for the patient

2. Improving access to psychological therapies

Universal exercise

As a group, explore how local pathways to psychological therapies work in your area. Consider:

■ Who can refer and to whom?
■ How long are the waiting times for treatment?
■ Is the CBT provided suitable for patients with a range of problems (e.g. post traumatic stress disorder, as well as more common mental health problems)?

Consider, also, the role of the voluntary sector in providing CBT and/or counselling. It might be useful to compile a local compendium of services that you have considered, contacted and ideally visited that can be regularly updated. Issues you might want to consider include:

■ Can people self-refer?
■ Are there associated costs with using the service?
■ How are issues of risk and confidentiality managed?

If based in England, you might also like to find out whether the IAPT programme is now running in your area, and reflect on the barriers and facilitators to implementation of the scheme in your locality.

Suggestions for further reading

1. Armstrong, E. (2002) *The guide to mental health for nurses in primary care*. Abingdon, Radcliffe Medical Press

   This is an easy to digest book with practical descriptions of the roles nurses can play in improving the care of people with mental health problems. It has disease-specific and more generic chapters, for example, on health promotion and stigma.

2. Elder, A. and Holmes J. (2002) *Mental health in primary care*. Oxford, Oxford University Press

   This thought-provoking four-part book is structured to reflect encounters in the consulting room, reflective practice, mental health thinking in the surgery and perspectives from secondary care (including chapters on postnatal depression, eating disorders, substance misuse and management of serious mental illness). There are beautifully written descriptions of the importance of using time, of bearing witness to patients' lives, of the importance of containment, of being a 'good enough' GP, of Balint's work on the function of the doctor as a drug, and gentle but pragmatic reminders of precipitating factors for burnout and ways to decrease the likelihood of this happening.

3. Cohen, A. (2008) *Delivering mental health in primary care*. London, Royal College of General Practitioners

   This edited book provides a practical introduction to many of the issues faced by practitioners trying to deliver high quality evidence-based primary care mental health. It is perhaps of most interest to GPs and practice nurses.

4. Gask, L. *et al.* (eds) (2009) *Primary care mental health*. London, Royal College of Psychiatrists

   This comprehensive edited book is international in its focus and includes chapters on clinical issues, research, epidemiology, the sociology of primary care mental heath, service organisation and delivery and how to stay healthy as a health or social care professional.

5. See also WHO Europe (2008): *Policies and practices for mental health in Europe: meeting the challenge* (available online via: www.euro.who. int/eprise/main/WHO/Progs/MNH/baseline/20080602_1?language) and WHO/WONCA (2008) *Integrating mental health into primary care: a global perspective* (available online via: www.who.int/mental_health/ policy/services/mentalhealthintoprimarycare/en/index.html).

4 Community Mental Health Services

In this chapter we discuss:

- The origins of community mental health care
- The development and roles of generic CMHTs
- The advent and impact of functionalised teams
- Alternative ways of providing community mental health services
- Social exclusion and mental health
- Positive practice in community inclusion

The origins of community mental health care

Although the term 'community' has been used in the English language since the fourteenth century (Williams, 1976), the precise origins of its meaning are difficult to pinpoint. It is similarly almost impossible to say, with any degree of accuracy, where the phrase 'community care' comes from. Titmuss claimed he had tried and failed to discover any precise social origin for the phrase but went on to reflect: 'institutional policies both before and since the Mental Health Act of 1959 have without a doubt assumed that someone knows what it means' (1968, p. 105).

At the beginning of the twenty-first century, most people in the UK, including those with serious mental illness, are now cared for in the community. They are seen by locality-based CMHTs rather than in outpatients in District General Hospitals and are likely to be treated in their own homes by specialised mental health teams when acutely unwell, rather than admitted to an inpatient ward. Indeed, the number of working-age adults recorded as admitted to an inpatient ward has consistently reduced during the last decade, with a reduction of nearly 9 per cent between 2005/6 and 2006/7 (CSIP, 2008).

There are multiple complex political and economic reasons underpinning the development of community care (see Chapter 2 for a detailed discussion) and the move towards our current community-based mental health care system has been slow and incremental. The rise of community care was probably heralded by the 1930 *Mental Treatment Act*, which enabled voluntary treatment in 'Mental Hospitals' for the first time and legitimised local authority spending on outpatient care. Perhaps the next significant step was the move by a handful of 'Mental Hospitals', just after the Second World War, towards an 'open-door' rather than a locked-ward system. At approximately the same time, a small number of hospital-based nurses were seconded to work within the wider community as prototype CPNs and the first mental health day hospital was opened in London in 1946 (Bierer, 1951).

CPN practice, as we might recognise it today, began at Warlingham Park Hospital (Croydon) in 1954. Dr Rees, the Physician Superintendent, decided that a pragmatic method of relieving pressure on hospital beds would be to develop a psychiatric nursing service within the community. Two outpatient nurses were therefore seconded to work in the community, initially for a six-month trial period, although Lena Peat, one of the first two nurses, recalls that she in fact stayed for 23 years (Peat, 1979)! Gradually, as the role spread to other hospitals and settings, CPNs became responsible for the administration of depot (injectable) medication in the community, running clubs in day hospitals, checking up on patients who failed to keep appointments and providing support to relatives (Royal College of Psychiatrists, 1997). Some CPNs also became involved in delivering forms of psycho-social care including family therapy and CBT.

This new, extended nursing role initially met with a mixed response. White and Brooker (2001, p. 62) suggest:

> The Regional Health Authority disclaimed knowledge of the development, provided no extra funds and refused to recognise that the nurses who worked outside the hospital were part of the official establishment. In some situations, District Nurses insisted that only they could administer drugs to patients in their homes resulting in two nurses visiting the same patient. Some General Practitioners welcomed the assistance of the psychiatric nurses while others would have nothing to do with them. Even consultant psychiatrists were divided.

The 1959 *Mental Health Act* made two key provisions that helped to establish community mental health services. First, it required outpatient follow-up for patients who had been detained (sectioned) and therefore, in some sense, began to recognise the importance of continuity of care. Second, the Act legislated for the involvement of social workers in the care of people with mental illness.

As the process of asylum closure continued during the 1960s and 1970s, day hospitals and inpatient units in District General Hospitals became the central planks of community reprovision for people with serious mental illness (Burns, 2004). The process was, however, much slower than the policy makers and planners might have hoped. Between 1962 and 1970, the time period over which the *Hospital plan* (Ministry of Health, 1962) proposed a 43.4 per cent reduction in asylum beds, the actual reduction was 14.8 per cent (Maynard and Tingle, 1975).

As we discussed in Chapter 2, the move towards community care was accompanied by concerns about the potential negative consequences of moving people out of long-stay wards into community accommodation. Perhaps the most influential and certainly the most detailed study of the outcomes of deinstitutionalisation was the Team for the Assessment of Psychiatric Services (TAPS) project. Established in May 1985 with the explicit purpose of evaluating the national policy of replacing psychiatric hospitals (in this case, Friern and Claybury Hospitals in north London) with district-based services, the study followed up 630 people who had been inpatients for a period of five years, giving a comprehensive picture of life and care in the community (see Box 4.1).

| Box 4.1 | **The outcomes of the TAPS project** |

- Nearly 80 per cent of people were discharged to staffed houses and two-thirds were still living in their original residence at the end of the five years
- 72 patients were considered to be too difficult to place in standard staffed homes and were transferred to high-staffed facilities. However, 40 per cent of this group were subsequently transferred to standard community homes by the end of the five years
- Reprovision did not increase death or suicide rates
- Four patients were estimated as lost to follow-up because of homelessness, giving a 'vagrancy' rate of 0.6 per cent over the study period
- There were 24 recorded criminal incidents committed by eighteen patients
- Psychiatric symptoms and social behaviour problems remained unchanged overall. The community homes were much less restrictive than the hospital wards with an average of ten rather than 26 rules. Although social networks did not enlarge, patients increased the number of people they could confide in
- Perhaps the biggest issue was that of readmission. The reprovision plans for the hospital closure included a reduction in beds in general hospitals which meant that, at times, there were no beds available for people in crisis. When admitted, many patients also found wards in general hospitals noisy, crowded and non-therapeutic
- The overall readmission rate was 38 per cent. Of these, one third of people remained in hospital for over one year, often because of a lack of rehabilitation services. These patients technically became long-stay patients once again
- Overall, there was little difference between hospital and community costs. Coupled with the outcome findings, the economic evaluation suggests that community-based care is more cost effective than long-stay hospital care

(Summarised from Leff *et al.*, 2000)

In parallel with the deinstitutionalisation agenda, multidisciplinary CMHTs began to be established across the country throughout the 1980s. CMHTs usually consisted of CPNs, psychiatrists, occupational therapists and psychologists with some form of integration with social services. A generic catchment area CMHT became available to over 80 per cent of the population by the early 1990s (Johnson and Thornicroft, 1993). The number of CPNs therefore increased from 717 in 1975 to 4351 in 1990 (White, 1990) and indeed now number over 9000. CMHTs were tasked with assessing and treating any adult patient referred to them, and supporting and advising local GPs. In fact, by 1993, CPNs were taking over 40 per cent of their referrals from primary care professionals (White, 1993). However, this also meant that CPNs and CMHTs began to focus on people with common mental health problems as well as people with serious mental illness.

In the last decade, and particularly since the publication of the *NSF for mental health* (NSF) (Department of Health, 1999a), community mental health debates have increasingly centred on the need for more specialised community-based mental health teams such as assertive outreach, crisis intervention/home treatment and early intervention teams. The findings from the TAPS project and the increasing recognition of so-called 'revolving door' patients (see Chapter 5) have also highlighted the effects of inadequate reprovision of beds for people who are 'difficult to place' and for the 'new long-stay' patients. The wider social inclusion agenda, particularly for people with serious mental illness, has also become a more prominent issue, since living within and being part of a community are very different outcomes. We explore these issues in more detail later in this chapter.

The development and roles of the generic CMHT

Since the 1980s, multidisciplinary generic CMHTs have been the main vehicle for delivering co-ordinated, comprehensive, community-based mental health services (Kingdon, 1989). A major tension, almost from inception, has been the caseload balance of people with short-term, more common mental health problems and those with serious and more enduring mental illness (Sayce *et al.*, 1991). The relatively disappointing effectiveness and cost-effectiveness outcomes in studies of CMHTs in the late 1980s (Gournay and Brooking, 1994,1995; Patmore and Weaver, 1991) and the fierce criticism in some quarters about CPNs' lack of appropriate training in treating people with common mental health problems helped convince policy makers in the 1990s that CPNs and CMHTs should focus on people with serious mental health problems. This was further reinforced by wider policy debates about care or control in the community (see Chapters 2 and 6) (Department of Health, 1994, 1998a), risk management and the introduction of the CPA (Department of Health, 1990a) (see Box 4.2).

Tensions over the most appropriate client groups for CPNs and for CMHTs were also increased by the advent of fund holding in the early 1990s, which enabled some practices to employ their own CPN and to then determine their role in mental health care provision (Monkley-Poole, 1995). CPNs were therefore left in a difficult position, torn between the different needs of client groups, employers and policy imperatives (Secker *et al.*, 2000).

The evidence base on the effectiveness of CMHTs is largely descriptive and relatively difficult to interpret because of variations in team structures and functions. As Burns (2004, pp. 49–50) suggests:

they evolved by word of mouth as clinicians tried to find ways of dealing with a changing health care system and rising expectations within fixed resources. As a result there have been many blind alleys along the way and enormous local variation in how they are managed, staffed and function … A consequence of this is that the 'feel' of CMHTs can vary enormously even if their core activities are fairly uniform.

However, the evidence suggests that, at least in comparison with a traditional psychiatric unit, CMHTs provide better quality care at both two and four years after referral (Gater *et al.*, 1997). Generic CMHT management also appears more effective than standard non-team hospital-orientated care for

---

Box 4.2   The Care Programme Approach

- CPA, introduced in 1991, became the cornerstone of the US-influenced 'case management' approach to care for people accepted by specialist mental health services. Outside mental health services, this type of care co-ordination was known as 'care management' and tended to fall under the remit of social workers rather than the NHS (Means *et al.*, 2008). Hardly surprisingly, this overlap led to a degree of confusion and duplication of effort, though changes in 2008 (see below) may go some way towards addressing this
- Led by health workers, CPA obliged health and other agencies to assess the individual needs of service users, construct care plans to meet these needs, identify a key worker to oversee each individual plan of care and undertake a regular multidisciplinary review of care, including issues of risk
- Revised guidance (Department of Health, 1999b) heralded the integration of CPA with care management to form a single care co-ordination approach, with health and social services jointly identifying a lead officer
- CPA was divided into two levels – standard and enhanced – until October 2008, when it was refocused, as part of the wider personalisation agenda, as a single new approach concentrating resources on those most at risk (e.g. people with complex needs and those requiring multi-agency input) (Department of Health, 2008d)
- It is interesting to note that a Cochrane Review (Marshall *et al.*, 1998) of case management for people with 'severe mental disorders' found no evidence that case management improves outcome on any social or clinical variable other than ensuring that more people remain in contact with psychiatric services (one extra person remains in contact for every fifteen people who receive case management)
- CPA does, at face value, appear to systematically assess health and social care needs, formulating a care plan, appointing a key worker and ensuring a regular review. However, some commentators argue that CPA is largely driven from a professional rather than user perspective and is focused on aspects of mental health and social needs that seek to keep people safe and well rather than adopting a holistic approach that seeks to help someone recover from mental illness on their own terms. Once again, it remains to be seen if recent changes in policy to address this by refocusing CPA are implemented in practice

people with serious mental illness, particularly in terms of accepting treatment and also in possibly reducing hospital admissions (Malone *et al.*, 2000).

CMHTs have also been criticised for having over-ambitious aims, and a tendency to neglect people with the most challenging health and social care needs (Patmore and Weaver, 1991). Their role in providing assessment and management of people with a range of needs and in integrating the health-led CPA with social services-led care management has meant that community mental health managers have had a difficult brokering role, often with no additional resources (Onyett *et al.*, 1997). The Sainsbury Centre for Mental Health (1998a) report, *Keys to engagement*, also noted that members of CMHTs frequently have caseloads that are too high to allow sufficient contact time to work effectively with people with serious mental illness.

Despite these controversies, CMHTs have flourished during the last twenty years, becoming the backbone of mental health services. Numbers have increased from 81 in 1987 (Sayce *et al.*, 1991) to 826 in 2006 (Centre for Public Mental Health, 2006) and their core roles have now been defined by the Department of Health (see Box 4.3 for a summary).

Box 4.3	The roles and responsibilities of CMHTs

1. Giving advice on the management of mental health problems by other professionals – in particular, advice to primary care and a triage function enabling appropriate referral.
2. Providing treatment and care for those with a time-limited disorder who can benefit from specialist interventions.
3. Providing treatment and care for those with more complex and enduring needs.

(Department of Health, 2002f)

There are, inevitably, a number of challenges for CMHTs in the coming years. The advent of practice-based commissioning may put pressure on them to develop services for people with more common mental health problems at the expense of their broader roles. The increasing policy focus on social inclusion, citizenship and rights will also add pressures both in terms of workload and resources to teams that have seen a net loss in nursing and social work staff since the advent of functionalised teams (Goldberg, 2008).

The advent of functionalised teams

Over time, the notion of a generic CMHT has been challenged and reassessed across the globe. Evidence from evaluations of service models in North America (Stein and Test, 1980) and Australia (Hoult, 1986) and successful remodelling of community mental health services in north Birmingham have been influential in the thinking and development of *functionalised* mental health teams in the UK. Functionalised teams are, in essence, specialist teams organised to provide for the needs of particular patient groups. This approach has been reinforced by the *NSF for mental health*, *The NHS plan* and a number of team-specific Policy Implementation Guides (Department of Health, 1999a, 2000a, 2001g). *The NHS plan*, for example, heralded the creation of 220 assertive outreach teams, 335 crisis resolution teams and 50 early intervention teams by 2004, with the *Mental health policy implementation guidance* (MH-PIG) describing the more detailed team structure and functions.

The MH-PIG on CMHTs states that 'Community Mental Health Teams will continue to be the mainstay of the system. CMHTs have an important and indeed integral role to play in supporting service users and families in community settings. They should provide the core round which newer service elements are developed' (Department of Health, 2002f, p. 3). Although the guidance is not prescriptive about the relationships between CMHTs and newer functionalised teams, it suggests that 'mutually agreed and documented responsibilities, liaison procedures and in particular transfer procedures need to be in place when crisis resolution, home treatment teams, assertive outreach teams and early intervention teams are being established' (2002f, p. 17). CMHTs are therefore seen as the central hub of mental health care, liaising with the more specialised teams as well as with primary care.

The roles and responsibilities of functionalised teams

Assertive outreach

Assertive outreach teams (AOTs) are the best developed, described and most evidence-based of the functionalised teams. They were first established in the late 1970s in Madison, Wisconsin, as the Programme for Assertive Community Treatment (PACT) (Stein and Test, 1980). This programme was essentially a form of intensive case management, with patients with serious mental illness who seemed likely to need an admission allocated either to intensive case management and given intensive help with social functioning and clinical care, or to standard treatment. A service evaluation found that patients in the PACT group were less likely to require inpatient admission, had improved clinical and social functioning and were more satisfied with their care. The service was also judged to be cost effective (see Box 4.4).

The funding for the original PACT ran out after fourteen months and the significant gains were lost almost as quickly as they were established, indirectly confirming the effectiveness of the programme. The programme was also replicated by a group in Australia (Hoult, 1986) with similar positive outcomes.

In the UK, the PRiSM (Psychiatric Research in Service Measurement) study was the first large-scale attempt to explore how community teams functioning in different ways might lead to different service outcomes (Thornicroft *et al.*, 1998a). PRiSM compared two contrasting service models

Box 4.4	The core components of PACT

The core components of PACT/AOTs were and continue to be:

■ Assertive follow-up
■ Small caseloads (ideally 10:1)
■ Increased frequency of contact (capacity to visit daily)
■ An emphasis on medication
■ Assertive engagement (tenacious, creative and innovative rather than aggressive)
■ Support for family and carers
■ Emphasis on relapse prevention
■ Crisis intervention
■ Availability twelve hours a day, seven days a week

for patients with psychosis: a standard generic CMHT and a more intensive two-team approach that incorporated a psychiatric acute care and emergency team and a psychiatric assertive continuing care team. The main study conclusion was that: 'on balance the results weigh slightly in favour of the two-team model for acute and continuing care in terms of clinical effectiveness, but the general model is almost as effective and is less expensive' (Thornicroft et al., 1998b, p. 423).

However, the results caused controversy when published, not least from proponents of functionalised models (Sashidharan et al.,1999). Marshall et al. (1999) also suggested that the PRiSM study had a number of flaws and in particular criticised it for evaluating a mixture of models of care. A Cochrane Review of assertive community treatment (ACT) for people with severe mental disorders (Marshall and Lockwood, 1998) also found that, compared to standard community care, patients receiving ACT were more likely to remain in contact with services, less likely to be admitted to hospital, spent less time in hospital and had better clinical and social outcomes in terms of accommodation, employment and satisfaction. The review also concluded that, when targeted on high users of inpatient care, ACT can substantially reduce the costs of hospital care. On balance, therefore, despite the equivocal outcomes of PRiSM, the evidence base for the value of an AOT approach is still relatively strong.

The MH-PIG (2001) suggests that AOTs are most appropriate for patients with:

■ Severe and persistent mental disorder associated with a high level of disability
■ A history of high use of inpatient or intensive home-based care
■ Difficulty in maintaining lasting and consenting contact with services
■ Multiple complex needs including self-harm, homelessness and substance misuse

This group has been estimated to be about 15,000 people at any one time in the UK (Sainsbury Centre for Mental Health, 1998a).

Although the AOT model has been well described, there were initially a number of uncertainties over how best to apply the core principles. A report from the Sainsbury Centre for Mental Health (Chisholm and Ford, 2004, p. vi) suggested that:

> Setting up AO teams means changing not merely structures and processes but cultures and attitudes within mental health services. Such a paradigm shift takes time and resources – it cannot be achieved overnight. It relies on an acceptance of the need for changes, good project management and a shared understanding of how services will be improved.

There are also potential tensions between fidelity to the AO model and individualised care and local flexibilities, and between assertive treatment and individual patient civil rights. As Burns (2004, p. 101) suggests, 'assertive outreach teams ... need to maintain a broad psychosocial approach to their patients while not losing sight of the central importance of evidence based medical practice. In short, their research based and prescribed approach is both their greatest strength and their Achilles' heel.'

Despite these concerns, considerable progress has been achieved in establishing new teams. By March 2004, 263 AO teams were in place (*The NHS plan* target was 220) and the number of staff recorded as either designated AO staff, or working within an AO team increased from 1742 in 2003 to 2762 in 2007 (CSIP, 2008). There are also high levels of satisfaction with services and good service user engagement, although research remains equivocal in terms of some hard outcomes such as number of days spent in hospital (Killaspy *et al.*, 2006). Interestingly, however, a recent systematic review of randomised controlled trials that compared the impact on the use of inpatient services of various forms of intensive case management (including assertive community treatment) with standard community mental health care found that the way in which the team organised its approach to the work and whether it was implemented in an area with high use of inpatient services accounted for the differences in findings (Burns *et al.*, 2007). Burns suggests that similarities in the organisation of the team between CMHTs and AO teams could explain the lack of efficacy in the UK, and concluded that case managers should work as teams rather than as individuals when caring for people with a severe mental illness. Killaspy (2007) has also suggested that the evidence base now highlights the critical success factors for AO as a team-based approach, extended hours and a high proportion of *in vivo* (home- or community-based) visits.

Crisis resolution (CR) and home treatment (HT) teams

CR teams have been in existence in the US and Australia since the 1980s. Just as the terminology with assertive outreach can be confusing, (PACT/ACT/AOT), the terms 'home treatment' and 'psychiatric emergency team' (PET) are sometimes used rather than 'crisis resolution'. Essentially, however, these services offer an alternative to inpatient care for people experiencing an acute mental health crisis. There have been two powerful drivers for developing CR/HT teams. Service users and carers have clearly asked for services to be available 24 hours a day, seven days a week (Minghella *et al.*, 1998), echoing the emphasis on quick response times (e.g. pain to needle time in chest pain) within the wider NHS. CR/HT have also been seen as a mechanism to reduce reliance on the ever-decreasing supply of inpatient beds.

Overall, the evidence suggests that CR/HT services may achieve reduced admissions and bed use (Glover *et al.*, 2006), better service retention and equal clinical outcomes to inpatient care (Johnson *et al.*, 2005). The services are also generally preferred by patients and relatives (Minghella *et al.*, 1998; Smythe and Hoult, 2000). Some, however, have suggested that such positive findings may reflect the commitment and charisma of the 'hero innovators' of home treatment and may be more difficult to replicate in everyday practice, particularly in rural areas (Burns, 2004; Coid 1994; Owen *et al.*, 2000).

The MH-PIG (Department of Health, 2001g) states that CR/HT should be targeted at adults (sixteen to 65 years old) with severe mental illness (schizophrenia, manic depressive disorders, severe depressive disorder) with an acute psychiatric crisis of such severity that, without the involvement of the CR/HT team, hospitalisation would be required (see Box 4.5).

Box 4.5	Core components of CR/HT teams

A CR/HT team should be able to:

- Act as a gate keeper to mental health services, rapidly assess individuals with acute mental health problems and refer them to the most appropriate services
- For individuals with acute severe mental health problems, for whom home treatment would be appropriate, provide immediate multidisciplinary community-based treatment 24 hours a day, seven days a week
- Remain involved with the person until the crisis has resolved and the service user is linked into ongoing care
- Have an assertive approach to engagement
- If hospitalisation is necessary, be actively involved in discharge planning and provide intensive care at home to enable early discharge
- Provide a time-limited intervention

(Department of Health, 2001g, pp. 11–12)

Teams are meant to cover approximately 150,000 people and have a case load of twenty to 30 service users shared between a multidisciplinary team of around fourteen people. The intensity of the service means that there is team but not necessarily health professional continuity of care. Although the guidance suggests patients should stay in contact with the team for three to four weeks, in practice it appears this may be as long as three to six months (Burns, 2004).

The National Audit Office (2007) reported that by 2007 there were 343 crisis resolution and home treatment teams across England (target 335) delivering over 95,000 episodes of care (target 100,000). They reported that the introduction of CR/HT has reduced pressure on beds as they support people that ought to be at home, and, in some cases, sped up discharge from hospital. They also reported favourable views of service users and carers about CR/HT, including the value of having this as an alternative to being admitted. However, they also reported a wide variety of development of CR/HTs nationally, with large differences in spending and on staffing levels between teams. They also estimated that full use of CR/HT services in appropriate cases costs approximately £600 less per crisis episode than one in which CR/HT is not available. Gate keeping by CR/HT services (being involved in all decisions of whether or not to admit a person to inpatient psychiatric care), is crucial to the success of services and indeed the ability to deliver effective and efficient returns to a local health economy. Department of Health guidance (2006d) defined full gate keeping as encompassing all requests for admission, including pending Mental Health Act assessments and assertive outreach. The National Audit Office, however, found that there was a significant way to go nationally for CR/HTs to be fully gate keeping. In a review of experiences of supporting CR/HTs, McGlynn (2007) also identified a number of problems including teams' lack of understanding of the role and their unrealistic expectations of other teams, rigid exclusion criteria and a lack of flexibility for those trying to access the system. The challenges now appear to be the need to isolate the key ingredients for success in CR/HTs, and then to implement teams in a way that makes sense within the wider local service context.

Early intervention services

Early intervention services (EIS) have been a feature of health care in Australia, Scandinavia and the US for over a decade. They have, however, only relatively recently become part of the landscape of UK mental health care. The policy imperative for EIS for young people with first-episode psychosis has been driven by user and carer dissatisfaction with existing poor quality services (Rethink, 2003a), health professional concerns about the state of services and a growing evidence base that links long duration of untreated psychosis (DUP) with poorer long-term prognosis (Norman and Malla, 2001). Evidence has also emerged in the last decade that the early phase following the onset of a first psychotic illness could be conceived of as a 'critical period', influencing the long-term course of the illness. Providing timely and effective interventions at this stage for the 7500 young people a year who suffer their first episode of psychosis (Department of Health, 2007e) might therefore alter the subsequent course of the illness and have a disproportionate impact relative to later interventions (Birchwood et al., 1998).

Evidence also suggests that patients' needs during the early phases of the illness differ from those of individuals with longer-standing illness and therefore require different treatment options (Norman and Townsend, 1999). Young people have to deal with the initial personal trauma of psychosis in addition to the normal anxieties associated with adolescence and young adulthood and have high hopes of returning to a normal level of functioning. Engagement, or the formation of a 'therapeutic alliance', is therefore crucial and can be fostered by developing youth-sensitive services in as flexible a way as possible.

Most of the EI evidence initially concentrated on justifying the need to provide services at an earlier stage in the illness. However the more recent evidence has focused on the effectiveness of EIS themselves. Data from the Lambeth Early Onset trial shows statistically significant differences in terms of relapse and rehospitalisation for young people in contact with the EIS compared to standard care (Craig et al., 2004). Early results from the OPUS trial, a large randomised clinical trial of integrated treatment versus standard treatment for patients with first-episode psychosis, also suggests that integrated treatment improves clinical outcomes and adherence to treatment at one- and two-year follow-up (Peterson et al., 2005). Lester et al. (2009) evaluated established and emerging EIS across the West Midlands and found high levels of service engagement at twelve months and of service user and carer satisfaction. The latest economic modeling of EIS suggests that over twelve months the EIS pathway for each individual is £5000 cheaper than standard care. Over three years, the saving is £14,500 for an EIS approach (CSIP, 2008). McCrone et al. (2008) suggest that the potential annual savings from expanding EIS could be in the region of £13–65 million for people with schizophrenia and £8–31 million for people with a bipolar disorder by 2026 because of a reduced need for services at a later stage. Despite this, there are still concerns about the need for a separate EIS at all (Burns, 2004; Pelosi and Birchwood, 2003) that perhaps reflect the age-old argument between the need for and relative value of specialists and generalists.

The MH-PIG (Department of Health, 2001g) states that EIS should be targeted at people aged between fourteen and 35 with a first presentation of psychotic symptoms during the first three years of psychotic illness. Key features of EIS in the MH-PIG are shown in Box 4.6.

The NHS plan originally suggested that there should be 50 EI teams across England and a national client total of 22,500 by December 2006. These targets were, however, missed. A mapping exercise jointly conducted by NIMHE and Rethink (Pinfold et al., 2007) found that funding difficulties were a barrier to development for at least half of the EIS contacted, exacerbated by new and inexperienced service commissioners in PCTs. The Department of Health therefore launched a recovery plan in 2006, to reconfirm EIS as a key government priority and get EI implementation back on track (Selbie, 2006). This appears to be having some effect, since EI recorded staffing increased from 206 in 2003 to 1136 in 2007 (591 per cent) with a further increase in staff between 2006 and 2007 of 25 per cent. It is also encouraging that

Box 4.6	Key features of EIS

EIS should be able to:

- Reduce the stigma associated with psychosis and improve professional and lay awareness of symptoms of psychosis and the need for early assessment
- Reduce the length of time young people are undiagnosed and untreated
- Develop meaningful engagement, provide evidence-based intervention and prioritise recovery during the early phase of illness
- Increase stability in the lives of service users, facilitate development and provide opportunities for personal fulfilment
- Provide a user-centred service – that is, a seamless service available for those from fourteen to 35 that effectively integrates child, adolescent and adult mental health services and works in partnership with primary care, education, social services and youth services
- At the end of the treatment period, ensure that care is transferred thoughtfully and effectively

(Summarised from Department of Health, 2001g, pp. 46–7)

Louis Appleby (mental health tsar) has gone on record saying that 'I now believe that early intervention will be the most important and far reaching reform of the NSF era. Crisis resolution has had the most immediate effect but I think early intervention will have the greatest effect on people's lives' (Appleby, 2008).

There remain plenty of challenges ahead for EI. The core components of an EIS are still not entirely clear, although the National Eden study will provide evidence in this area in 2011. There is also work to be done around relationships with adjacent teams, particularly entry points from Child and Adolescent Mental Health Services. As EI matures and more young people exit 'gold standard' services, discharge policies into usual care within a primary care setting also need to be carefully considered.

New ways of working

Linked to these changes, the former Care Services Improvement Partnership, the Royal College of Psychiatrists and the Department of Health brought out joint guidance on the roles and responsibilities of consultant psychiatrists (CSIP/NIMHE/Changing Workforce Programme/Royal College of Psychiatrists, 2005). *New ways of working* suggested that psychiatrists use their skills, knowledge and experience to the best effect by concentrating on service users with the most complex needs, acting as a consultant to multidisciplinary teams and promoting distributed responsibility and leadership across teams (see Box 4.7).

Box 4.7	Objectives of *New ways of working*

- To tailor the role of consultants and all mental health professionals to the new values and service configuration which were described in the NSF (Department of Health, 1999a) and *NHS plan* (Department of Health, 2000a) and which aim to address current expectations of service users
- To eliminate overworking of consultant psychiatrists, reduce their caseloads and allow them greater focus on more complex and higher risk cases
- To respond to the increasing aspirations and ability of non-medical mental health professionals for autonomy in clinical decision making and responsibility for patients
- To build multidisciplinary teams that can provide patients with the widest possible range of skills in assessment and care programme provision
- To ensure all professionals have the continuous support from and surveillance by other professionals that safe practice requires
- To eliminate current confusion over the responsibilities that consultant psychiatrists hold

(Summarised from CSIP/NIMHE/Changing Workforce Programme/Royal College of Psychiatrists, 2005)

New ways of working has required a significant culture change within mental health services and raised concerns around the ability of other disciplines to take on new roles given up by psychiatrists (Lelliott, 2008). Craddock *et al.* (2008, p. 8) go one step further, commenting that:

> It is easy to understand how we have arrived at the model of distributed responsibility and leadership as a pragmatic, short term response to recent crises in staffing and morale in general psychiatry. However we should not assume that this pragmatic emergency solution is an ideal, or even a desirable state of affairs. Although distributed responsibility may make life easier for psychiatrists and appears to be the cheaper option, it does not follow that this is in the best interest of patients.

A recent survey by the Royal College of Psychiatrists found that 66 per cent of psychiatrists across all areas of England reported that the principles of *New ways of working* were being adopted and applied in their Trusts (Kennedy, 2008), which suggests that, despite reservations from some quarters, implementation has been a relative success.

Alternative service provision within the community

As we discuss in Chapter 5, users frequently report negative inpatient experiences. Hospital beds are also a relatively scarce and expensive form of service provision. Yet government policies that emphasise patient choice mean that alternatives to inpatient wards, and indeed to the essentially medical model off the CR/HT team, are needed. Against this background, there are a small but growing number of alternatives to inpatient units, although few have been subject to rigorous evaluation or are widely available. Within a whole systems approach, users and their families, who particularly since *The NHS and Community Care Act* (1990) have shouldered the main responsibility for everyday care in the community, should ideally be offered a number of alternatives to acute admission, including crisis resolution/home treatment teams, user-led crisis houses, day hospitals and halfway hospitals/community inpatient units (see Box 4.8).

Box 4.8 **Some alternatives to inpatient care**

User-led crisis houses

There are a small number of user-led crisis houses in England, staffed or managed by service users or people with experience of crisis. An evaluation of three such houses by the Sainsbury Centre for Mental Health (2002a) found that in Anam Cara, a four-bed crisis house in Birmingham, 100 per cent of those interviewed felt the service met all their needs, and that it was more cost effective than inpatient care. Users particularly valued support from recovery guides with similar experiences and the non-judgemental atmosphere of the house. It should, however, be noted that such initiatives are often fragile in terms of funding streams and Anam Cara is no longer providing this service.

Day hospitals

Evidence suggests that up to 40 per cent of people in need of hospital admission could be treated successfully in a day hospital setting with few differences in clinical or social outcomes (Creed *et al.*, 1990) and that the costs associated with day hospital care are less than inpatient care (Creed *et al.*, 1997; Marshall *et al.*, 2001). Day hospital treatment for voluntary psychiatric patients in an inner-city area also appears more effective in terms of reducing psychopathology in the short term (Preibe *et al.*, 2006).

Community inpatient units

Community inpatient units or halfway hospitals provide a service for patients who require admission but not the high intensity of supervision that an acute ward would provide. They can also act as a support facility between the acute ward and the community to enable respite and asylum in a therapeutic environment for people with acute mental illness (Boardman and Hodgson, 2000).

A further hopeful development in community services is the expansion of direct payments. Under the *Community Care (Direct Payments) Act* 1996, since April 1997 social services departments can make cash payments to a range of different adult user groups in lieu of directly provided social services (and in some children's services). Research in this area suggests that direct payments give recipients greater choice and control, are more cost effective than directly provided services and lead to greater user satisfaction, a more creative use of resources, greater continuity of care and fewer unmet needs (see Glasby and Littlechild, 2009, for a summary). Since April 2003, it has been a legal duty for councils to make direct payments to individuals who are eligible and wish to receive a direct payment, and numbers have continued to rise – by 2007–8 there were some 67,000 direct payment recipients in England (Information Centre, 2008d, p. 1).

However, direct payments have yet to make a significant impact on mental health services in many areas. In 2000 there were no mental health direct payment recipients in Scotland at all, while in 2003 in England only five local authorities had ten or more direct payment recipients with mental health problems (and 57 per cent had no recipients with mental health problems at all) (Spandler and Vick, 2004; Witcher et al., 2000). By 2005, almost a quarter of all local authorities in England were still not making any direct payments and a further half were making only between one and five. Despite a series of pilot projects and additional guidance (Department of Health, 2006e), there remain a series of longstanding barriers to greater uptake in mental health (see Box 4.9).

Box 4.9	Direct payments and mental health

Barriers to direct payments for people with mental illness include:

- The emphasis of the 1996 Act on the needs of people with a physical impairment
- A lack of information for users, carers and staff
- Low expectations of social services due to previous poor experiences
- A tendency for people with mental health problems to have contact with the NHS (where direct payments were not initially available) rather than with social services
- Difficulties which people with mental health problems may have managing money when ill and an awareness of being perceived as people not trusted to take care of themselves
- A sense of 'catch 22', where people feel they are either too well to qualify for assistance, or so unwell that they are not deemed capable of managing their own support

(Summarised from Glasby and Littlechild, 2009; see also Ridley and Jones, 2002; Spandler and Vick, 2004).

In spite of slow progress with direct payments in mental health, the more recent development of personal budgets seems to offer further grounds for optimism. At their most simple, personal budgets involve being clear with the person from the outset how much money is available to spend on their needs and allowing them a greater say in how this money is spent. Beyond this, options for how the money is controlled can vary from the full amount being taken as a direct payment, right the way through to the person's social worker managing the money on their behalf (with several other options in between). Unlike direct payments, personal budgets can also be used to purchase public services (as well as private and voluntary services), and this spectrum of control could be especially relevant for some mental health service users. Although it remains early days, the emerging evidence suggests that personal budgets are a particularly effective way of increasing choice and control, of allowing people to make desired changes in their lives and of connecting people more fully to their communities (see Glasby and Littlechild, 2009; Poll et al., 2006;

Hatton *et al.*, 2008; Glendinning *et al.*, 2008, for further discussion). Indeed, such has been the early success of personal budgets that the government has taken them up with enthusiasm, rolling them out across the whole of adult social care and pledging to pilot them for forms of health care.

More recently, the Darzi Review has pledged to extend direct payments and personal budgets to some forms of health care, and a series of pilots are currently being developed. While these ways of working are likely to prove very counter-culture in some areas of the NHS, there is a possibility that mental health *could* be an early beneficiary. Certainly, the principles of both direct payments and personal budgets link well with concepts such as recovery, user-led crisis services, advance directives and developing alternatives to acute care – and access to some sort of crisis and/or recovery budget could be a powerful new approach to more genuinely rebalancing the current system.

Social exclusion and mental health

Community-based mental health services have enabled literal care in the community. However, as Prior (1993) suggests, people are not accepted 'more openly and readily by the community at large simply because they have a new mailing address' (p. 192). The significance of moving beyond the meaning of community as acknowledged in communitarian theory (see Chapter 2) is that people with mental illness who are often in most need of community care may be just those who are most excluded from participating in communities of interest. Indeed, there is plenty of evidence to suggest that people with mental health problems are multiply excluded and that the situation is particularly difficult for people with serious mental illness. In this final part of the chapter, we therefore look at the nature, origins and realities of social exclusion and argue that it is not enough to be treated in the community where the meaning is simply geographical (*out* of hospital) but that people also need to be *included within* society as part of a community of interest.

Promoting the social inclusion of people with mental health problems continues to be a key focus of UK government policy (ODPM, 2006). However, social exclusion is both poorly defined and hard to measure. Sayce (2001, p. 121) has focused attention both on the impact of impairment and societal responses, and has described social exclusion as:

> the inter-locking and mutually compounding problems of impairment, discrimination, diminished social role, lack of economic and social participation and disability. Among the factors at play are lack of status, joblessness, lack of opportunities to establish a family, small or non-existent social networks, compounding race and other discrimination, repeated rejection and consequently restriction of hope and expectation.

Morgan *et al.* (2007) reviewed the conceptual and methodological literature in this area and concluded that social exclusion is an enforced lack of participation in key social, cultural and political activities.

On virtually any indicator of social exclusion, people with serious mental illness are among the most excluded in British society (ODPM, 2004; Sayce, 2001). Part of the difficulty in teasing out what we mean by, and how we can address, issues of social exclusion within the context of mental illness is that many of the precipitating factors for social exclusion such as unemployment, lack of social networks and poverty can be both a cause and a consequence of mental illness. Stigma and negative stereotyping and attitudes all have a significant role to play in the generation of discrimination and prejudice (see Box 4.10).

Box 4.10	Key concepts in social exclusion and mental health

- 'Stereotype' describes the picture in peoples' heads of various social groups, and can be positive or negative
- 'Stigma' refers to socially constructed negative stereotypes related to the characteristics of a person
- An 'attitude' is a psychological tendency that is expressed by evaluating a particular issue in a positive or negative way
- 'Discrimination' is being treated unfairly or denied opportunities
- 'Prejudice' is public fear, misunderstanding and intolerance

Box 4.11	Attitudes towards people with mental illness

- In 1993, the Department of Health survey found that 30 per cent of people thought anyone with a history of mental problems should be excluded from public office and that 43 per cent thought that most women who were once patients in a mental hospital could not be trusted as babysitters. However, 92 per cent of people agreed that we need to adopt a far more tolerant attitude towards people with mental illness in our society (Department of Health, 1993)
- In 1997 (Department of Health, 1997b), the survey found strong support for community care services but only 13 per cent of people would be happy if their son or daughter were going out with somebody with schizophrenia
- In 2000, just under 20 per cent of respondents were frightened to think of people with mental illness living in residential areas (compared to 25 per cent in 1997). However, 90 per cent also agreed that we need to adopt a far more tolerant attitude towards people with mental illness in our society and 92 per cent believed that virtually anyone can become mentally ill (Department of Health, 2000b)
- The proportion of people agreeing 'people with mental illness have for too long being the subject of ridicule' has dropped from 82 per cent in 1994, to 72 per cent in 2007 (ONS, 2007)
- In 2003, only 83 per cent of people agreed that we need to adopt a far more tolerant attitude towards people with mental illness in our society (Department of Health, 2003d)

The Department of Health has been tracking popular attitudes to mental health since 1993 and, although certain aspects of the British public's attitudes have become a little more positive in recent years, there are still many examples of negative stereotyping (see Box 4.11).

Link and Phelan (2001) have suggested the following process of exclusion for people with mental illness: we label a person as different, but then, at least in the context of mental illness, associate that label with negative attributes (that is, we negatively stereotype the person as being dangerous or incompetent). We then separate out 'them' from 'us' and so differentiate ourselves from people we perceive as 'other' (see Box 4.12 for a quote which summarises this process). Finally, 'they' become the thing that they are labelled, so they become not a person with schizophrenia, but a 'schizophrenic'. This leads to a loss of status and discrimination, and then, quite quickly, to exclusion.

Box 4.12	**The otherness of mental illness**

'There is a vast and very complicated unwritten constitution of conduct which allows us to move with confidence through public spaces, and we can instantly and by a very subtle process recognise someone who is breaking that constitution. They are talking to themselves; they are not moving at the same rate; they are moving at different angles; they are not avoiding other people with the skills that pedestrians do in the street. The speed with which normal users of public places can recognise someone else as not being a normal user of it, is where madness appears.'

(Miller, in Laurance, 2003, p. 43)

The realities of social exclusion

The reality of social exclusion for many service users is that of multiple interlocking factors that can impact on every aspect of life (see Box 4.13).

People with mental health problems also have fewer social networks than average, with many of their contacts related to health services rather than sports, family, faith, employment, education or arts and culture. One survey found that 40 per cent of people with ongoing mental health problems had no social contacts outside mental health services (Ford *et al.*, 1993). Fear of stigma and discrimination can also lead to severe loss of confidence.

Perhaps the biggest issue for people with mental health problems is that of unemployment and the consequent risk of financial hardship. In the general working age population, 70–90 per cent of people are economically active. However, in England, only 24 per cent of people with mental health problems are currently in work (the lowest employment rate of any group of people), and only 8 per cent of those with severe mental health problems are in employment (ONS, 2003). People with mental health problems also earn

Box 4.13	Social exclusion and mental illness

- People with mental health problems have more than double the risk of losing their job than those without (Burchadt, 2003)
- People with mental health problems are nearly three times as likely to be in debt (Meltzer *et al.*, 2002)
- It has been estimated that someone with a serious mental illness is four times more likely than an 'average' person to have no close friends (Huxley and Thornicroft, 2003)
- One in four tenants with mental health problems have serious rent arrears and are at risk of losing their homes (Shelter, 2003)
- People with mental health problems have, until recently, been barred from being school governors and ineligible for jury service (ODPM, 2004)
- People with a severe mental health problems are three times more likely to be divorced than those without (Meltzer *et al.*, 2002)

only two-thirds of the national average hourly rate (ONS, 2002). The costs to society of workforce exclusion are also considerable. Mental illness costs employers an estimated £26 billion each year; over £8 billion a year in sickness absence; £15.1 billion a year in reduced productivity at work; and £2.4 billon a year in replacing staff (Sainsbury Centre for Mental Health, 2007b). The total number of people on Incapacity Benefit due to mental and behavioural disorders in 2006 was roughly 1 million, representing 40 per cent of total Incapacity Benefit recipients.

Studies show a clear interest in work and employment activities among users of mental health services, with up to 90 per cent wishing to go into or back to work (Grove and Drurie, 1999). In 2001, however, fewer than four in ten employers said they would consider employing someone with mental health problems compared to over six in ten for a physical disability (ODPM, 2004). Read and Baker (1996) found that 34 per cent of people with mental health problems had been dismissed or forced to resign from their job, and that almost four in ten people with mental health problems felt they had been denied a job because of their previous psychiatric history.

Employment also provides latent benefits such as social identity and status, social contacts and support, a means of occupying and structuring time and a sense of personal achievement (Shepherd, 1998). Lack of work therefore exacerbates the paucity of available social contacts and networks.

It is also interesting to reflect that in 1995, a MORI public attitudes survey found that while the public are most likely to accept people with mental illness as road sweepers, actors and comedians, they are less likely to accept them as doctors or police officers (that is, with jobs requiring greater 'responsibility'). It will be interesting to see if more recent reports of people in positions of power and influence who have had episodes of depression (such as a previous President of the Royal College of Psychiatrists in the UK and the Prime Minister of Norway) will have any effect on this.

Positive practice in community inclusion

The test of a good society, we would suggest, lies in the care and support it offers to its most disadvantaged members. The importance of tackling social exclusion, particularly for people with mental illness, is becoming increasingly widely recognised. Standard One of the *NSF for mental health* (Department of Health, 1999a) acknowledged the importance of combating stigma and the *NSF for mental health – five years on* (Department of Health, 2004b) highlighted the need to 'tackle social exclusion in people with mental health problems, improving their employment prospects and opposing stigma and discrimination' (p. 1). The Royal College of Psychiatrists and voluntary sector organisations continue to campaign for better understanding of mental health issues. Indeed, the Social Exclusion Unit report (ODPM, 2004) on mental health and social exclusion has proposed a 27-point action

Box 4.14	Encouraging community inclusion

- Mechanisms that appear useful in changing public attitudes towards people with mental illness include encouraging contact between users and non-mental health service users in a positive way, for example, by employing users and ex-users as staff in mental health services; ensuring users have training and support to speak to the media; targeting young people in particular with images and labels that they don't necessarily associate with mental illness and challenging negative attitudes
- Training and employment opportunities are also a key part of promoting social inclusion. People with long-term mental health problems can work effectively given the right support and adjustments (for example, someone to talk to or a quiet space). Prevocational training (a period of preparation before entering competitive employment) and supported employment (placement in competitive employment while offering on the job support) are both ways of helping people with severe mental illness obtain work. A systematic review of the evidence in this area found that supported employment is more effective than prevocational training in helping people obtain and keep competitive employment (Crowther *et al.*, 2001) and there is also some evidence that supported employment is cost effective (Grove *et al.*,1997)
- Initiatives like Support Time and Recovery workers (Department of Health, 2003e) and PCGMHWs (Department of Health, 2003b) offer positive examples of developing jobs where lived experience of mental illness is a positive asset rather than a gap on the curriculum vitae. See also Chapter 8.
- Campaigns that include positive images/messages of active contribution and participation, rather than depicting people with mental illness as victims, appear to have most effect in challenging and changing peoples' attitudes (Thornicroft, 2006)

plan involving a range of government departments and other organisations in a concerted effort to challenge attitudes and significantly improve opportunities and outcomes for people with mental illness (see Box 4.14). The White Paper *Choosing health* (Department of Health, 2004d) also highlighted the need to work with non-government organisations in the voluntary and community sector and deliver services in settings where people live their lives. *Choosing health* in particular adopted a broad definition of community, beyond that of traditional communitarianism, in talking about the potential of community action:

> Individuals belong to a range of overlapping communities – their local neighbourhood or state, a faith or age group, communities relating to common interests or social networks … communities are vital in improving health and can play a significant role in promoting individual self-esteem and mental wellbeing and reducing exclusion. (Department of Health, 2004b, pp. 78–9)

Conclusion

Community mental health care has developed in a piecemeal fashion, influenced by a range of factors including economic constraints, difficulties in partnership working between health and social care and public concerns over safety. The closure of asylums and the development of mental health teams within the community 'have occurred unevenly across the country … in no instance however has a psychiatric hospital simply withered away because all its functions were replaced by a network of community services' (Leff, 1997, p. 189).

A range of generic and more specialised community-based mental health teams are now being developed across the UK. New functionalised teams have certainly had additional finances during the last few years, but the continued development of acceptable, appropriate, accessible and effective user-centred services is complex and requires all key stakeholders to understand both their own and each others' roles and responsibilities within the wider health and social care system. We also need to continue to test the evidence base for both CMHTs and functionalised teams and ensure the 'black box' element of what works best, for whom and in which context, is better understood.

Many people now living in the community who might, in previous generations, have lived within long-stay institutions, have not necessarily been able to access adequate health or social care or housing or employment opportunities. Geographical inclusion (physically living in the same street) does not mean an individual automatically participates in the social life of that community or in the activities of wider society. Public concerns and policy focused on risk and safety rather than on quality of life for individuals have exacerbated social exclusion. Good community mental health care requires individuals as well as wider society to recognise these inequalities and work towards a culture of inclusion.

Reflection exercises

1. Working practices between teams

Exercise for community-based mental health staff, social services and primary care

Think about the ways in which you communicate with the other mental health teams, primary care services and social care in your area.

- Are patient pathways between sectors well co-ordinated? If not, why not and what can you do to improve the situation?

Consider the entry points for your service:

- Does your team have a gate-keeping role or are all referrals accepted from other mental health teams and/or primary care? Discuss the strengths and weaknesses of both ways of working.

Now consider the exit points from your service:

- Try to map the patient pathways of a number of clients who have been discharged and then re-referred to your service during the last 24 months. In particular, think about the reason behind the re-referral – was this something that could have been avoided through better communication or discharge planning?

2. Promoting social inclusion

Exercise for all staff

Think about the ways in which your organisation and you as an individual can promote access and inclusion for people who use your service:

- What skills do you think are key to building a positive and affirming relationship with your service users and patients?
- What strategies can you use and what resources can you call on or direct people towards to help them feel more included within their local community?
- How would you measure whether your ideas for improving inclusion for service users have had any effect?

You may find it helpful to look at the Inclusion website (www.ndt.org.uk/projectsN/SI.htm) and read Hacking and Bates' (2008) description of issues around the measurement of social inclusion.

Suggestions for further reading

1. Burns, T. (2004) *Community mental health teams: a guide to current practices.* Oxford, Oxford University Press

   This book, written by Professor Tom Burns (who has a long and distinguished career as both a researcher and consultant psychiatrist), describes a personal view of the current state and future challenges facing the generic CMHT with the newer functionalised teams.

2. Hannigan, B. and Coffey, M. (eds) (2003) *The handbook of community mental health nursing.* London, Routledge

   This edited collection from leaders in the field is a comprehensive and easy to read resource for practising community mental health nurses. It includes chapters that contextualise the area, as well as interesting and thought-provoking contributions on a broad range of issues, including ethics and the law.

3. The *Mental health policy implementation guidance* describes the functions and standard operating procedures for different mental health teams, and can be downloaded free of charge from: http://www.dh.gov.uk/en/Publicationsandstatistics/Publications/PublicationsPolicyAndGuidance/DH_4009350

4. ODPM (2004) *Mental Health and Social Exclusion.* London, ODPM

   This excellent, evidence-based practical report can be downloaded free of charge from: www.cabinetoffice.gov.uk/media/cabinetoffice/social_exclusion_task_force/assets/publications_1997_to_2006/mh_summary.pdf

5. Thornicroft, G. (2006) *Shunned: discrimination against people with mental illness.* Oxford, Oxford University Press.

   This book, which includes numerous personal accounts of stigma and discrimination, clearly describes the nature and severity of discrimination against people with mental illness and, importantly, what we can do to help reduce this.

6. For the latest government views on action to improve the quality and accessibility of services for people with mental health problems, see www.newhorizons.dh.gov.uk

For more on social inclusion and the wider personalisation agenda, go to http://www.ndt.org.uk/projectsN/SI.htm

5 | Acute Mental Health Services

In this chapter we discuss:

- The role of acute care
- Trends and pressures in inpatient services
- The hospital stay
- Hospital discharge
- Grounds for optimism

The role of acute care

Despite their apparent popularity with the public and the media, hospitals can be ambiguous places. If you are suddenly or seriously ill, then having immediate access to skilled professionals trained in managing your condition can be, quite literally, a matter of life and death. For people who have become ill over a longer period of time, then finally realising that someone is going to take care of you and (hopefully) make you better can also be a major relief – prompting feelings of extreme gratitude. However, some people probably did not want to end up in hospital in the first place, and for them the same process can be much more distressing and intimidating. Often, they can feel scared, unsure what is happening and desperate to do anything they can to get home. Nationally, there have been debates about the availability of single-sex wards, the nature of the built environment, the quality of hospital food and the cleanliness of wards – all of which can vary significantly and which have a major impact on the health and well-being of the individual concerned. As people get better and begin to prepare to leave, moreover, they can become increasingly frustrated by the institutional nature of many ward routines. For those with ongoing needs, there have also been longstanding debates about how best to organise follow-up support, so that people are not set up to fail by being kept in hospital too long, by being discharged too soon, or by being sent home before appropriate community support is in place.

In a similar way, the role of hospital services within the broader NHS can also be ambiguous. While hospitals have a key role to play, they are only part of the overall network of services needed to respond to the nation's ill health.

Unfortunately, because they provide such specialist and intensive services, hospitals also tend to be very expensive and resource-intensive places. Although this is appropriate when people have very serious needs, the way in which the NHS has evolved over time has tended to mean that a number of services continue to be based within hospitals when arguably they could be better provided in community-based settings. As part of the 'care closer to home' agenda, therefore, the government has sought to encourage a shift away from some hospital-based services (see Box 5.1 for an example from recent policy), and the role of hospitals seems to be changing. With advances in medical technology, it is possible that future hospitals may move away from the traditional 'district general' model to a situation in which health care is provided much more locally for some conditions and in much larger, regional centres of excellence for other conditions. While hospitals will still be a crucial part of the spectrum of care, they will be working alongside more specialist community services and are likely to be working more flexibly, rather than as standalone services. As a result, a range of current policies are designed to keep people living more independently in the community, reduce emergency hospital admissions, ensure swift and effective discharge for people once they are medically fit to leave and concentrate specialist services in larger units. For all these reasons, hospitals can often seem like part of the solution or part of the problem – depending on your point of view – and the ongoing reform of hospital services remains controversial.

Box 5.1	Care closer to home

'Our longer-term aim is to bring about a sustained realignment of the whole health and social care system. Far more services will be delivered ... in settings closer to home ... Year on year, as NHS budgets rise, we will see higher growth in prevention, primary and community care than in secondary care, and also resources will shift from the latter to the former.'

(Department of Health, 2006a, p. 17)

If hospital services can arouse contradictory feelings within the wider NHS, then this is even more the case in mental health. Because of the nature of people's conditions and previous contact with services, it is particularly important that we are clear about the proper role of hospital care within the broader spectrum of support available and that we make this a positive experience. As the Sainsbury Centre for Mental Health (1998b, p. 9) observes:

> If and when people with severe mental health problems can no
> longer manage to live in the community ... they, their relatives, and
> society expect care to be available in a therapeutic and humane place.
> In practice, this means admission to an acute psychiatric ward and

inevitably losing some degree of freedom and privacy. Most people suffering from a severe mental illness will have been in hospital at some stage in their lives. A considerable proportion will have been admitted against their will under the Mental Health Act because they were judged to be a danger to themselves or others. At the point of admission people become patients, and will be in a severe state of crisis, both personally and mentally. Imagine being transported to a frightening unknown place, possibly in an ambulance or police car, while suffering from deep despair or confusion. It is unlikely that at any point in their life anyone could feel more vulnerable, and would be more in need of high quality and sensitive care.

Trends and pressures in inpatient services

Traditionally, services for people with mental health problems have been dominated by institutions, with many people being placed in long-stay hospitals or asylums. As discussed in Chapter 4, however, this emphasis on institutional care was replaced in the second half of the twentieth century with a recognition of the need to care for more people in the community, either in their own homes or in community-based settings which are as homely as possible. As a result, the number of hospital beds for people with mental health problems has fallen considerably (both in the UK and elsewhere). In 1954, there were 154,000 residents in UK mental hospitals. By 1982, this figure had fallen to 100,000 and, by 1998, to 40,000. This number has continued to decline, with the number of inpatients recorded in national census falling to 32,023 in 2006 and 31,187 (CSIP, 2008).

Another way of looking at this is that the number of psychiatric beds per 100,000 population has fallen from 131.8 in 1990 to 62.8 in 2001 (Priebe *et al.*, 2005). In some countries the degree of the deinstitutionalisation has been even greater. For example, in Italy between 1968 and 1978, the asylum population fell from 100,000 to 50,000. In the US, although relatively few psychiatric hospitals have been closed (26 in 17 states since 1970), there has been a similar dramatic reduction in the number of inpatients over the last four decades from 560,000 people in 1955 to 77,000 in 1995 (see Goodwin, 1997; Rogers and Pilgrim, 2001; Centre for Mental Health Services, 1995, for all statistics quoted).

However, this does not necessarily mean that the number of hospital admissions has been decreasing. On the contrary, the number of admissions increased from 155,000 in 1964 (347 per 100,000 population) to 192,000 in 1984 (409 per 100,000 population) and 224,000 in 1993–4 (462 per 100,000 population) (Payne, 1999, p. 247). More recently there have been indications of a new process of 'reinstitutionalisation' (see Chapters 2 and 6) with an increase in certain types of bed (for example, the number of NHS medium secure beds increased from 1750 to 2060 between 1998–9 and 2002–3 – an increase of 18 per cent; see CSIP, 2008). However, the overall trend for many years has been one of decline, with the number of hospital beds falling at the same time as admissions were increasing. As is also the case for other user groups, this has been achieved by:

- A reduction in the length of hospital stay (see Box 5.2 for a quote to illustrate this trend).
- Changes in community services to work with people with increasingly high-level needs. In older people's services, this is often described in terms of people being discharged from hospital 'quicker and sicker' (Neill and Williams, 1992, p. 17), with community services having to support a growing number of people who would previously have been cared for in an acute setting. Such changes also require a shift in the thinking from inpatient services, so that they see themselves as part of a broader spectrum of care rather than as a standalone service.

Box 5.2	**Pressures in acute care**

'Many recent studies have highlighted the enormous pressures currently facing acute psychiatric wards. There has been a dramatic decline in hospital beds for mental health care since their peak at 155,000 in the mid-1950s. The number of available beds in NHS hospitals has more than halved in the last decade or so to around 37,000 ... At the same time demand has been rising. Throughput in mental health beds has more than doubled ... Referrals of patients appear to be rising while at the same time the severity of problems of people treated in hospital has also increased ... [Thus], studies have reported increasing numbers of patients on wards with drug or alcohol abuse problems, people referred by court diversion schemes (aimed at keeping mentally ill people out of the prison system) and people needing accommodation in low or medium secure units.'

(Sainsbury Centre for Mental Health, 1998b, p. 10)

Hardly surprisingly, this puts extra pressure on hospital services (to treat and discharge people as quickly as possible) and on community services (to support people with increasingly significant and complex needs). This not only means that community services have a heavier caseload, but that those people who are admitted to hospital are likely to have particularly severe needs and that the whole service becomes increasingly intensive in its focus. This has a number of implications which are discussed in further detail throughout the remainder of this chapter. As Quirk and Lelliott (2001, p. 1567) observe:

The emergent picture is that:

- The reduction in bed numbers has created a 'concentrating' effect whereby the threshold for admission has increased ...
- High bed occupancy rates mean that quality of care is compromised. Some people have to be admitted to distant hospitals with subsequent loss of continuity; nurses spend most of their time managing crises rather than giving care

- Because of the concentrating effect, wards are disturbed places where 'violence breeds violence' ...
- Unavailability of beds compromises the quality of community care which requires easy access to beds for short-term management of crises or for respite.

Interestingly, however, the statistics above do not tell the full story. As Payne (1999, p. 248) explains, some of this increase in psychiatric admissions is actually the same people being admitted and readmitted to hospital:

> The pattern for many patients, however, is one of admission to psychiatric hospital and discharge which is then followed by subsequent readmission at a later date. If one compares figures for first admissions ... with figures for total admissions it is clear that the vast majority of the increase in psychiatric admissions ... is accounted for by the readmission of those who have already been treated as in-patients and discharged from hospital – the phenomenon of the so-called 'revolving door.'

Although the concept of the 'revolving door' admission is discussed in more detail below, it is significant to note that these trends within mental health can also be seen in services for other user groups. As an example, the Audit Commission (1997, 2000a) describes a 'vicious circle' in services for older people (see Figure 5.1) in which the number of hospital admissions is rising, lengths of hospital stays are declining, opportunities for rehabilitation are reduced, there is an increased use of expensive residential/nursing home care and less money for preventative services, thereby leading to more hospital admissions. As a result, there are concerns that older people could be discharged from hospital too quickly, only to be readmitted again at a later stage when their initial medical problems recur or due to a breakdown in hastily assembled community support arrangements (see, for example, Glasby, 2003).

Hardly surprisingly, one of the main results of the decline in the number of psychiatric beds and rising demand has been a significant increase in pressure on hospital services. In response, the tendency has been for mental health services to seek to treat more people with fewer resources by increasing bed occupancy rates (more people seen per bed). This can be done using a variety of tactics, all of which are 'unsatisfactory' (Quirk and Lelliott, 2001, p.1566; see also Box 5.3). Despite this, the answer may not necessarily lie in expanding hospital services. This is the result of a number of factors:

- Occupancy rates are not uniform throughout the country, and the evidence suggests that pressures are particularly strong in the south of England (especially London) and in inner-city areas (see, for example, Audini et al., 1999; Greengross et al., 2000; Shepherd et al., 1997). As a result, it may be that local agencies may need to reassess the level of their provision with a view to increasing bed availability in some areas, but not in others.

■ There is evidence to suggest that some admissions to hospital may be inappropriate. In North Cheshire, for example, 35 out of 520 people were admitted to hospital as a result of social problems (Cawley *et al.*, 1997), while national research undertaken by the Sainsbury Centre for Mental Health (1998b) found that one in ten people were admitted for social reasons or for respite care. In two London hospitals, a project to develop a Bed Requirement Inventory found that 17 per cent of patients had been inappropriately admitted (Tyrer *et al.*, 2006). Elsewhere, a systematic review of the appropriateness of acute bed use cites two studies which suggest that just under one third of admissions may be inappropriate (McDonagh *et al.*, 2000). Key factors contributing to inappropriate admissions may include inadequate assessments undertaken by junior and non-specialist staff in Accident and Emergency and general wards, inadequate community services and a lack of alternatives to hospital outside office hours (Auckland *et al.*, 2000; Minghella and Ford, 1997). As noted above, moreover, other patients may experience 'revolving door' admissions to hospital due to breakdowns in community services or as a result of services treating outward symptoms of mental illness rather than tackling the underlying causes (see Box 5.4). Taken together, findings such as these suggest that it may be possible to reduce the number of hospital admissions by making more accurate initial assessments of people's needs and by developing community-based alternatives to inpatient care.

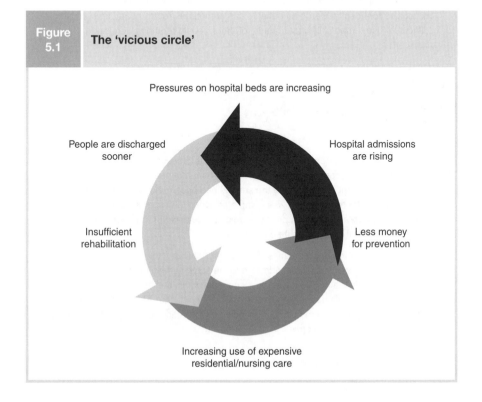

Figure 5.1 **The 'vicious circle'**

Pressures on hospital beds are increasing

People are discharged sooner

Hospital admissions are rising

Insufficient rehabilitation

Less money for prevention

Increasing use of expensive residential/nursing care

Box 5.3	Dealing with pressures in acute care

Tactics for managing rising acute pressures include (summarised from Quirk and Lelliott, 2001):

- Transferring patients to hospitals outside the local area (a practice traditionally known as extra-contractual referrals or ECR, sometimes referred to as 'out of area transfers' or 'individual patient placements')
- Maintaining waiting lists, with people needing inpatient care waiting in settings such as general medical wards, community settings, prison or police cells
- Sending some patients home on short-term leave (sometimes prematurely and often at short notice) in order to free up beds for others

As a result of this, the bed occupancy rate (when all those in the above categories are added in) can frequently exceed 100 per cent – clearly, the implications of such pressure on beds can be extremely serious:

- Quality of care can be compromised by admitting patients to hospitals at a long distance from their homes, discharging or sending people on leave early and not admitting other patients
- The use of ECRs is not only unpopular with service users, but is also very costly, diverts money away from community services and disrupts continuity of care
- Sending people out on leave can also can create significant administrative difficulties for hospital wards as patients can sometimes return at any time, making it difficult to use temporarily vacant beds for other people requiring admission

Box 5.4	Revolving door admissions

In one London health authority, researchers studied the process of care for a sample of 100 consecutive discharges from acute wards in two mental health trusts (Minghella and Ford, 1997). Overall, three-quarters of the sample had been in hospital before and many were readmitted after the research was completed. Despite this, around half did not have a recorded care package or had a package which broke down prior to admission. Elsewhere, a national study of acute care found that:

> 89 per cent of admissions were classified as emergencies. However, 40 per cent of the patients had previously been admitted to the same service in the last 12 months, 20 per cent within the last 90 days and 13 per cent within the last six weeks, confirming the so-called 'revolving door' of mental health care. This high rate of people returning to acute care in a crisis indicates the difficulties community services experience in preventing admission or finding alternative forms of care for people with mental health problems.

(Sainsbury Centre for Mental Health, 1998b, p. 16)

The hospital stay

Once in hospital, some people will receive high quality services that meet their needs. Despite this, many accounts of inpatient care suggest that some service users have very poor experiences of hospital services, with few people having 'anything good to say about acute hospital care' (Royal College of Psychiatrists, 2002b). In 2000, a national survey carried out by Mind revealed a series of extremely worrying findings (see Box 5.5), which paint 'a grim picture of life on many psychiatric wards – a depressing environment, unsafe, dirty, with illegal drugs easily available, minimal contact with staff, not enough to do and not enough access to food, drink, bathing facilities, interpreters if needed, telephones and fresh air' (Baker, 2000, p. 31).

Box 5.5	Mind national survey

In 2000, the mental health charity Mind published the results of a national survey of 343 people with experience of hospital services:

- More than half (56 per cent) of patients said that the ward was an untherapeutic environment
- Just under half (45 per cent) said that ward conditions had a negative effect on their mental health
- Just under half (45 per cent) said they found the atmosphere on wards 'depressing' and bleak
- Almost a third (30 per cent) of patients said that they found the atmosphere on wards unsafe and frightening
- Just under a third (30 per cent) said illegal drugs were being used on the wards. Two-thirds of these patients (66 per cent) said that drugs were easily available to patients
- Almost two-thirds (64 per cent) of patients who needed an interpreter did not get one
- More than half (57 per cent) said they didn't have enough contact with staff. Only 35 per cent said they did
- The vast majority (82 per cent) of patients who said they didn't have enough contact with staff said that they spent fifteen minutes or less with staff each day
- Almost one in six (16 per cent) of patients said they had experienced sexual harassment on the ward. 72 per cent of those patients who complained said that no action was taken to prevent it happening again
- Almost two-thirds (60 per cent) of patients had problems getting a restful night's sleep
- Just under half (45 per cent) of patients said they didn't have enough access to food, and 31 per cent said they didn't have enough access to drinks
- A quarter (26 per cent) of patients said the toilets weren't clean

(Summarised from Baker, 2000, p. 6)

Unfortunately, many of these findings are mirrored in other studies, suggesting that they may not be unique to the Mind survey (see Boxes 5.6–5.8 for further examples). Over time, key recurring issues from the literature include:

- High levels of staff vacancies and the use of workers employed on a casual basis (Ford *et al.*, 1998)
- Staff dissatisfaction with rapidly increasing administrative duties and reduced contact with patients (Higgins *et al.*, 1999)
- Volatile environments in which there can be frequent violence, substance misuse, bullying and fear (Phillips and Johnson, 2003; Kumar *et al.*, 2001; Ireland and Snowden, 2002). As one service user commented in Quirk *et al.*'s (2004, p. 2577) study of users' responses to risk and violence in acute care: 'You are always under the threat of violence. You never know when it's going to occur and so you live on a knife edge.'
- Widespread boredom among patients (Warner *et al.*, 2000a; Walton, 2000)
- Disempowering regimes that promote a culture of infantilisation (Barnes *et al.*, 2000)
- A lack of involvement from community services (Sainsbury Centre for Mental Health, 1998b)
- A lack of information for users and carers (Watson, 2001)
- Increasing concerns about the experiences and well-being of younger people placed on adult mental health wards (see, for example, McDougall *et al.*, 2009; 11 Million, 2007; Royal College of Psychiatrists, 2009).

Box 5.6	Acute concerns – the views of social work students

In Merseyside, social work students observing local psychiatric wards highlighted the following issues (Walton, 2000):

- *Institutional aimlessness*: Patients are often bored, do little other than watch TV and are regularly moved round by cleaning staff. Ward routines have become ends in themselves and the physical atmosphere is debilitating. The limited activities on offer are seen as being very patronising, but users take part to try to demonstrate that their mental health has improved and secure an early discharge
- *Poor staff – patient relationships*: Most staff time is spent on administrative tasks, talking to each other in the office and watching patients rather than engaging with them
- *Narrow approaches to mental health*: Staff see patients as being 'ill' and pay little attention to users' social backgrounds. As a result, the presenting problem is often seen as the issue to be addressed with no consideration of the factors that may have caused this problem in the first place. There is an almost total reliance on psychiatric drugs as the solution to mental health problems
- *Indifference to civil and human rights*: Staff tend to treat all patients the same way irrespective of whether or not they have been admitted as compulsory patients. Some people have little knowledge of the law and have had no training at all in this area. Ward routines are very rigid and some are unnecessarily stressful (such as denying people drinks outside set times even though dry mouths are a common side-effect of medication or the oppressive nature of ward rounds, with patients unable to contribute due to the large number of professionals that come to see them)

| Box 5.7 | Ongoing concerns about acute care |

In 2004, Mind conducted a second national survey as part of its 'Ward Watch' campaign. Based on 335 responses from people with recent or current experience of mental health inpatient services, the survey found that (Mind, 2004 p. 3):

- 23 per cent have been accommodated in mixed sex wards (two years after a government target to eliminate mixed-sex wards). 31 per cent did not have access to single-sex bathroom facilities
- 27 per cent said they rarely felt safe in hospital
- 51 per cent reported being physically or verbally abused, with 20 per cent reporting physical assault
- 18 per cent reported sexual harassment, 7 per cent reported being subject to harassment due to their race and 10 per cent reported harassment due to their sexuality
- 53 per cent thought the hospital surroundings had not helped their recovery. 31 per cent thought it had made their health worse
- Only 20 per cent felt they were treated with respect and dignity by staff, while 17 per cent said they were never treated with dignity and respect by staff

Also in 2004, the Sainsbury Centre for Mental Health carried out a survey of acute mental health inpatient wards in England (2004b, p. 2):

- The national average vacancy rate for qualified nurses on acute wards was 13 per cent
- The national average sickness rate among ward staff was 6.8 per cent
- The national average use of bank and agency staff per week per ward was 152 hours (equal to more than four full-time staff)
- 26 per cent of wards had lost staff to community teams in the past year
- 12 per cent of ward managers had no administrative support
- 48 per cent wards did not have a lead consultant and 13 per cent had no ward manager or nurse above grade F
- 18 per cent of ward managers reported they did not have access to a Psychiatric Intensive Care Unit (PICU)
- Communication with community teams was felt to be poor during patient admissions by 16 per cent ward managers
- Cognitive behavioural therapy was available on fewer than 20 per cent of wards
- Three-quarters of managers believed their wards offered a good environment for mental health care, while 86 per cent said their wards were safe places to be
- 55 per cent of wards had a cultural sensitivity policy, but in a quarter of wards no staff had had cultural sensitivity training

In 2005, the former Healthcare Commission (2005b) published results of a national audit of violent incidents in mental health and learning disability wards and units. Key factors felt to be contributing to violent incidents included: unsafe environments, inadequate staffing, overcrowding, substance misuse, high levels of boredom, and limitations in staff training in the prevention and management of violence.

Box 5.7	Ongoing concerns about acute care (*continued*)

In 2008, the former Healthcare Commission (2008b) reviewed the quality and safety of care provided by all 69 NHS Trusts providing mental health acute inpatient care. Despite many positives, no Trust scored 'excellent' on all four of the key criteria (acute care pathway, whole person care, involvement of service users and carers, and safety), 39 per cent were scored weak on involving users and carers and around one in nine Trusts were scored weak on whole person care and safety. Although progress had been made in some areas, the audit identified four key priority areas:

- Putting a greater focus on the individual and care that is personalised
- Ensuring the safety of service users, staff and visitors
- Providing appropriate and safe interventions
- Increasing the effectiveness of the acute care pathway

Box 5.8	Service user experiences of acute care

Service users in Mind's (2004) *Ward watch* survey were asked about their experiences of acute mental health care. Responses included:

- 'I had to spent the first night on a fold-up bed in the male wing because there were no beds on the female dormitory.'
- 'I was too scared to sleep.'
- 'I was disgusted by the way I was treated by my consultant. I felt bullied and threatened. I was a voluntary patient but when I decided to leave the hospital I was threatened with being sectioned.'
- 'A staff member said "cheer up, at least you're not black or gay".'
- 'They did absolutely nothing when I was sexually molested and didn't even write it down.'
- 'The complete absence of any meaningful daily activity led my condition to worsen.'
- 'There was little therapy apart from smoking and television.'
- 'The ward was dirty and unkempt. Carpets were badly stained and burnt. Furniture was damaged. My room smelt of urine. Doors were locked, even though it was an open ward. The whole environment gave out a clear message that you were not worth caring about and did not deserve to be looked after.'
- 'The staff did not encourage patients to participate in the few therapeutic activities that were available. They often overreacted to situations, which made them worse. Making sure that patients were given access to fresh air and exercise was not considered a priority.'
- 'The staff were go, go, go all day. They were pushed by management to breaking point.'
- 'The whole ward should be demolished and started again. It is unsafe. Drugs are being bought and sold in the ward. Staff do not seem interested in their jobs. Patients are left to wander around with nothing to do (it is a long day). The place smells like an old ashtray. Service users all feel demoralised and get little help from staff.'

(Mind, 2004, pp. 6–19)

Since the 2000 Mind campaign, moreover, a series of additional national surveys have continued to reveal similar themes and issues (see Box 5.6). However, behind such national overviews lie a multitude of service user stories and experiences which often illustrate the key issues much more effectively than the statistics alone (see Box 5.8 for examples; see also further reading at the end of this chapter). While many of the negative aspects of the hospital stay relate to the trends and pressures in acute care described above, Quirk et al.'s (2006) study of three acute psychiatric wards in London makes a fascinating contribution to this debate through the notion of a 'permeable institution'. While mental health hospitals are often seen as closed environments, Quirk et al. demonstrate how much interaction there is with the outside world – including turnover of patients (with increasingly short stays and high turnover), patients' links to families and friends, other professionals visiting the ward, etc. Although this is positive in so far as it reduces the danger of institutionalisation, it can also cause risks, with unwanted people coming onto the ward (for example, a former patient returning to threaten staff, drug dealing, etc). As a result, staff face a series of legal, ethical and practical dilemmas, including (Quirk et al., 2006, p. 2116):

- How to respect the freedom of movement of informal patients while detaining those held involuntarily under mental health legislation
- How to provide acceptable accommodation for people with a prolonged stay as well as acute care for people in a crisis
- How to prevent informal patients from engaging in criminal or antisocial activity
- How to help people maintain positive links to the outside world while also preventing the intrusion of damaging or antisocial influences

In response to all these issues, a number of commentators have suggested that this may, in part, be the result of a tendency to focus on the development of community-based services, effectively turning something of a blind eye to conditions in acute care. Thus, Higgins et al. (1999, p. 52) have argued that:

> In recent years, political and managerial attention has focused predominantly on the consequences of the failure of National Health Service community services to provide effective care to people with severe mental illness in the United Kingdom ... However, what happens inside hospitals has received less scrutiny. Not since the reports and inquiries of the 1960s and early 1970s into the poor standards of nursing care provided in some long-stay psychiatric hospitals has hospital care been under the spotlight.

Similarly, Ford et al. (1998, p. 1823) have claimed that:

> The combination of increasingly pressured acute wards and high levels of casual staffing cannot be good for the care of patients. These problems

are most severe in London, where patients have more severe problems …
The policy, managerial, and training focus has been on developing
community services. This has resulted in a relative neglect of inpatient
settings. [This study] has shown that attention must be given to inpatient
wards, which are an essential and major element of mental health care.

As the Sainsbury Centre for Mental Health (1998b, p. 11) concludes:

> There is scant evidence about the effectiveness and quality of care of acute
> wards in dealing with people with psychiatric problems. Relatively little
> is known about exactly who are the people who stay on acute psychiatric
> wards and what happens to them while they are there. There is a sense
> that hospital care is a black box, with people entering and leaving, and
> we have high but vague expectations about what happens in between. The
> issue about quality and effectiveness of care is crucial, however, not least
> because acute inpatient treatment is the most intensive and expensive form
> of mental healthcare – but also because patients on acute wards have to
> sacrifice both privacy and freedom during their stay. Moreover, they are
> unpopular with many of these patients. It is crucial, therefore, that hospital
> stays are used to best advantage, treating the patients who need and benefit
> most from this regime and for the shortest necessary time.

Hospital discharge

Although hospital discharge can be problematic for other user groups such as
older people, it is also a central concern in acute psychiatric inpatient services. In 1999, for example, a Department of Health-funded study of acute
psychiatric nursing care found that the pressure on beds meant that patients
were discharged from hospital before they had sufficiently recovered and were
often quickly readmitted after their community services broke down (Higgins
et al., 1999). At the same time, research by the Sainsbury Centre for Mental
Health (1998b) indicates that discharge arrangements were often dealt with in
an *ad hoc* way during ward rounds, with only one third of patients receiving a
formal or separate meeting to plan for leaving hospital. Most patients had very
little notice of their discharge and had little involvement in discussions about
their futures. Involvement from carers and community staff was also limited
(Sainsbury Centre for Mental Health, 1998b, p. 6):

> Discharge is often unplanned with inadequate involvement of
> community staff, patients and carers … Only 34 per cent of patients had
> a discharge planning meeting and most patients had no idea that they
> were to be discharged until a few days before they left, and had little
> involvement in discussions about their future.

Although some patients may be discharged from hospital prematurely, others
may remain in hospital much longer than they need to because of a lack

of community services. In 1999, a review of alternatives to acute psychiatric beds found that between 20 and 60 per cent of patients could be better placed (although the latter figure was produced by a study outside the UK) (Bartlett *et al.*, 1999). The following year, a systematic review of the appropriateness of acute bed usage found that between 24 and 58 per cent of days of care were not considered appropriate (McDonagh *et al.*, 2000). In both studies, key factors contributing to delayed discharges were found to include a lack of housing, a lack of community services (such as group homes), a lack of rehabilitation services and, in a small number of cases, the need for higher levels of care. At a national level, the Department of Health estimates that around 10 per cent of psychiatric beds are unavailable because of delayed discharges (CSIP, 2007, p. 3), at a potential cost of over £110 million per year (Gould, 2007, p. 24). Similar findings have also been produced by a range of other commentators, suggesting that a substantial number of people would be able to leave hospital if community alternatives were more readily available (see Table 5.1 for an overview).

Table 5.1	Delayed hospital discharges	
Study	**Rate of delayed discharge**	**Causes/possible alternatives**
Fulop *et al.* (1992)	37 per cent	Lack of accommodation and long-stay hospital care
Lelliott and Wing (1994)	61 per cent	Lack of continuing care provision, rehabilitation, supported group homes or low-staffed hostels
Fulop *et al.* (1996)	23 per cent	Professional support in the patient's home, housing/more appropriate housing, group homes, rehabilitation
Koffman *et al.* (1996)	24 per cent	Residential and/or nursing home care, total dependency psychiatric care, community services (such as day care or home care), housing
Connolly and Ritchie (1997)	54 per cent in 1994 46 per cent in 1995	Some patients with stays of three months or more could have been discharged to other NHS services (for people with complex needs), supported accommodation or mainstream housing

Table 5.1	Delayed hospital discharges *(continued)*	
Beck *et al.* (1997)	42 per cent	Of patients with stays of at least 60 days, some could have been discharged to alternatives such as a non-acute low-level observation inpatient facility, the patient's own home, a group home, day hospitals and support by a CPN
Minghella and Ford (1997)	10 per cent	Problems finding suitable accommodation (including forensic care)
Shepherd *et al.* (1997)	27 per cent	Lack of supported housing/ rehabilitation services, secure accommodation and specialist services
Sainsbury Centre for Mental Health (1998b)	19 per cent (after one week)	Lack of accommodation, home-based support and rehabilitation, and patients requiring higher levels of supervision
Bartlett *et al.* (1999)	Systematic review	A spectrum of provision is required, including support at home as well as residential care staffed by specialist nurses
McDonagh *et al.* (2000)	Systematic review	Delayed discharge could be reduced by services such as more appropriate housing/housing plus support, group homes, rehabilitation and services with higher levels of supervision
Paton *et al.* (2004)	46 per cent	Insufficient specialist resources for placement or return home, lack of money to finance placements, no alternative to acute ward and users and carers refusing placements/ refusing to pay for care
Lewis and Glasby (2006)	Average of 7 per cent beds (or 1691 bed days) lost per Trust	Lack of funding, awaiting residential/ nursing home, awaiting further NHS care, awaiting assessment, awaiting domiciliary package and/or patient/ family exercising choice
Tyrer *et al.* (2006)	39 per cent	Not explored in detail

Source: Adapted/updated from Glasby and Lester, 2004

Grounds for optimism?

To date, much of the research on inpatient services has been extremely negative and raised serious concerns about quality of care. While these are significant issues, it is important to emphasise that there have been a number of national initiatives to improve acute care. At a local level, there are also a range of activities underway to tackle some of the problems identified in this chapter, and these should not be overlooked. As Quirk and Lelliott (2001, p. 1571) observe:

> [Research to date has] generated much useful information about what happens on acute psychiatric wards ... However, such accounts are limited by the fact that they tend to present an unremittingly bleak picture of life on the wards – something that is unlikely to be the case for all the patients all of the time and across all wards.

One example is the Sainsbury Centre for Mental Health's *Acute solutions* project (2006a), which has sought to build on previous negative research findings by working in depth with four case study sites to find ways of improving acute mental health care. Their summary of *The search for acute solutions* helpfully describes the approach taken, the results produced and the lessons learned, seeking to demonstrate what can be achieved in the current system by enabling staff and service users to make changes at ward level. At a national level, moreover, there has been additional guidance, extra investment and a series of policy and practice developments (see Box 5.9 for a summary). Even more important has been an explicit acknowledgement that problems exist within acute care, that inpatient services have not received the same emphasis as community services in the past and that this needs to change (Rooney, 2002, p. 3):

> Too often acute inpatient services are not working to everyone's satisfaction. A range of reports and surveys and the reported experience of service users and staff have clearly and consistently demonstrated a high level of criticism and dissatisfaction with current provision ... It is clear that the physical, psychological and therapeutic environment of care must all be attended to.

Despite these grounds for optimism, a number of doubts must still remain about what the future holds for acute inpatient care. In particular, the persistent and longstanding nature of many of the issues outlined above suggest that the problems associated with acute inpatient mental health services are extremely complicated and entrenched. As an example, Box 5.10 compares findings from the hospital scandals of the 1960s and 1970s with a 2003 Commission for Health Improvement report on mental health services, providing a stark reminder of the relatively low base from which acute care is starting and a traditional lack of progress in hospital services. While this 2003 report predates many more recent changes, the fact that so many of the key issues have remained so difficult to tackle over many years suggests that an even bigger shift in thinking may be required in future if current changes are to be truly effective.

Box 5.9	Positive developments in acute care

Star Wards is a national project run by the charity Bright to work with mental health trusts to improve mental health inpatients' daily experiences and treatment outcomes. It currently has over 400 wards as members (see www.starwards.org).

The NHS Institute is supporting trusts to improve the effectiveness, safety and reliability of mental health wards through its *Productive Mental Health Ward: releasing time to care* initiative (see www.institute.nhs.uk). Around 80 per cent of trusts have signed up.

National and regional work has been undertaken in order to improve ways in which inpatient services are reviewed, improve workforce development, promote good practice, to improve the sexual safety of mental health service users, to improve the management of violence and to promote race equality (see CSIP/National Mental Health Partnership/DH, 2006).

Some wards have been introducing changes to working practices based on concepts of recovery and on techniques such as Wellness Recovery Action Planning (WRAP – see www.mentalhealthrecovery.com).

The Royal College of Psychiatrists has developed AIMS (a standards-based accreditation service to improve the quality of care in psychiatric wards – see www.rcpsych.ac.uk/clinicalservicestandards/centreforqualityimprovement.aspx).

There has also been much greater recognition of the needs of young people in adult mental health inpatient services, with this issue highlighted nationally by the Children's Commissioner for England (11 Million, 2007) and through new standards developed by the Royal College of Psychiatrists (2009).

Conclusion

Despite recent positive developments, acute mental health services seem to be starting from a low base with a recent history characterised by relative policy neglect. Following official commitments to community care, the nature and quality of acute services appears to have been overlooked to a certain extent, with evidence of a range of serious issues rising over time. Thankfully, this is now beginning to change, and a number of new initiatives have sought to tackle some of the longstanding issues at stake. However, in seeking to respond to the many issues raised above, it seems clear that there are few 'easy answers' and that the way forward may lie in taking a whole systems approach that considers the full range of mental health services (see, for example, Lee and Bradley, 2000; Minghella and Ford, 1997; Shepherd *et al.*, 1997). Many of the problems of over-occupancy, poor quality acute care and delayed discharges cannot be resolved in isolation, but require concerted action across the full range of available services (see Box 5.11 for quotes summarising these arguments). Ultimately, as Higgins *et al.* (1999, p. 61) observe:

Without close examination of what is happening in hospitals … and without suitable remedial action, it is conceivable that hospital care

Box 5.10	Longstanding problems in acute care

Inquiries into the hospital scandals of the 1960s and 1970s identify a range of contributing factors, including (Martin, 1984):

- The isolated nature of some acute services (including not only geographical isolation, but also staff being left in charge of large numbers of people and lack of visits by medical staff)
- Closed, institutional settings and a tendency to suppress complaints
- A corruption of care – focusing on the maintenance of order and routine rather than on providing care
- Failures of leadership
- Staff shortages and inadequate training

The Commission for Health Improvement (2003a) identified a very similar list of issues, suggesting a considerable lack of progress over time. Examples include:

- The isolated nature of services
- Institutional environments
- Low staffing levels and high use of bank and agency staff
- Closed cultures
- Poor clinical leadership and supervision

Box 5.11	The need for a whole systems approach

'In the short-term, better bed management at every stage – at admission, throughout the patient's stay and at discharge – can relieve some of the pressures [on hospital services]. To solve the problems of over-occupancy and costly delayed discharges in the longer term, a range of care options, with several ... alternatives for different levels of need and different kinds of problems, must be considered. Acute inpatient care should be viewed as one component of such a spectrum, operating a specific, well-defined function – that is to provide intensive 24-hour care for those patients whose needs are for intensive assessment, immediate treatment and stabilisation of symptoms.'

(Moore and Wolf, 1999, p. 22)

'More important than beds is the total range and quality of services. Inpatient services and community services must be provided together to meet people's needs. The quality of clinical decision-making helps people access appropriate services. We may need more beds, especially in the hardest-pressed inner city areas. But we also need more community mental health services, and to invest in a comprehensive range of inpatient and community services that work together in flexible and integrated ways.'

(Lee and Bradley, 2000, p. 31)

might once again be subject to the scrutiny and criticism that cast a shadow over psychiatric services in the 1960s and 1970s. Nurses and other mental health professionals need to work together to prevent such circumstances arising and to develop the full spectrum of services required in each locality.

While much of this is about resources, about collaboration and about policy focus, it is also about values and attitudes – and these may be even harder to change. Despite some recent grounds for optimism, it remains to be seen whether the recent rediscovery of acute care and the many shortcomings that exist in inpatient services will be sufficient to tackle the scale and complexity of the problem. As a psychiatrist in Hardcastle *et al.*'s (2007, pp. 82–3) study of the views of service users, carers and professionals has suggested:

> Many of our hospitals are now frankly scandalous. We can only guess at the horror of patients and carers as they walk (or are dragged) into a ward that is filthy, offers no sexual privacy and has an atmosphere of predatory violence. Partly this is a matter of resources. The impression has grown that community care equals success and in-patient care equals failure; so all the fancy new money and creative thinking has gone into community teams. Hospital staff and patients have been left behind, demoralised and institutionalised, cut off from the worlds outside the walls. Ideally, hospital and community should be complementary parts of one mental health service, equally well resourced, with the integration of patients' and carers' needs, across the boundaries. And there are plenty of examples now of in-patient care broken down into smaller, modern, short-stay units nearer to patients' homes. We should not have to put up with old-style, isolated 'bins', where I did most of my training decades ago. But it is also a matter of attitudes too.

Reflection exercises

1. Hospital services

Exercise for all workers

If possible, walk round the mental health hospital that serves your area (or talk to staff and service users from the hospital):

- How welcoming, safe and supportive does the hospital feel?
- How good a building is this as a place for trying to make people feel better?
- How clean are wards?
- What are staffing levels like and what sort of relationship can you see between staff and patients?
- What access is there to food/drink, single-sex accommodation and everyday social and leisure opportunities?
- How would you feel if you or a family member were admitted here?

2. Hospital services

Exercise for hospital staff

- What is good about the service you currently offer?
- What would you like to change about your hospital to make things better for users and carers?
- What would you like to change to make things better for staff?
- What can you do on your ward or with your team to build on the positives and minimise the limitations?

3. Hospital services

Exercise for community staff

- How much do you know about local hospital services and how could you find out more? If hospital staff were asked the same question about your service, what might they say?
- How does your service try to support people as they move in and out of hospital?
- What opportunities exist locally for you to meet and get to know some of the staff from the hospital?
- Talk to hospital staff and to service users who have been hospital inpatients – what is life like on the wards?
- How would you feel if it was you being admitted to this hospital?

Suggestions for further reading

1. National overviews of mental health inpatient care are provided by the former Healthcare Commission (2008a, b), the National Patient Safety Agency (2006) and the Sainsbury Centre for Mental Health (2004b). From a service user and voluntary sector perspective, Rethink, Sane, the Zito Trust and the National Association of Psychiatric Intensive Care Units (2006) have produced their *Behind Closed Doors* summary of the current state and future recommendations for acute mental health care.

2. The Sainsbury Centre for Mental Health has produced an initial report, *Acute problems* (1998b) based on a survey of the quality of care in acute psychiatric care (see also Sainsbury Centre for Mental Health, 2004b). Subsequently, its *Acute solutions* Project has sought to respond to the issues identified. Further details of relevant publications are available via www.scmh.org.uk and via a series of project publications (see, for example, Sainsbury Centre for Mental Health, 2002b–d, 2006a).

3. The Department of Health's *Mental health policy implementation guide: acute adult inpatient care provision* reviews current problems with acute care and makes a series of recommendations about future policy and practice (Rooney, 2002). An additional guide focuses on education, training and continuing professional development (Clarke, 2004). A 2006 update on the National Acute Inpatient Project is also available, summarising both actions and aspirations around service improvement in acute inpatient care (CSIP/National Mental Health Partnership/DH, 2006). More recently, CSIP's (2007) *A positive outlook* provides a good practice toolkit to improve discharge from inpatient mental health care.

4. The former Care Services Improvement Partnership has hosted a 'virtual ward' (www.virtualward.org.uk), with examples of good practice from admission to aftercare and recovery, access to relevant policy and helpful tools/examples.

5. The Royal College of Psychiatrists' Centre for Quality Improvement has developed a system of accreditation to identify and acknowledge wards that have a high standard of organisation and patient care (Accreditation for Acute Inpatient Mental Health Services (AIMS) – see www.rcpsych.ac.uk/crtu/centreforqualityimprovement/aims.aspx). The Royal College also runs a Quality Network for Inpatient Child and Adolescent Mental Health Services (QNIC) – for further details, visit www.rcpsych.ac.uk/researchandtrainingunit/centreforqualityimprovement/qnic.aspx).

6. Above all, the user-centred accounts of hospital services cited in this chapter give a clear indication of users' priorities for change and provide very powerful and graphic descriptions of people's experiences as inpatients (see, for example, Sainsbury Centre for Mental Health, 1998b; Goodwin *et al.*, 1999; Kumar *et al.*, 2001; Quirk *et al.*, 2004). Within this, Mind's national surveys

of people's experiences of acute inpatient care are particularly revealing (Baker, 2000; Mind, 2004). The latter campaign was accompanied by a competition for mental health service users to produce a work of art based on the theme of 'being an inpatient' (see http://www.mind.org.uk/News+policy+ and+campaigns/Campaigns/Ward+Watch/Artcomp/index.htm for examples). An excellent resource is Hardcastle *et al.*'s (2007) *Experiences of mental health in-patient care* – an edited collection of accounts by service users, carers and mental health professionals which provides a rich and challenging insight into the positives and negatives of current services.

6 Forensic Mental Health Services

In this chapter we discuss:

- Mental health and risk
- The 'mad' v 'bad' debate
- Forensic mental health services
- Mental health needs in prison
- Inappropriate placements in secure services
- Possible ways forward

Mental health and risk

There is a common public misconception, often reinforced by the media, that mental health is equated with dangerousness and with crime. A good example is the 'not in my back yard' approach, whereby many people recognise the need to move away from institutional forms of care, but resist attempts to locate new community services near to where they live (see also Chapter 5). More recently, there has also been an enormous public outcry about the presence of people with personality disorders, who have typically been portrayed as 'fiends' and 'perverts' (Markham, 2000, p. 28). That such fears are not always well founded on fact and an accurate assessment of risk is demonstrated by events in South Wales, where a children's doctor was hounded out of her home because neighbours confused 'paediatrician' with 'paedophile' (Hall, 2001).

At its most extreme, a key image is of the 'axe-wielding maniac' waiting on street corners to attack unsuspecting passers-by (see Box 6.1 for a quote which illustrates this issue). Research suggests that two-thirds of all British press and television coverage of mental health includes a link with violence, while around 40 per cent of daily tabloids and nearly half of the Sunday tabloids contained derogatory references like 'nutter' and 'loony' (ODPM, 2004, p. 26). In the most part, such media stereotypes have been fuelled by a small number of very high profile and brutal murders (for example of Jonathan Zito or Megan and Lin Russell). While these are human tragedies, they are clearly not representative (as evidenced by the substantial media coverage which they received) – albeit that they do raise important questions about the nature and management of risk.

| Box 6.1 | Violence, mental health and the media |

'Violence is firmly linked to mental illness in media coverage ... Different specific "panics" have emerged in different countries, states and cities, often attaching the fear of madness to other potent concerns of the moment: violence in the workplace – almost none of which is in fact perpetrated by people with mental health problems – an American panic fuelled by one heavily publicised case of a "crazed" Post Office employee who turned a gun on colleagues; infanticide – a Chicago panic, stemming from the killing of a child by a woman with mental health problems, which exacerbated concerns about the safety of public agencies' decision making; and random street violence, a British panic, fuelled by the emblematic, but highly atypical, British case of Christopher Clunis, a man with mental health problems who killed a total stranger in a London Underground station.

In different localities, "stories" emerge and succeed each other in varying patterns, not in line with actual trends in crime or other social phenomena but according to subtler cultural shifts. Some countries have a stronger record in including positive "stories": in Italy, the push for "democratic psychiatry" enabled users to appear somewhat heroic, of interest for their successes in getting out of institutions rather than for more "demonic" qualities (Ramon, 1996). British and American experiences are not, however, unique, and globalisation of the media is likely to make "stories" increasingly international, as framed by more influential nations. This could mean a spread of moral panics – rather as movie watchers internationally are influenced by American films, which make frequent links between madness and violence.'

(Wahl, 1995, in Sayce, 2000, p. 7).

Despite public concerns, there is substantial evidence to suggest that the association between violence and mental health is weak:

1. Very few people with mental health problems commit homicides (perhaps 40 or 50 instances each year) (see Taylor and Gunn, 1999 for all statistics in this paragraph). While this is clearly 40 or 50 cases too many, it should be compared to other risks (for example, some 600 to 700 people are murdered each year, there are an additional 300 deaths from danger-ous driving and some 3500 to 4000 deaths per year in road accidents). As Taylor and Gunn (1999, p. 13) suggest:

   On average, every week someone in the UK wins the jackpot on the National Lottery. About 54,999,999 people do not. On average, rather less than one person a week loses their life to a person with mental illness, generally his/her mother, father, sibling, spouse, child or other close contact; 54,999,999 remain safe from this threat.

2. Most homicides carried out by people with mental health problems are committed against family members or people they already know.

According to the National Confidential Inquiry into Suicide and Homicide (2001, 2006) – so-called 'stranger homicides' (where the perpetrator and victim do not know each other) are relatively rare and the risk to the public is not increasing.

3. While mental health is a factor in a small number of deaths, other factors such as substance misuse may be much more significant (Swanson *et al.*, 1990; Steadman *et al.*, 1998; Walsh *et al.*, 2002; Walsh and Fahy, 2002; National Confidential Inquiry into Suicide and Homicide, 2006). This is often referred to as dual diagnosis and is frequently a key factor in mental health homicide inquiries. Indeed, such is the link between substance misuse and the very small number of mental health homicides that some commentators suggest that the focus of attention should not necessarily be on mental health, but on the alcohol or drug problems that compound mental health problems and can sometimes lead to violence (personal communications).

4. About 95 per cent of violent crime is committed by people without mental health problems (Sayce, 2000, p. 33).

5. People with mental health problems are more likely to be the victims rather than the perpetrators of crime (Jewesbury, 1998; McCabe and Ford, 2001; ODPM, 2004; Sayce, 1997, 1999).

6. Between 1957 and 1995, there has been little fluctuation in the number of people with mental health problems committing homicide, but their contribution to the overall homicide rate has been falling by 3 per cent annually (Taylor and Gunn, 1999). Thus, as more and more people were being discharged from long-stay hospitals, the homicide rate for people with mental health problems actually fell.

We also know from the wider literature that people with mental health problems face considerable discrimination, poverty and social exclusion (see Chapters 4 and 9), factors known to contribute to criminal activity in the wider population. Moreover, some people with mental health problems probably commit some crimes knowing that what they are doing is illegal – in such situations, the criminal activity may be little different from crimes committed by people without mental health problems and should be punished through the criminal justice system. According to Sayce (2000, p. 226), therefore, there are a number of key messages which we need to test out on the public and the media:

- Most crime is committed by people without mental health problems
- People with mental health problems often commit crimes for the same reasons as everyone else (poverty, drink and drugs, family/relationship frustrations)
- It is extremely rare for people with mental health problems to attack someone they don't know
- People with mental health problems are more often victims than perpetrators of crime
- People with mental health problems can usually be held responsible for their crimes

A final consideration is the difficulty (if not the impossibility) of predicting risk. While violence is rare and while services may try their best to take into account issues of risk when assessing patients, it is difficult to predict risk with any degree of accuracy. A key finding from a range of mental health enquiries has been that many violent incidents committed by people with mental health problems have been hard to predict. As Peck (quoted in Chamberlain, 1998, p. 2) observes: 'The assessment of risk and dangerousness is an art not a science and a difficult art which requires practitioners to balance past and present behaviour with predictions of interventions and the civil liberties of the patient.' Further details about risk assessment and different predictive tools are provided by Blumenthal and Lavender (2000) in their review of violence and mental disorder.

The 'mad' v. 'bad' debate

When someone commits a crime that the public finds particularly hard to understand, an immediate response is often to question if the person concerned is either 'mad' or 'bad': did they behave as they did because they are 'evil', or are they experiencing some form of mental health problem? Whereas many would see the need to punish the 'bad', they may often feel that someone with a mental health problem may not have been 'in their right mind' and hence not responsible for their action. As a result, such a person should receive treatment and care in the health service, rather than punishment in prison.

In practice, such distinctions are sometimes hard to make (especially where the crime is horrific and difficult to comprehend). Examples include infamous figures such as Ian Brady, Myra Hindley, Harold Shipman and Ian Huntley. While these are extreme cases, they nevertheless illustrate the complexities at stake, as someone with a mental health problem assessed as not responsible for their actions will 'escape' prison and be treated in a health rather than a penal setting. Of course, whether entering the mental health system in such circumstances is an 'escape' is a moot point. Arguably, the stigma of using forensic mental health services is so significant that many would consider it as bad as or worse than the stigma of having been in prison. However, the fact remains that the initial assessment is crucial to establish why someone acted as they did, whether or not they were responsible for their actions and what should happen to them next.

Forensic mental health services

While the association between mental health problems and violent crime is vastly overstated in the public imagination, there is a small minority of people with serious mental health problems who do pose a risk to the public and who do commit crimes – sometimes very serious ones. Although high quality community and hospital services will be sufficient to meet the needs of many people with mental health problems, there may always be a small group of people who require even greater levels of support and supervision than is possible in these settings. These people fall under the remit of forensic mental health services. As McFadyen (1999, pp. 1436–7) explains:

> Forensic mental health services deal with those mentally ill people whose presentation has been assessed as requiring a more focused level of expertise and/or increased levels of physical security. Some of these people will have exhibited behaviours which present major challenges, with or without associated violent conduct, beyond the capabilities of general psychiatric services. Others will be mentally disordered offenders who have broken the law or who are deemed to have the propensity to do so. Some patients will have been identified at the level of general NHS psychiatric services and some via the criminal justice system. Of the latter, some will be on remand ... Others, however, will be convicted prisoners ... who are subsequently transferred from prison during the course of their penal sentence.

From this initial quote, a number of key issues are immediately apparent that are explored in more detail later in this chapter:

- Forensic mental health services are extremely complex, with many different routes in and a wide range of service users
- Forensic services potentially involve a large number of agencies (such as health care, social care, probation and the prison service)
- By definition, forensic services will be working with people who may display extremely challenging behaviour and who may have been found to be too difficult to work with in other settings prior to their referral to forensic care

This complexity and difficulty is also emphasised by McCann (1999, p. 65):

> Mentally disordered offenders ... span the range of mental health problems and diagnoses, and the spectrum of criminal offences. Often their needs are complex and involve a number of agencies ... Invariably there is also an element of political or media interest ... This pressure on services to make the 'right' decisions, often with inadequate information, places professionals in a vulnerable position, both clinically and personally. It is understandable therefore that professionals are cautious, treading carefully the narrow path between their roles as therapist and custodian. Generally however the needs of mentally disordered offenders are no different to any other individual with mental health problems, and they require access to a similar range of services.

As McCann (1999) continues, forensic mental health services are typically divided into three different categories depending on the level of service users' needs (see Box 6.2 for some overall facts and figures):

1. Low security services tend to be based near general psychiatric wards in NHS hospitals, but often have higher staffing ratios (also known as psychiatric intensive care units or PICUs).
2. Medium secure services often operate on a regional basis and usually consist of a number of locked wards with a greater number and a wider range of staff.
3. High security services are provided by the three special hospitals (Ashworth, Broadmoor and Rampton). These are characterised by much greater levels of security and care for people with mental health problems who pose an immediate and serious risk to others.

Box 6.2	Forensic mental health facts and figures

- In July 2007, there were 3723 people detained in forensic mental health services (an all time high), with admissions increasing year on year. As national policy focuses on 'care in the community' and 'care closer to home', these rises seem ironic to say the least – with some commentators seeing this as a form of 're-institutionalisation' (see Chapter 2)
- Of these, 88 per cent were men and 12 per cent women
- Although 7.9 per cent of the general population are from a non-White ethnic group, the numbers in forensic services are 29 per cent of those directly transferred from prison following a custodial sentence, 56 per cent of those transferred while on remand or awaiting trail, and one third of those transferred directly from court
- An average of 42 prisoners per quarter waited more than three months for transfer from prisons to forensic services. In 2006 the most common reason for delay was 'lack of bed availability'
- More than half (53 per cent) stay in forensic services for less than five years and one in five people stay between five and ten years
- The main offences committed are violence against the person (36 per cent of the total), criminal damage (14 per cent, mostly for arson) and robbery (10 per cent)
- The most common discharge destinations are 'conditional discharge to the community' (32 per cent), discharge by the court (not into the community) (27 per cent), remaining in hospital unrestricted (14 per cent) and return to prison (10 per cent)
- Recalls to forensic services after a conditional discharge represent 13 per cent of total admissions
- Reoffending rates for those first discharged from forensic services to the community are very low (compared to rates for people released from prison)

(Summarised from Rutherford and Duggan, 2007)

In addition, a range of new services are slowly being developed to meet the needs of mentally disordered offenders in the community, either with a forensic specialist working with a community mental health team (an *integrated* model) or with forensic specialists working as a separate specialist team (a *parallel* model) (Judge *et al.*, 2004; Mohan *et al.*, 2004; Mohan and Fahy, 2006). These have received particular impetus following the creation of Multi-agency Protection Arrangements (MAPPAs), statutory local partnerships introduced and then strengthened under 2000 and 2003 *Criminal Justice Acts* to assess and manage the risk of violent and sexual offenders.

Over time, a series of official reviews have emphasised the principles that should underpin forensic services. Most build on a series of longstanding concepts first articulated as part of Reed Report (Department of Health/ Home Office, 1992, p. 7). This stated that services should be provided:

- With regard to the quality of care and proper attention to the needs of individuals
- As far as possible, in the community, rather than institutional settings
- Under conditions of no greater security than are justified by the degree of danger they present to themselves or others
- In such a way as to maximise rehabilitation and the chances of sustaining an independent life
- As near as possible to their own homes or families

In seeking to deliver these aspirations, more recent policy has also tended to emphasise:

1. The concept of 'equivalence' (Department of Health/HM Prison Service/ National Assembly for Wales, 2001, p. 5) – a recognition that people in prison should nevertheless 'have access to the same range and quality of services appropriate to their needs as are available to the general population through the NHS'.
2. Diversion schemes to ensure that people with mental health problems are moved away from the criminal justice system towards the NHS so that their needs can be more appropriately met (Home Office, 1990). This can happen at a number of key stages, including on arrest, during interview, after a court appearance or while on remand/bail. Although such schemes can be effective and are often well regarded, there is ongoing evidence of a failure to identify and refer relevant people, problems around training and a lack of knowledge, and more general concerns about the experience of people with mental health problems within the criminal justice system, both as suspects and as witnesses (see, for example, Independent Police Complaints Commission, 2008; NACRO, 2005; Thompson *et al.*, 2004; Vaughan *et al.*, 2001; Watson, 1997).

In many ways, this chapter reflects similar themes to the rest of the book. As with hospital services, there is considerable evidence to suggest that many people in forensic mental health services may be inappropriately placed and many of the issues highlighted in Chapter 5 apply equally here. At the same time, delivering effective forensic services requires a high degree of partnership working (Chapter 7) and raises particular issues with regard to gender and ethnicity (Chapter 9). In many ways, indeed, forensic services are at the 'extreme' end of the mental health system, and any findings from general psychiatric services will probably apply to an even greater extent in forensic mental health, where the issues at stake are even more complex and high profile. To supplement this material, the remainder of this chapter explores three key issues:

■ The prevalence of mental health needs in prison
■ Inappropriate placements in secure services
■ Possible ways forward

Mental health needs in prison

Despite attempts to divert people with mental health problems away from the criminal justice system, there remains a very large number of people in prison with mental health needs (see Table 6.1). According to official figures (Department of Health/HM Prison Service/National Assembly for Wales, 2001, p. 3), around 90 per cent of prisoners have a diagnosable mental illness, substance abuse problem or, often, both. For young people, the numbers are even higher (95 per cent of young offenders). Of 4500 women in prison in England and Wales, 5 per cent are mothers, and research suggests that women in prison mother and baby units might also have a series of unmet mental health needs (which could also have an impact on the development of the children concerned – see, for example, Birmingham *et al.*, 2006). While most prisoners with mental health problems have common conditions, some have much more severe needs.

Table 6.1	Mental health needs in prison	
	Prevalence among prisoners – 16 years + (Singleton *et al.*, 1998)	Prevalence in general population (16–64) (Singleton *et al.*, 2001)
Psychosis	8 per cent	0.5 per cent
Personality disorder	66 per cent	5.3 per cent
Neurotic disorder	45 per cent	13.8 per cent
Drug dependency	45 per cent	5.2 per cent
Alcohol dependency	30 per cent	11.5 per cent

Source: Sainsbury Centre for Mental Health (2009c, p. 2) – reproduced with permission

Box 6.3	Safer prisons

According to a study of 157 prison suicides (1999–2000), the *National Confidential Inquiry into Suicides and Homicides by People with Mental Illness* (Shaw *et al.*, 2003) concluded that:

- Thirty (21 per cent) were known to have been victims of bullying
- Thirty-two (21 per cent) did not take part in any prison activities
- Fifty-seven (42 per cent) had received no visits prior to death
- Nineteen (18 per cent) had experienced a recent family bereavement or terminal illness in a family member
- One hundred and ten (72 per cent) had at least one psychiatric diagnosis
- Ninety-five (62 per cent) had a history of drug misuse
- Forty-six (31 per cent) had a history of alcohol misuse
- Seventy-eight (53 per cent) had a history of self-harm
- Eighty-nine (57 per cent) had symptoms of psychiatric disturbance on reception to prison
- Forty-six (30 per cent) had a history of contact with NHS mental health services

While many of these people had been referred to a health professional, admitted to the prison health care inpatient unit or placed on medium or high levels of observation, there were a number of concerns. For example:

- It was unusual for information to be requested from a GP or from mental health services
- Fifteen per cent had no further contact with health care staff after reception
- Twenty-two (15 per cent) of suicides were seen by health staff as preventable
- There were a range of antecedents, including expressions of suicidal ideas, deliberate self-harm, adverse life events, bullying, bereavement and family/relationship problems
- In seven cases a transfer to an NHS hospital was awaited
- Between 1996 and 2000, 354 people died within a year following release from prison. Eighty (23 per cent) died within the first month following release, suggesting the need for better follow-up in the community

Altogether, 141 (90 per cent) of the 157 suicides in this study could have been seen as 'at risk' at reception to prison because of a history of previous NHS mental health care, a lifetime history of mental disorder, current symptoms, current treatment, a history of drug misuse, alcohol misuse or self-harm (p. 43).

Clearly, such figures raise serious questions about the role that prisons may be being asked to play in caring for people with mental health problems and the extent to which prison staff are equipped to fulfil this role. While a detailed consideration of prison health care is beyond the scope of this book, the government has recognised that this is a real problem (Department of Health/HM Prison Service/National Assembly for Wales, 2001, p. 5; see also Box 6.3):

The way mental health services are currently organised ... do not meet prisoners' needs. Ineffective and inflexible services that do not match identified health needs inevitably result in poor outcomes for prisoners, wasted resources and de-motivated staff. There are too many prisoners in too many prisons who, despite the best efforts of committed prison health care and NHS staff, receive no treatment, or inappropriate treatment … from staff with the wrong mix of skills and in the wrong kind of setting.

In response, there have been a number of key policy initiatives developed to improve prison health care, including:

- The publication of *Changing the Outlook*, a joint Department of Health/Prison Service programme to improve mental health care in prisons
- The transfer of responsibility for commissioning health services for prisoners from the Prison Service to the NHS (completed in 2006)
- The development of in-reach services to support prison-based staff and to focus on prisoners with the most severe mental health problems
- The creation of a National Health and Social Care in Criminal Justice programme

At the same time, some of these positive trends appear to have been undermined, at least in part, by broader developments within current approaches to law and order. While these issues are beyond the scope of this book, a number of commentators have expressed concern that recent reforms of the criminal justice system may be having a disproportionate affect on people with mental health problems. A recent example is the policy of Imprisonment for Public Protection (IPP), whereby a 'dangerous' offender receives an indeterminate sentence, going before a panel after a minimum period to consider whether or not they can be released. If they are, they remain on licence (subject to a recall to prison) for life. Contrary to the diversion schemes that have historically tried to take people with mental health problems out of the criminal justice system, therefore, this could represent a form of 'reverse diversion' (Rutherford, 2008) in which government penal policy, whether deliberately or in an unintended way, treats people with mental health problems more punitively than others.

The level of inappropriate placements in secure services

An additional factor that may contribute to high levels of unmet mental health needs in prison may be an inappropriate use of existing bed capacity in secure services (see Box 6.4 for two quotes illustrating this issue). With the current system having developed piecemeal over many years, there remains something of a fragmented approach. According to a number of commentators, somewhere between 37 and 75 per cent of patients in maximum security

> | Box | |
> | --- | --- |
> | 6.4 | **Inappropriate placements in secure services** |
>
> 'Acute psychiatric units are serving an increasing number of more severely disturbed patients detained under sections of the Mental Health Act of 1983 … Patients whose needs cannot be met within local acute care units often have to wait several weeks before transfer to a more secure environment. Access to appropriate care and treatment may require recourse to expensive and often private out-of-area placements many miles from the patient's home and family. Other patients may become 'stuck' in high security placements that were suitable at the time of referral but have become inappropriate for their current needs. Their move to a less restrictive placement may be delayed, often for a considerable time, due to the scarcity of suitable accommodation at lower levels of security' (Badger *et al.*, 1999, p. 1625).
>
> '[The inappropriate placement of people in medium secure units is extremely expensive]. However the financial cost is just part of the problem. The cost to individual patients in terms of unnecessary incarceration and all that entails should not be ignored. Absence of appropriate and adequate community facilities means many people are inappropriately detained in medium secure units who could otherwise be enjoying more fulfilled lives in the community. This also has a knock-on effect on others in the chain. People are kept inappropriately in high security hospitals because there are no medium secure beds available, and people in prison with mental health care needs are left untreated because available high security beds are similarly blocked' (McIntyre, 1999, p. 382).

hospitals may not need the services provided there (see, for example, Coid and Kahtan, 2000; McCann, 1999; McKenna *et al.*, 1999; Vaughan, 1999) – and similar problems of inappropriate placement seem to exist within low and medium secure services too (see, for example, Dabbs and Isherwood, 2000; Dolan and Lawson, 2001; McIntyre, 1999; Beer *et al.*, 2005). When capacity problems occur, patients have to wait to access the services most appropriate for their needs and increasing use is made of independent sector provision (Coid *et al.*, 2001; Lelliott *et al.*, 2001; Polczyk-Przybyla and Gournay, 1999), often some distance away from the area in which the individual concerned lives. This is not only expensive, but also contravenes the stated aim of supporting service users in their own homes or under conditions of no greater security than are justified by the degree of danger they present to themselves or others. As McIntyre (1999, p. 382) observes:

> The inappropriate placement of people in … secure services has long been recognised. The need to develop services that more appropriately meet the needs of these people … has similarly long been recognised. However progress is slow … Absence of [alternative service provision] represents a significant drain on precious financial resources; it forces people needlessly and without clinical justification to be required to live in conditions of significant security and curtailment of liberty, potentially in breach of civil rights. It has to be asked how much longer this will continue unchallenged.

Possible ways forward

As highlighted throughout this book, the provision of effective mental health services requires a wide range of agencies to work closely together (see also Box 6.5 for additional quotes illustrating this issue). While the more general issue of partnership working is discussed in detail in Chapter 7, the literature highlights considerable barriers that will need to be overcome if successful partnerships are to be developed and sustained in forensic mental health. A good example is provided by Vaughan *et al.* (2000), whose study of community teams providing support to mentally disordered offenders in Wessex found that this user group had complex and multiple needs which often fell outside the range of skills and services that individual teams could offer. As a result, community mental health teams felt deskilled, unsupported and frustrated by the reluctance of some support services to accept referrals for this group. Team members also highlighted a lack of interagency communication and co-operation, with each agency reluctant to accept ownership of mentally disordered offenders. From the perspective of probation teams, however, mental health services were seen as difficult to access, slow to respond and poor at sharing information. As a result, many individual teams adopted something of a 'siege mentality', reluctant to offer a service to people outside their normal referral criteria and spending a significant amount of time disputing responsibility for 'borderline' cases (pp. 580–1). Neither probation nor the community mental health team had formal links with special hospitals or the local medium secure unit, and the community mental health team had no formal relationship with the prison service. As a result, teams often relied on the discretion of individual workers to

Box 6.5	**Partnership working in forensic mental health**

'The system of care for offenders with mental disorders in the United Kingdom has developed piecemeal over the years, and responsibilities have been divided between the criminal justice system, the National Health Service, and ... social services departments. The specialized secure facilities have also evolved in an ad hoc way throughout the country, without standardized models of service delivery' (Badger *et al.*, 1999, p. 627).

'In this survey, most community services were not organized in a way that facilitates contact with mentally disordered offenders, who tend to shun services. For the most part, teams ... operate within their own strict boundaries and there is a general reluctance to work with other client groups. Each group has its own distinctive cohort of mentally disordered offenders but often cannot meet all of their needs due to limitations within each service. Because of the compartmentalized nature of the services, gaining access to a wider range of skills is difficult. Accordingly, many mentally disordered offenders are denied a comprehensive range of interventions and sometimes get only partial help for their problems' (Vaughan *et al.*, 2000, p. 583).

make contact with these institutions and there was little continuity of care or sharing of information as individual users moved through services.

Similar themes have also emerged from Hill *et al.'s* (2007) study of psychiatrists' attitudes towards forensic psychiatry, with some of the former feeling that forensic services should have a lower admission threshold, that they have been over-funded compared to other services, that they should integrate more closely with non-secure psychiatric services and that they should offer more community services rather than focusing on inpatient care. As one psychiatrist commented (in a particularly hard-hitting interpretation) (p. 223):

> Are forensic services and prisons the new asylums? Society is increasingly risk averse and forensic services are the 'beneficiaries' of the increased money being spent to allay these anxieties. How this affects perceptions and stigma of mental illness and medicalisation of character traits can only be negative. It also means that other more preventative measures remain under resourced and developed.

In response to such issues, there is an increasing recognition that the issues at stake are so fundamental that only a whole systems approach will suffice (see also Chapters 4, 5 and 7 for similar findings). Thus, for Maguire (1999, p. 21), there is a need for 'a clear pathway from the point of entry into a service, through to the point of discharge, incorporating community and mainstream mental health services' (see also Markham, 2000; McFadyen, 1999). This is echoed by Vaughan (1999, p. 562), who suggests that 'in order to facilitate a flow-through of patients in the system as a whole, adequate provision is required at every stage of a person's illness'. Unfortunately, such a spectrum of support may be a long way from fruition in some areas, with a range of ongoing pressures preventing a more holistic approach from being developed. As an example, Coid and Dunn (2004) describe a forensic mental health system in one health and social care community only able to respond reactively to referrals from other agencies, making no sessional commitments to probation services, prisons or court diversion schemes, providing no dedicated aftercare, relying heavily on private sector provision, accumulating growing waiting lists and unable to reduce the number of people detained in maximum security hospitals who no longer require this level of supervision.

In addition to a whole system approach, there is also a need for a longer-term perspective which moves away from episodic approaches to ones which support people over time as their needs change. As an example, Davies *et al.* (2007) explored the long-term outcomes of people admitted to a medium secure unit from 1983 to 2003. Of 554 people, the researchers found that (p. 73):

> After discharge the outcome for patients was poor, with a mortality rate that was six times that which one might expect; that almost half of those discharged had at least one reconviction; that almost two-thirds

were readmitted within 5 years after discharge; and that their capacity to obtain and retain gainful employment was very limited.

Perhaps most significant of all, however, is the need to develop approaches which draw more fully on the experience of service users and their families. In other chapters in this book, there are detailed accounts from a service user and/or carer perspective that provide a powerful critique of some aspects of current services. In contrast, service users and carers often only appear in the forensic mental health literature as statistics in large-scale audits of patient populations, and (with a few notable exceptions) hardly ever as real people with feelings, preferences and experiences to contribute to the debate about what works and what does not work in mental health. As McCann (1999, p. 67) observes:

> There is a need to foster closer working relationships with the people for whom ... services are being provided. For too long forensic services have ignored the views of users and excluded their families from becoming involved. Future work should aim to build mechanisms and services that seek the involvement of users and carers, and respond to their views. It is to be hoped that this will improve as services take steps to meet their obligations to be sensitive to the needs of the communities they serve.

Against this background, there seem a number of possible areas for further exploration. Although user and carer involvement is even harder in forensic services, there are a number of studies that have managed to achieve a degree of meaningful engagement, illustrating the power of this way of working (see, for example, Durcan, 2008; Spiers *et al.*, 2005; see also Box 6.6). While this seems an important thing to do in its own right, it is also possible that such an approach will yield different results to more traditional approaches. As one example, there is very little emphasis in the literature on the scope for preventative work (despite the fact that people in secure services have often had significant contact with mental health services in the past and have sometimes committed a number of crimes prior to their admission to forensic services; see, for example, Lelliott *et al.*, 2001; Maden *et al.*, 1999a, 1999b). Against this background, a fascinating insight is provided by MacInnes (2000), whose review of the literature suggests that carers often detect changes in users' behaviour before offending or admission to forensic services, but that health services do not react to carers' concerns as users are beginning to become unwell. A similar insight is provided by a small exploratory study by Ryan (2002), who examines the risk management strategies developed by carers. Although it must remain conjecture, both these contributions raise the possibility that more genuine user and carer involvement might be a way of gaining an insight into more effective means of preventing a crisis in the person being cared for.

Box 6.6	Experiences of prison mental health care

As an example of what is possible, the Sainsbury Centre for Mental Health has conducted research into experiences of prison mental health care based on interviews with 98 prisoners (Durcan, 2008). Through this approach, the study provides an insight into life before prison, arrival, life in prison, prison health care, experiences of in-reach services and release from prison, underpinned by some fascinating but harrowing personal stories (which often emphasise the importance of the issues at stake much more than would be possible in a more traditional research study).

Conclusion

Overall, there is clear evidence of a need for reform in forensic mental health services. Despite significant recent attention and progress, there remains a sense that we all too often have the wrong people in the wrong settings at the wrong time. While there seems to be greater recognition than in the past of the need for a long-term and whole systems approach that builds on the expertise of service users and carers, longstanding concerns about unmet mental health needs in prison, inappropriate placements in secure services and insufficient interagency collaboration remain. Ultimately, these overarching issues are probably more to do with ongoing debates about risk, public protection and 'mad v bad'. Until we can achieve a degree of consensus about these as a society, then solutions to some of the more service-specific tensions within forensic mental health care may well remain elusive.

Reflection exercises

1. Mental health and risk

Exercise for all workers

- Reading the papers and watching the news, how often do stories about mental health appear? Are they predominantly positive or negative?
- How much risk do you think is posed by the people you work with, and is this similar to public perceptions and media portrayals?
- What can you or your team do to start to change public attitudes?

2. Prison mental health

Exercise for all staff

- When someone with a mental health problem is admitted to prison, do you know where to go for support?
- What additional needs might someone with a mental health problem have in prison?
- What can you do to improve the current system bottom-up?

3. Secure services

Exercise for staff in secure services

- Could some of the people you care for be supported in less secure settings?
- If so, what barriers prevent this from happening?
- What could you and your service do to reduce these barriers and limit the impact of the situation on service users?

4. Partnership working

Exercise for all staff

- To what extent does your team liaise with others involved in forensic mental health services?
- What opportunities exist to improve local working relationships?
- Where possible, visit a local/regional secure service and/or prison – what do staff, service users and prisoners have to say about the mental health system as a whole and how might their insights help to change your practice?

Suggestions for further reading

1. The *National Confidential Inquiry into Suicide and Homicide by People with Serious Mental Illness* has produced a range of useful publications which shed light on issues of risk, dangerousness and suicide (www. national-confidential-inquiry.ac.uk).

2. The Sainsbury Centre for Mental Health has published a series of helpful overviews, including a summary of key facts and figures, a briefing on prison mental health care, a review of London's prison mental health services, a discussion paper on primary care mental health in prisons, an exploration of access to employment for people in forensic mental health services, responses to recent policy and an analysis of spending on prison mental health care (Rutherford and Duggan, 2007; Sainsbury Centre for Mental Health, 2006b, 2006c, 2007c, 2007d, 2008, 2009a, 2009b). More recently, their briefing on *Mental health care and the criminal justice system* is a helpful summary of key issues (2009c) and they have produced *10 top tips for PCT boards* when commissioning mental health care within criminal justice (n.d.).

3. *Changing the outlook* is the government's strategy for improving the quality of mental health services in prisons (Department of Health/HM Prison Service/National Assembly for Wales, 2001). The Department of Health and NIMHE (2005) have also produced an offender mental health care pathway to provide best practice guidance for providers and commissioners of mental health services. A summary of policy for improving offender health is available via: www.dh.gov.uk/en/Healthcare/Offenderhealth/index.htm.

4. See www.probation.homeoffice.gov.uk/output/Page30.asp for details of MAPPA annual reports.

5. The National Forensic Mental Health Research and Development programme was established in 1999 and has commissioned a range of research studies to support the provision of services for mentally disordered offenders (www.nfmhp.org.uk).

6. Of all the sources cited in this chapter, one of the most powerful is Durcan's (2008) study of prison mental health care, based on the experiences of prisoners themselves.

7 Partnership Working

In this chapter we discuss:

- The importance of partnership working
- The health and social care divide
- Different models of partnership working
- Lessons from the mental health literature
- Possible ways forward

The importance of partnership working

In 1942, William Beveridge published his report on *Social insurance and allied services*. Often viewed as the founding father of the UK welfare state, Beveridge identified *five giants* or social problems that would need to be resolved in the post-war world: Want, Disease, Ignorance, Squalor and Idleness (p. 6). Although this language may seem old-fashioned, the issues Beveridge identified remain key features of government policy today and have traditionally tended to be handled by large-scale and very hierarchical departments of government (see Table 7.1). As an example, we have tended to respond to the *giant* of 'want' by paying social security benefits to people with low incomes, disabled people, the unemployed and older people

Table 7.1	The five giants and the welfare state

Beveridge's giants/social problems	Government response/service
Want	Social security
Disease	NHS
Ignorance	Education
Squalor	Housing and regeneration
Idleness	Employment and leisure

via the Department of Social Security (now the Department for Work and Pensions).

Of course, the problem with this way of organising services is that it does not necessarily take account of the complexity and the overlapping nature of many social problems. Thus, many people living in poverty will also live in poor housing in deprived areas and may also experience poor education services, unemployment and ill health. This complexity can be problematic for a number of reasons:

- Some problems are so multifaceted that services need to work together to make any inroads at all. Thus, no one service is able to tackle crime and disorder, prevent social exclusion, eradicate substance misuse or tackle teenage pregnancy – these are all issues that require a number of agencies to co-operate and pool their respective resources and expertise to provide even a partial solution
- There is scope for considerable duplication of effort and a waste of scarce resources. Thus, one family with a child who has been in trouble with the police, in the local community and at school might receive input from a large number of welfare agencies, including the education system, the police, social services, the housing department, the youth offending team, the local regeneration initiative, child and adolescent mental health, a behaviour support team, special educational needs services, the youth service and so on. With such a large array of services, there is clearly scope for some sort of co-ordination to provide a more appropriate and less labour-intensive input into this one family
- At the same time, there is scope for services to fail to meet the needs of particular individuals. There are many instances of this in the UK, but examples would include a high profile child death in which police, education, social services and the NHS failed to work together or to share information (see Box 7.1), or a frail older person who is considered too sick for social services, but not ill enough to require NHS care

Put simply, people tend not to live their lives according to the categories we create in our welfare services.

In addition, there is a common tendency to conceive of the welfare state solely in terms of the public sector. However, this ignores the fact that we have always had a mixed economy of care in which welfare is provided by a range of different groups and organisations:

- By family, friends and neighbours (the informal sector)
- By voluntary organisations and self-help groups (the voluntary and community sector)
- By private companies (the private sector)
- By the state (the public sector)

Thus, in the nineteenth century local authorities were responsible for the water supply, sewage and sanitation, while voluntary agencies offered services

Box 7.1	Failures to work together

In 2003, Lord Laming published the results of an official inquiry into the death of Victoria Climbié, a young girl who had been killed by her great-aunt and her great-aunt's partner (Marie-Therese Kouao and Karl Manning) in 2001. In his inquiry, Lord Laming described the horrific treatment which Victoria had received (p. 1):

'At his trial, Manning said that Kouao would strike Victoria on a daily basis with a shoe, a coat hanger and a wooden cooking spoon and would strike her on her toes with a hammer. Victoria's blood was found on Manning's football boots. Manning later admitted that at times he would hit Victoria with a bicycle chain. Chillingly, he said, "you could beat her and she wouldn't cry … she could take beatings and the pain like anything".'

While a wide range of factors and mistakes contributed to Victoria's tragic death, the inquiry identified a lack of communication and poor interagency working between the large number of organisations who knew Victoria as key contributing factors (pp. 4, 6):

'In his opening statement to the Inquiry, Neil Garnham QC listed no fewer than 12 key occasions when the relevant services had the opportunity to successfully intervene in the life of Victoria.'

'Not one of the agencies empowered by Parliament to protect children in positions similar to Victoria – funded from the public purse – emerge from this Inquiry with much credit. The suffering and death of Victoria was a gross failure of the system and was inexcusable.'

'The single most important change in the future must be the drawing of a clear line of accountability, from top to bottom, without doubt or ambiguity about who is responsible at every level for the well-being of vulnerable children. Time and again it was disappointing to listen to the "buck passing" from those who attempted to justify their positions.'

such as community nursing services, befriending and financial assistance to the poor. GPs at this time were private practitioners who charged a fee for their services, and a lot of support was provided by neighbours and communities. In the twenty-first century, this is little different (although the balance of services has shifted in favour of the state): in older people's services, for example, the state funds and provides health care, voluntary organisations such as Age Concern provide lunch clubs and meals services, the private sector operates a range of home care services and residential homes, and family and friends provide considerable informal support. As a result, when we talk about the need to work in partnership, this often refers not only to public sector agencies, but also to partnerships across the mixed economy of care.

The health and social care divide

In response, successive governments have sought to encourage services to work more effectively together, both across agency boundaries (such as health care, social care and housing) and across sectors (public, private and voluntary). This is true in a range of different services, but is particularly the case in health and social care (which are often seen as two sides of the same coin and inextricably interlinked). Traditionally, the post-war welfare state is based on the assumption that it is possible to distinguish between people who are sick (health needs) and those who are merely frail or disabled (social care needs). This was enshrined in two pieces of 1940s legislation (the *NHS Act* 1946 and the *National Assistance Act* 1948) and continues to form the basis of service provision in the early twenty-first century (Glasby and Littlechild, 2004). As a result, two separate systems have developed, each with different ways of working, different structures and different priorities (see Box 7.2).

Box 7.2   **The health and social care divide**

Key features of social care include:

- Councillors democratically elected at a local level
- Local government is overseen and monitored by the Department for Communities and Local Government (although the Department of Health has a significant role in the oversight and monitoring of social care)
- Subject to means testing and charges
- Based on specific geographical areas
- Traditional focus on social factors contributing to individual situations and on choice/empowerment
- Strong emphasis on social sciences

Key features of NHS care include:

- Non-executive directors appointed by central government
- Overseen and monitored by the Department of Health
- Free at the point of delivery
- Boundaries are based on GP practice registration
- Traditional emphasis on the individual and on medical cure
- Strong emphasis on science

Of these, perhaps the most significant difference for members of the public is that health care tends to be provided free at the point of delivery, while social care tends to be subject to a means test and to charges (which are sometimes very significant). Thus, whether something is defined as health or as social care can be extremely important for the individual concerned and their family.

More recently, this state of affairs has been recognised as problematic for a number of key reasons:

1. The distinction between health and social care can often appear rather abstract and arbitrary. A famous example is the provision of bathing services: if the bath is for a 'health' reason (such as a skin condition or if the person has specialist

lifting and handling requirements), they may receive a bath from the NHS free of charge; if it is simply a 'social' bath then this will be provided by social services and the person will have to pay. Arguably this is a distinction which may not seem very meaningful to the service user (who simply wants a bath, irrespective of who provides it) (Glasby and Littlechild, 2004).

2. Different professionals bring different skills and experiences which, if combined, could lead to a much better, more holistic service. This is often encapsulated in the notion that the whole is frequently greater than the sum of its parts.

3. Considerable time and energy can be expended in deciding whether a particular case is the responsibility of health or of social care, when a more efficient use of resources may be to work together to avoid such 'turf wars'.

4. When resources are scarce, there is a tendency for eligibility criteria for services to be restricted. In such a situation, overstretched departments have a vested interest in trying to define individual cases as the responsibility of the other agency (often known as buck-passing or cost shunting). As an example, it is not uncommon for people with learning difficulties and mental health problems to be passed backwards and forwards between mental health and learning difficulty services, with each agency feeling that the other is responsible for the person concerned (see also Chapter 9).

As the Department of Health (1998c, p. 3) suggests:

> All too often when people have complex needs spanning both health and social care good quality services are sacrificed for sterile arguments about boundaries. When this happens people, often the most vulnerable in our society ... and those who care for them find themselves in the no man's land between health and social services. This is not what people want or need. It places the needs of the organisation above the needs of the people they are there to serve. It is poor organisation, poor practice, poor use of taxpayers' money – it is unacceptable.

To prevent the dangers of overly compartmentalised service provision, successive governments have emphasised the importance of partnership working. Over time, responses have ranged from the Joint Consultative Committees, joint care planning teams and joint finance initiatives of the 1960s and 1970s to attempts to ensure greater co-ordination with mechanisms such as care management and the Care Programme Approach in the 1990s. Despite these changes, significant divisions in health and social care remained in practice throughout the rest of the 1990s, with greater consultation and liaison between health and social care, but ongoing professional divisions, demarcation disputes and financial difficulties (see, for example, Hudson *et al.*, 1997; Hudson and Henwood, 2002). Since 1997, however, the election of New Labour has led to much greater emphasis on partnership working, with new legal powers to work more flexibly across boundaries and the option to create new integrated health and social care organisations (see Box 7.3).

Box 7.3	New Labour innovations: the *Health Act* 1999 and Care Trusts

Under the *Health Act* 1999 (since updated by the *NHS Act* 2006), local partners have three new 'flexibilities' which they can choose to use (either alone in combination):

1. *Pooled budgets* – health and social services put a proportion of their funds into a mutually accessible joint budget. Unlike previous joint finance initiatives, contributions lose their health or social care identity and can be used on either health or social care as appropriate. The newly created joint budget is administered by a pool manager, supervised by a committee made up of representatives from each partner agency.
2. *Lead commissioning* – one authority transfers funds to the other who then takes responsibility for purchasing both health and social care. Services that might benefit from such an approach could be those for people with mental health problems or those with learning difficulties.
3. *Integrated provision* – one integrated organisation provides both health and social care.

In particular, many mental health services are now delivered by some form of Partnership Trust, using the Health Act flexibilities (see Glendinning *et al.*, 2002a for an early evaluation; see also Phelps and Regen, 2008).

The *Health and Social Care Act* 2001 introduced the concept of a Care Trust – an NHS body with social care responsibilities delegated to it. Care Trusts can either be PCT-based (both commissioning and providing) or based on an NHS provider trust (just providing). Despite initial enthusiasm in some localities, there are still very few Care Trusts nationally – see Glasby and Peck, 2003, for further discussion.

Box 7.4	More recent partnership initiatives

Whereas some policies in the early 2000s seemed to suggest the need for significant organisational changes, more recent developments have tended to be more flexible about the shape of local services, while also making it clear that failing to work together is not an option. Key policies include:

- Various legal duties for health and social care to collaborate (including the *Health Act* 1999, the *Children Act* 2004 and the *Local Government and Public Involvement in Health Act* 2007)
- A new duty for health and local government to conduct a Joint Strategic Needs Assessment of their local area, thereby jointly understanding the current and future needs of local people
- Guidance around joint commissioning for health and well-being (Department of Health, 2007)
- The creation of a new Care Quality Commission, based on a merger of previous health care, social care and mental health regulators
- A requirement for local agencies to develop new Local Area Agreements to set out local priorities for the area that require joint action (see www.communities.gov.uk)

More recently, these policies have been supplemented by additional legal duties to collaborate, a more integrated approach to regulation, inspection and performance management, and a new duty to jointly assess the needs of the local population (see Box 7.4).

Box 7.5	The Somerset innovations

'In 1996, Somerset Health Authority and Somerset County Council issued the findings of a review of mental health services which catalogued a series of problems that would have been familiar to most localities around England at that time. However, the response of the Health Authority and County Council to this report was without precedent. They decided to introduce joint commissioning (through the establishment of the Joint Commissioning Board – JCB) and integrated provision (through the creation of the Somerset Partnerships Health and Social Care NHS Trust – the Trust) simultaneously on 1st April 1999. Almost as unusually, the two agencies also commissioned an evaluation of the impact of these innovations during the first thirty months from the Centre for Mental Health Services Development, King's College London ....'

The aims of the evaluation were 'to identify the impact of joint commissioning and combined service provision' through:

■ Identification of the impact of the changes on service users and carers
■ Assessment of the impact of changes on the professional staff involved
■ Identification of aspirations and beliefs of the agencies involved for joint commissioning and joint provision of mental health services in Somerset, and how these changed over time

Over time, the research involved regular interviews with service users and carers, a self-administered survey of all staff members involved with adult mental health service provision, exploratory workshops with self-selected members of staff, semi-structured interviews with senior managers of health and social services and non-participant-based observation of the Joint Commissioning Board.

Key findings include:

■ For staff, the changes initially led to a reduction in morale, role clarity and job satisfaction, although there were some signs of improvement by the end of the evaluation.
■ For service users and carers, there was little change: while some felt that services were better co-ordinated, there were fears that therapeutic/support groups would become more limited as buildings changed into offices for co-located teams, concerns about changes in key workers and a perceived reduction in personnel. Crucially, there were also ongoing concerns for some users and carers throughout the study about the attitudes of some staff members, the quality of acute care, the lack of user involvement in drawing up care plans and a failure to consider the needs of carers.

Adapted from Peck *et al.* (2002a, 2003, pp. 39–40)

However, perhaps the most famous example of partnership working under New Labour is the Somerset Partnerships Health and Social Care NHS Trust. Cited as a good practice example in *The NHS plan* (Department of Health, 2000a, p. 71), the Trust was the first integrated mental health trust in the UK and took the unprecedented step of commissioning a long-term and independent evaluation of its work (see Box 7.5). The final report of this study (Peck *et al.*, 2002a) represents the most in-depth and substantial contribution to our knowledge of health and social care partnerships, and is a crucial document for anyone wishing to explore this topic in more detail. Significantly, this research painted a rather different picture to the positive spin of *The NHS plan*, suggesting that the positives of integration in Somerset may also have been accompanied by some negatives (see later in this chapter for further discussion).

As a result of these changes, there is a fear among some social care staff in particular about a potential loss of identity and the danger of being dominated by a much larger and more powerful NHS. In some ways, this has been true over a period of time – although this book adopts a multidisciplinary approach, there is sometimes a tendency to equate mental health services with the NHS and with health care practitioners, overlooking the social care contribution. With current mental health partnerships increasingly located within NHS bodies (such as Care Trusts or Partnership Trusts), some social care staff are currently concerned about the future of social care (see also O'Sea, 2004; Carpenter *et al.*, 2003 for further discussion of the role of social workers in interagency mental health services). For these practitioners, we suggest Blinkhorn's (2004) study of the role of the social worker in multidisciplinary teams and the work of the Social Perspectives Network (www.spn.org.uk) to develop new approaches to mental health practice that reflect the needs and hopes of service users and that build on a more holistic understanding of mental distress (see also, ADASS, 2008; Tew, 2005). Also useful will be Reflection exercise 1 at the end of this chapter to help social care workers think through and be confident about the contribution they have to make and the value base they bring with them in health and social care partnerships.

Different models of partnership working

As a result of the current emphasis on partnership working, there is a growing literature which seeks to define what we mean by the term *partnership* and identify the factors that may help and hinder interagency working. However, a useful definition is offered by Sullivan and Skelcher (2002), who see partnership working in terms of its emphasis on:

1. A shared responsibility for assessing the need for action, determining the type of action to be taken and agreeing the means of implementation.
2. Negotiation between people from different agencies committed to working together over more than the short term.
3. An intention to secure the delivery of benefits or added value which could not have been provided by a single agency acting alone.

In terms of barriers to successful partnership working and possible ways forward, common frameworks include those developed by the Nuffield Institute for Health (Hudson *et al.*, 1997) and Poxton's *partnership readiness framework* (see Boxes 7.6 and 7.7), both of which seek to identify those factors that can facilitate or hinder effective partnerships.

Box 7.6	Partnership working: what helps and what hinders?

Barriers:

- *Structural* (the fragmentation of service responsibilities across and within agency boundaries)
- *Procedural* (differences in planning and budget cycles)
- *Financial* (differences in funding mechanisms and resource flows)
- *Professional* (differences in ideologies, values and professional interests)
- *Perceived threats to status, autonomy and legitimacy*

Principles for strengthening strategic approaches to collaboration:

- *Shared vision*: specifying what is to be achieved in terms of user-centred goals, clarifying the purpose of collaboration as a mechanism for achieving such goals, and mobilising commitment around goals, outcomes and mechanisms
- *Clarity of roles and responsibilities*: specifying and agreeing 'who does what' and designing organisational arrangements by which roles and responsibilities are to be fulfilled
- *Appropriate incentives and rewards*: promoting organisational behaviour consistent with agreed goals and responsibilities, and harnessing organisational self-interest to collective goals
- *Accountability for joint working*: monitoring achievements in relation to the stated vision, holding individuals and agencies to account for the fulfilment of predetermined roles and responsibilities, and providing feedback and review of vision, responsibilities, incentives and their interrelationship

(Summarised from Hudson *et al.*, 1997)

A further contribution is made by Glasby (2003), who sees partnerships as operating at three interrelated but separate levels of activity: that of the individual practitioner (I), that of local health and social care organisations (O) and that of national policy and the structure of the welfare state (S). These categories have been presented diagrammatically (see Figure 7.1) to illustrate the way in which individual workers can be influenced by the organisations in which they work and the structure of services nationally. At the same time, however, the way services are structured and the way in which local organisations relate to each other depend ultimately on the individuals working on the ground. As a result, Glasby argues that only a multifaceted approach which seeks to tackle the individual, the organisational and the structural level all at once can ever hope to achieve more effective partnership working. This model draws on the work of Thompson (2006) with regard to anti-discriminatory practice (see Chapter 9).

Box 7.7	The Partnership Readiness Framework

Successful partnerships depend on the nature and history of local services.
For example, to what extent do partners have a proven track record when it comes to:

1. Building shared values and principles
2. Agreeing specific policy shifts
3. Being prepared to explore new service options
4. Determining agreed boundaries
5. Agreeing respective roles with regard to commissioning, purchasing and providing
6. Identifying agreed resource pools
7. Ensuring effective leadership
8. Providing sufficient development capacity
9. Developing and sustaining good personal relationships
10. Paying specific attention to mutual trust and attitude?

(Summarised from Poxton, 2003, p. 17)

Figure 7.1	Different levels of partnership working

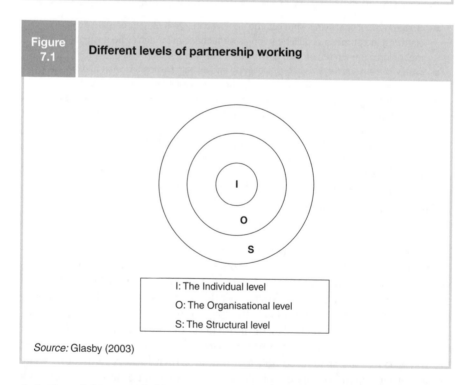

I: The Individual level

O: The Organisational level

S: The Structural level

Source: Glasby (2003)

A final model is provided by Peck (2002), who suggests that partnerships tend to pursue either depth or breadth. As demonstrated in Figure 7.2, organisations can either pursue a strong relationship between a small number of partners (such as the NHS and social services) or a wider relationship with a larger number of partners (such as the NHS and the wider local authority and voluntary sector). What is currently unclear is the extent to which local partners could seek to achieve both depth and breadth simultaneously.

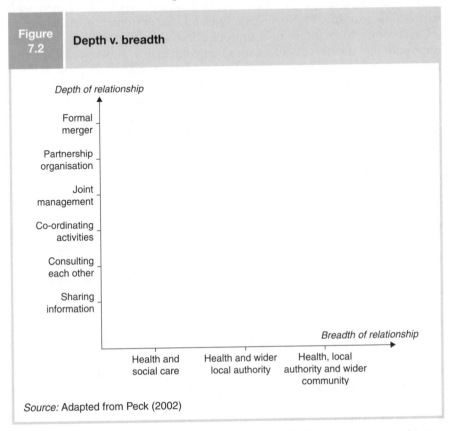

Figure 7.2 **Depth v. breadth**

Source: Adapted from Peck (2002)

Whatever approach is taken to developing more effective interagency and interprofessional relationships, the partnership literature is clear about the danger of trying to achieve positive change through structural reorganisation alone. While this is a bigger topic than can be dealt with here, the Somerset study above is a good example of the way in which a change in structures can easily become an end in itself (that is, the aim becomes having a merged organisation, not necessarily about improving outcomes for people who use services). Indeed, all the available evidence suggests that structural change by itself rarely achieves stated objectives, does not save money, can damage staff morale and can distract senior managers – often for several years after the initial integration (see Glasby and Dickinson, 2008b, for a summary; see also Reilly *et al.*, 2007, for discussion of the strengths and limitations of structural integration in Northern Ireland). Instead, the partnership literature is clear about the importance of paying significant attention to organisational and professional culture – warning that failure to do so can often lead to problematic interprofessional relationships and even to organisational failure (see, for example, Peck and Dickinson, 2008).

Lessons from the mental health literature

Throughout the partnership literature, different commentators are almost unanimous in identifying a multitude of potential benefits associated with partnership working. In North–East England, for example, an evaluation of a Community Mental Health Team found that an integrated team approach improved the transfer of information, encouraged a pooling of expertise, led to enhanced creativity in problem solving and resulted in more responsive services (Cook *et al.*, 2001). In Somerset and Northumberland, service reviews have emphasised the importance of a service with a single point of contact (Gulliver, 1999), while staff in Leeds feel that multidisciplinary working leads to pooled knowledge and to the opportunities to experience areas of work outside individuals' normal professional roles (Millar, 2000). At the same time, work undertaken by the Sainsbury Centre for Mental Health (2000, pp. 12–14) suggests that partnership working is a 'must do' for mental health services for a range of political, financial and practical reasons:

- Mental health is complex with a range of different agencies involved (including health care, social care, housing, welfare advice and employment services)
- Many mental health service users are vulnerable and have limited capacity to negotiate complex bureaucracies. They therefore need services that are well integrated at the point of contact, are easy to negotiate and are focused on their needs
- Resources are scarce, but the task is broad. It therefore makes sense for agencies to work together to achieve the vision for mental health set out in official policy documents
- There are strong perverse incentives in mental health, with evidence of, for example, 'bed blocking' due to the lack of community alternatives (see Chapter 5)
- Integrating the CPA and care management has historically been a high priority and is simpler and more effective when joint working arrangements are sound (see Chapter 4)
- Partnership working can help to minimise bureaucracy and duplication as well as maximising integration for service users and staff

Above all, partnership working is deemed to be beneficial for service users and their carers, who can often experience fragmented services, a lack of continuity and conflicting information in situations where local agencies fail to collaborate effectively. This has been described by Preston *et al.* (1999) in terms of being 'left in limbo', with users and carers feeling that they are failing to make progress through the mental health system:

> Separate clinics don't talk to each other or ring each other. I find the whole thing incredible the length of time it takes; it's just been horrendous, waiting weeks to see a consultant to be told 'I don't know why you've been referred to me' … It can make you feel very insignificant. (Service user, quoted in Preston *et al.*, 1999, p. 19)

Despite these potential benefits, the partnership literature identifies a series of barriers to more effective interagency collaboration. As well as the general barriers identified earlier in this chapter, there are a range of additional factors within mental health services that are also of significance. Thus, Norman and Peck's (1999) study of the views of leading members of professional organisations highlights issues such as a loss of faith by mental health professionals in the system within which they work, strong adherence to uni-professional cultures, the absence of a shared philosophy for community mental health services and mistrust of managerial solutions. For Nolan *et al.* (1998), key obstacles to collaboration include individual practitioners' lack of knowledge of other professionals, a tendency to stereotype other workers, defensive attitudes and a lack of certainty over one's own role. Engaging members of particular professions can also be problematic, as can looking beyond health and social care to include a wider range of partners (see Box 7.8). Also significant may be ongoing tensions between care and control within mental health services, which may deprive staff and their organisations of the shared vision of the way forward so necessary for effective partnerships (see Box 7.6 above). A lack of a common language and terminology can also be key barriers (see, for example, Salmon and Rapport, 2005).

Box 7.8	**Engaging 'hard to reach' professional groups**

Sometimes, it can be difficult to engage members from particular professions in partnership working:

- GPs may not necessarily see mental health issues as a priority and most are independent practitioners with very different contractual arrangements from other health and social care services (Cook *et al.*, 2001; Hancock and Villeneau, 1997; Poxton, 1999)
- Psychiatrists sometimes see themselves as being responsible for the work of the whole multidisciplinary team and may not support the view that team membership implies equality of status and some form of democratic decision making. This can lead to high levels of psychological stress, generate conflict among team members and inhibit team relationships (Norman and Peck, 1999; Peck and Norman, 1999)
- Psychologists may sometimes perceive themselves as relatively autonomous, high status practitioners and may be ambivalent about being too closely identified with multidisciplinary teams (Peck and Norman, 1999)
- Practice nurses have different employment arrangements from other groups and can feel isolated from other professional colleagues (Nolan *et al.*, 1998)
- Non-executive board members and local authority councillors are key decision makers, but are felt by some mental health practitioners to have a poor understanding of mental health issues (Hancock *et al.*, 1997)

In addition to these groups, partnerships may sometimes fail to reach out to services beyond health and social care (such as housing) or to keep other partners (such as services users or voluntary agencies) fully informed of what is happening (Hancock *et al.*, 1997).

Possible solutions

In order to overcome these barriers, researchers and policy analysts propose a wide range of possible solutions (see Box 7.9). Sometimes, the existence of a key power broker (often a consultant psychiatrist) can facilitate greater collaboration in a local area, although the resultant partnership is very vulnerable if this person leaves (Norman and Peck, 1999). Personal and leadership styles can also be important, with partnerships dependent on the attitude of senior managers and a willingness to pioneer new approaches (Sainsbury Centre for Mental Health, 2000). In contrast to this emphasis on key individuals or on personal characteristics, other commentators emphasise the need for more formal approaches to partnership working such as interprofessional education (Roberts and Priest, 1997) or interagency agreements about how to prioritise and allocate referrals (Maunder *et al.*, 2001; McDermott and Reid, 1999). For Gulliver (1999), the focus should be on more strategic issues such as securing senior management commitment, developing a shared vision, investing time in staff, owning each other's difficulties and recognising that partnerships are a means to an end rather than an end in themselves. Elsewhere, progress towards more effective partnerships seems to

Box 7.9	Improving partnership working

Work undertaken by the Sainsbury Centre for Mental Health (2000, pp. 6–9) suggests that successful partnerships may depend upon:

- Avoiding organisationally defensive routines
- Taking into account the user movement
- Understanding changing organisational cultures
- Understanding the key components of effective dialogue
- Taking account of well-understood success factors such as having a clear strategic purpose for the partnership
- Creating alliances which form part of the everyday functioning of organisations
- Developing a supportive internal infrastructure
- Looking at external factors when planning and acting
- Taking specific account of key issues such as governance arrangements, performance management, information systems, workforce issues, charging policies, complaints procedures and user involvement

For Norman and Peck (1999, p. 224), the way forward is to:

- Draw upon users' aspirations as an explicit philosophy for guiding the development of the partnership
- Clarify accountability and responsibility of staff
- Clarify staff roles
- Develop a framework to explore the relationships between multidisciplinary groups
- Draw upon existing theories for understanding team effectiveness

have been made by adopting a more developmental approach which seeks to explore the perceptions which different practitioners have of colleagues from other disciplines and working through these preconceptions in multiagency settings (see, for example, Nolan *et al.*, 1998; Peck and Norman, 1999; see Reflection exercise 1 for practical suggestions as to how practitioners can engage in such an activity). In contrast, research into the implementation of a Scottish integrated care pathway found that positive views among workers about joint working were not enough by themselves to tackle wider organisational barriers (with integration therefore dependent on a mix of staff ownership/involvement and strategic input; see Rees *et al.*, 2004).

Conclusion

Overall, the diverse range of issues discussed above would seem to support an assertion by the Sainsbury Centre for Mental Health (2000, p. 27) that 'there are no "quick fixes", and no magic solutions to complex health and social problems'. Ultimately, it seems as though the way forward may lie in an incremental approach, whereby individual partners make use of whatever avenue they think may be beneficial and locally appropriate to travel closer to the overall goal of more effective partnership working. Hopefully, some of the concepts and frameworks presented in this chapter may help to provide a way of understanding and engaging with the complexities that partnership working entails. However, this is probably little consolation to those busy practitioners frustrated with the restraints of the current system or to someone using mental health services (who does not distinguish between 'health care' and 'social care', but just needs support – irrespective of where it comes from).

Given all these difficulties, one option for future joint working is to focus on the *outcomes* that services and professions are seeking to deliver – for those who use services, for staff and/or for local organisations. All too often, public services seem to concentrate on issues of *process* and of *structure* (what should we call the partnership, who does it report to, what does it look like, etc.?). In many ways, this seems to come from our tendency to respond to pressure with a 'there's a problem, what do we do' approach. Understandable though this is, the risk is that we may not fully understand the nature of the problem (and could therefore be focusing merely on the symptoms rather than the cause) and that we have little idea of what success would look like. To counter this tendency, the framework in Figure 7.3 encourages potential partners to ask themselves what it is they are trying to achieve for local people (outcomes) and how well current services do this already (context). It is then (and only then) that discussion can turn to issues of process – what we do and how we design it in such a way as to achieve the outcomes we wish to deliver. While this is inevitably an over-simplification, we would argue that a health and social care community that has a genuinely shared understanding of where it wants to get to and of where it is now ought, at the very least, to be better equipped to decide together what best to do next.

Figure 7.3   Focusing on outcomes

Reflection exercises

1. Professional roles and identity

Exercise for all workers

- What is it that distinguishes your profession from other disciplines and what do you value about this?
- What do you admire about other professions and what bemuses you (i.e. confuses you, angers you, frustrates you)?

Consider this question with regard to psychiatrists, psychologists, nurses, social workers, general practitioners, local councillors and NHS non-executive board members. If possible, ask professional colleagues from different backgrounds to complete the same exercise and share your answers:

- What does this teach you about how others view your profession?
- Do you agree with others' views about you and do they agree about your views of them?
- If you do not understand something about another profession, can they explain it to you?
- Are there any key contributions that each of the professions make that you can all agree on?
- How can you build on the strengths of each profession and minimise any perceived limitations?

2. Barriers and success factors

Exercise for all workers

Using the frameworks in Boxes 7.6 and 7.7, reflect on a local health and social care partnership:

- To what extent has it experienced the barriers suggested by these frameworks?
- How has it tried to overcome them?
- To what extent is there local evidence of some of the success factors suggested by these frameworks?
- How can these be developed and built upon?

3. Focusing on outcomes

Exercise for all workers

Using the framework in Figure 7.3, reflect on a piece of joint working you have undertaken or read about recently:

- How easy is it to describe what outcomes this partnership was trying to achieve?
- How well do current services achieve these outcomes by themselves?
- What needs to change and how in order to get from where you are now to where you want to be?
- What role can you play in helping to bring about this change?

Suggestions for further reading

1. Introductory textbooks on partnership working include:

   - Balloch, S. and Taylor, M. (eds) (2001) *Partnership working: policy and practice*. Bristol, Policy Press
   - Barrett *et al.*'s (2005) *Interprofessional working in health and social care*. Basingstoke, Palgrave Macmillan
   - Glasby, J. and Dickinson, H. (2008b) *Partnership working in health and social care*. Bristol, Policy Press
   - Glendinning *et al.*'s (2002b) *Partnerships, New Labour and the governance of welfare*. Bristol, Policy Press
   - Sullivan, H. and Skelcher, C. (2002) *Working across boundaries*. Basingstoke, Palgrave

2. Glasby and Dickinson's (2008a) *Better partnership working* series is a collection of five books published by The Policy Press in association with *Community Care* magazine. Designed as a series of accessible 'how to' books, they provide a short, easy to use but research-based introduction to some of the key concepts and issues.

3. Peck *et al.*'s (2002a) evaluation of the Somerset Partnership Trust is still a key resource and remains one of the most comprehensive studies there has been of partnership working over time and of organisational and professional culture (see also Freeman and Peck, 2006, for further discussion of linked research in a second UK site). Building on this, Peck and colleagues have continued to explore issues of organisational/professional culture and strategies for managing during organisational mergers. Key resources include:

   - Peck and Crawford's (2004) discussion paper on organisational culture for the Integrated Care Network (see below for a link to the ICN website).
   - Peck and Dickinson's (2008) summary of the international literature (from both public and private sectors) on organisational culture.
   - Dickinson *et al.*'s (2006) review of the literature on managing organisational transitions (available free online via www.hsmc.bham.ac.uk).

4. For a discussion of the role of social workers in multidisciplinary teams and in services which are increasingly based in the NHS, see Blinkhorn (2004). For further discussion of social care-related issues, see ADASS (2008). Tew's (2005) edited collection on social perspectives in mental health is an extremely helpful contribution which brings together a range of more socially orientated perspectives.

5. The Integrated Care Network (www.integratedcarenetwork.gov.uk) produces a large number of publications and other resources designed to promote more effective partnership working.

6. Key journals with articles on interagency issues include the UK's *Journal of Integrated Care*, the *Journal of Interprofessional Care* and the *International Journal of Integrated Care*. The latter is a free online journal available via www.ijic.org

7. The Centre for the Advancement of Interprofessional Education (CAIPE) promotes interprofessional learning and has a range of information, publications, case studies and links available on its website (www.caipe. org.uk).

8. Following changes in policy outlined in Chapter 2, the role of several mental health professionals is also changing – and this is likely to have a key impact on future joint working (see, for example, Department of Health, 2005e, 2006g, 2007g, 2007h).

8 User Involvement

In this chapter we discuss:

- Different definitions of the term 'mental health service user'
- The history and current status of user involvement in mental health services
- The importance of user involvement in developing mental health services
- Key barriers and examples of positive practice
- The importance of organisational culture and personal attributes
- Future directions in user involvement

What is meant by the term 'mental health service user'?

The language used to describe service users is perhaps more varied in mental health than in any other sector of health and social care. User, survivor, patient, customer, citizen, consumer: all imply different notions of the roles and responsibilities of people with mental health problems and the relationship between services and users. Pilgrim and Rogers (2005) have described a useful four-part typology of users as consumers, survivors, providers or, perhaps most commonly, as patients.

'Consumerism' is a relatively new ideology within the public sector, linked, as we discussed in Chapter 2, to the rise of general management principles in the NHS in the 1980s and the development of a market economy through the introduction of an internal market. It is also linked to the growing acknowledgement of the importance of customer satisfaction with users of health and social care as customers who can exercise an informed choice about the services they receive and, if not satisfied, take their 'business' elsewhere. However, as Rogers and Pilgrim point out:

> Many psychiatric patients do not ask for what they get – it is imposed
> on them. Various sections of the 1983 *Mental Health Act*, like its
> legal predecessors, are utilised to lawfully impose restraints and
> treatments on resentful and reluctant recipients. In such circumstances,
> mental patients could be construed to be consumers if being dragged
> off the street and force fed was a feature of being a customer in a
> restaurant. (Rogers and Pilgrim, 2001, p. 169)

Poverty can also limit choice with private sector mental health services out of bounds, while, at times of crisis, the ability and motivation to obtain information about a range of services and select between them can be difficult (Lester *et al.*, 2004). Choice also implies a possibility of exit from the system, a notion that is difficult to sustain in a society whose courts recognise the validity of advanced directives only when they prospectively authorise treatment, not when they are used to reject the possibility of treatment (Szasz, 2003). Choice, then, as a central part of consumerism, appears to be a relative concept if you are a mental health service user.

In contrast, the user as 'survivor' is linked to the growth in the early 1970s of collective activities of mental health service users, initially in the Netherlands and the US. Recognising the wisdom of the dominant Trade Union philosophy of the time that 'Unity is Strength', organisations such as the Campaign Against Psychiatric Oppression and the British Network for Alternatives to Psychiatry were formed. The image and term 'survivor' is very particularly chosen by groups such as Survivors Speak Out, the UK Advocacy Network (UKAN) and the Hearing Voices Network to portray a positive image of people in distress as those who had the strength to survive the mental health system. 'Survivor' also implies a notion of rejecting forms of professionally led and produced information.

Linked to this, the conceptualisation of users as 'providers' is reflected in the development of user-led services that are found in the voluntary and statutory sector across the UK. The range of user-led activities includes a spectrum of involvement from patients being mutually supported in professionally led services to projects that are managed and staffed by users themselves. The latter include safe houses and drop-in day centres and often reflect the user movement priorities of voluntary relationships, alternatives to hospital admissions and personal support.

However, Pilgrim and Rogers suggest that the main way in which users have been portrayed is as 'patients' – as 'passive objects of study' (2005, p. 217). With this representation, users are seen in terms of their illness, perceived as irrational and therefore as incapable of having a valid view. Patients and relatives are assumed to share the same perspective and where they do not, relatives' views often take precedence.

A further way of thinking about the meaning of the word 'user' is as a citizen. This is a fluid concept that incorporates a cluster of meanings including defined legal and social status; a means of signifying political identity; a focus of loyalty; a requirement to perform duties; expectations of rights; and a yardstick of behaviour (Heater, 1990). Marshall's (1950) classic influential analysis of the development of the meaning of citizenship over time is summarised in Box 8.1.

A recent shift in the meaning of citizenship is that it entails not only rights but also a moral duty to 'to take part in constructing and maintaining the community' (Meehan, 1993, p. 177). Barnes and Walker (1996) similarly suggest that citizenship is closely allied to the concept of empowerment rather than consumerism, and includes the right to interactive participation and to share power with health and social care professionals.

Box 8.1	Elements of citizenship

Marshall (1950) defined citizenship rights as comprising:

■ Legal or civil rights which enable the individual to participate freely in the life of the community. These rights include property and contractual rights, and rights to freedom of thought, freedom of speech, religious practice, assembly and association
■ Political rights which entitle the citizen to participate in the government of the community: the right to vote and to hold political office
■ Social and economic rights to the circumstances which enable the individual to participate in the general well-being of the community. They include rights to health care, education and welfare

(From Barnes and Bowl, 2001, p. 14)

However, with respect to mental health service users, we would argue that citizenship rights are eroded in a number of different ways. The potential for compulsory detention, community treatment orders and medical treatment administered without consent are all constraints on legal and civil rights. Above all, aspects of the social exclusion experienced by many people with mental illness severely impact on their social and economic rights (Sayce, 2001).

The history of user involvement in mental health services

Although user involvement became more prominent in the late twentieth-century, protest and dissent have been a feature of the relationship between madness and medicine throughout the ages. Campbell (1996), for example, cites 'The Petition of the Poor Distracted People in the House of Beldam' in 1620 as an early example of collective protest. The Alleged Lunatics' Friends Society, a lobbying and campaigning organisation, was formed by 'ex-patients' in 1845 and is credited with extricating the poet John Clare from a Victorian asylum, possibly one of the first examples of peer advocacy. Occasionally, users' voices have also been heard in terms of individual experiences and treatment in early asylums (see Box 8.2). It is interesting, if disheartening, to note that despite the passage of nearly two hundred years, hopes and desires for treatment remain essentially unchanged.

During the early part of the twentieth century, individual descriptions of life in asylums continued to emerge, often in the context of the treatment of shell shock during and after the First World War. However, most were again individual accounts and there was little sense of a collective user voice. It was not until the 1960s and early 1970s that the convergence of a number of different related influences from both within the UK and internationally led to a slow but progressive change in the way in which users perceived themselves, and

Box 8.2	Early user voices

In 1838, John Perceval published 'A narrative of the treatment experienced by a gentleman during a state of mental derangement: designed to explain the causes and the nature of insanity and to expose the injudicious conduct pursued towards many unfortunate sufferers under that calamity'.

He described how, as a patient in Brislington House, 'men acted as though my body, soul and spirit were fairly given up to their control, to work their mischief and folly upon … I mean that I was never told such and such things we are going to do: we think it advisable to administer such and such medicine in this or that manner. I was never asked, Do you want anything? Do you wish for, prefer anything?'

(Perceval, 1838, quoted in Porter, 1999, p. 182)

were perceived by society. For example, social movements such as the women's movement started to develop powerful critiques of the assumptions underpinning social policy. Academic analysis of the nature and impact of the institution (Goffman, 1961) also created an impetus to think differently about patients and their environment. Parallel developments, particularly a series of reports on hospital scandals, similarly focused on the poor care and inadequate living conditions of institutionalised patients (see Chapter 2). The 1960s also saw the rise of the anti-psychiatry movement, a large professionally led movement that opposed the traditional medical model of thinking about mental illness and suggested that the symptoms of mental distress reflected an individual's life experiences. The anti-psychiatry movement proposed that the focus should move from symptoms, to the meaning behind them, and that this could only be achieved by listening to the voice of the people experiencing the distress. In the 1970s, a rising concern about individual freedom and the civil rights of the individual, with the National Campaign for Civil Liberties taking a leading role in this respect in the UK, also helped to shape the form and function of the mental health service user movement.

By the mid-1980s, user-based organisations included the Nottingham Advocacy Group, Survivors Speak Out and the UK Advocacy Network, while more traditional voluntary organisations also began to include a greater number of user representatives in their work. Patient councils and user groups became increasingly widespread within mental health services themselves as service providers sought feedback directly from users. However it is also important to remember that, in 1985, the total number of mental health service user groups only numbered around a dozen (Sainsbury Centre for Mental Health, 2005).

The recent policy context of user involvement

The last twenty years have been characterised by a rapid growth in a range of different user involvement activities underpinned by a plethora of policy directives. Since the establishment of Community Health Councils in 1973, the rhetoric of user involvement has become a central component of UK health and social policy. In 1990, the *NHS and Community Care Act* was the first piece of UK legislation to establish a formal requirement for user involvement in service planning. Subsequent key policies in the early 1990s included *The patient's charter* (Department of Health, 1991) and *Local voices* (NHS Management Executive, 1992) which aimed to make services more responsive to patients' needs, but stressed consumerism rather than partnership or participation.

Encouragement for user involvement in the context of mental health at that time was provided in documents such as *The health of the nation* (Department of Health, 1992), the Mental Health Nursing Review, *Working in partnership* (Department of Health, 1994) and *Building bridges* (Department of Health, 1995). Indeed, *Working in partnership* declared: 'The work of mental health nurses rests upon the relationship they have with people who use services. Our recommendations for future action start and finish with this relationship' (Department of Health, 1994, p. 5).

Since 1997, 'patient and public involvement' in health care has become one of the central tenets of the Labour government's NHS and social care reforms. This emphasis has been driven by a number of different agendas (see Box 8.3).

Box 8.3	Current drivers for greater user involvement

- Democratic right as tax-paying citizens
- Consumerist principles and the patient choice agenda
- The desire to increase accountability within the NHS
- The cross-policy partnership agenda

The justification for user involvement can be made on the basic democratic principle that, since 1948, the NHS has been paid for by the taxpayer, so they should have a choice in what is funded and how services are delivered. However, as noted earlier in this chapter, the principle of consumerism has also been a strong justification for user involvement for at least two decades, with users as consumers enabled to exercise choice to ensure their needs are met.

More recently, the patient choice agenda fuelled by the wider availability of information, more treatment options, a slowly growing private sector as well as consumerism (Appleby *et al.*, 2003) has become a particularly strong political imperative. *Building on the best* (Department of Health, 2003g) set out a series of measures to extend patient choice across primary, secondary and community care (although mental health is mentioned only briefly).

The desire to increase the accountability of the NHS and the professionals who work within it is a further strong driver for increased user involvement.

Medical practitioners who fail in their duty of care to patients are perhaps best represented in the collective public consciousness by Harold Shipman, the GP found guilty of murdering fifteen of his female patients in 2000, and by the Bristol Royal Infirmary cardiologists. While it is tempting to argue that Shipman at least has little to do with the reality of health care in the UK, the 198 recommendations in the Bristol Royal Infirmary Inquiry (2001) and other cases have come to symbolise the unchecked autonomy of the medical profession, and, allied to a growing momentum within the medical profession itself to increase accountability, helped create the patient and public involvement aspect of the broader clinical governance agenda. More recently, this has been demonstrated by the creation and indeed recreation of a series of quality control bodies such as the Care Quality Commission (http://www.cqc.org.uk/) and the emphasis given to professional revalidation.

The notion of partnership is a further strong driver and is a concept that has cut across a range of New Labour policy areas including local government, health care, education and crime and disorder (see Chapter 7). Crucially, ensuring effective partnerships includes engaging users and other local people in ways that make sense to them and that have an impact on resources and decision making.

Under New Labour, the user involvement agenda was formalised in policy terms through *The NHS plan* (Department of Health, 2000a), which emphasised the government's commitment to creating a patient-centred NHS with users' needs central to service design and delivery (see also Box 8.4):

> Patients are the most important people in the health service. It doesn't always appear that way. Too many patients feel talked at, rather than listened to. This has to change. NHS care has to be shaped around the convenience and concerns of patients. To bring this about, patients must have more say in their own treatment and more influence over the way the NHS works. (Department of Health, 2000a, p. 88)

In 2006, the Department of Health published *A stronger local voice: a framework for creating a stronger local voice in the development of health and social care services* (Department of Health, 2006f). This set out plans that were introduced via the *2007 Local Government and Public Involvement in Health Act*. Chief among these were a strong commitment to place patients' voices at the heart of the commissioning process and the creation of Local Involvement Networks (LINks), one in each local authority. Their role is to find out what citizens want from local services, to monitor and review the care they provide and to tell those who run and commission services what the community thinks.

However, despite the new raft of policies and legislation, a series of intended and unintended consequences are beginning to emerge. A national survey in 2008 on the current state of patient and public involvement in NHS Trusts across England found that implementation of LINks had caused the stalling of PPI activity more generally. Definition of and the resources underpinning the activities varied greatly and there were few examples of

Box 8.4	Current policies to encourage patient and public involvement in the NHS

- New statutory duties placed on NHS organisations by the *Health and Social Care Act* 2001 now ensure that patients and the public are consulted at an early stage about the planning and organisation of services (Department of Health, 2003h)
- Local authority Overview and Scrutiny Committees, made up of elected councillors, now have powers to scrutinise the NHS. The committees can review any aspect of NHS care locally and call NHS managers to account for their actions. They have the power to refer significant changes in service provision to the Secretary of State for Health for a final decision
- A national network of Independent Complaints Advocacy Services provided locally but operating to national standards was set up in 2003 to support people when they want to complain about the NHS
- The public can become involved in the running of NHS foundation trusts by becoming members, eligible to vote for board members (Department of Health, 2002g)
- In 2006, the NHS Centre for Involvement was set up to support and encourage the NHS and other organisations to involve patients and the public in health and social care decision making. In 2009 it was replaced by FONTIS (www.fontis.org.uk)
- From April 2008, LINks are gradually being developing in each local authority

the impact or influence of patient and public involvement (NHS Centre for Involvement, 2008). While improving choice has enormous popular and political appeal, the entire agenda raises a number of additional issues and creates particular tensions for people with mental health problems who, as we have already discussed, are rarely seen or treated as 'consumers' of services.

Mental health service user involvement in theory and practice today

User involvement, like the concept of user itself, encapsulates a range of different ideas (Braye, 2000) from active participation at the micro level of individual decision making, to more macro-level involvement in service planning and evaluation and, increasingly, in training and research. A range of different models to describe and conceptualise user involvement have been proposed. Hoggett (1992, p. 9, quoted in Means and Smith, 1998, p. 89), for example, tries to distinguish between the degree of participation/control available and whether a user is involved as an individual or through collective action (see Figure 8.1).

The four-way Pilgrim and Rogers formulation discussed at the beginning of the chapter reflects in part Arnstein's classification of citizens' participation (1969) along an eight-point ladder of participation from being informed (patient) through consultation and negotiation (consumer) to transfer of power (user-led services). The Pilgrim and Rogers categories also correlate with

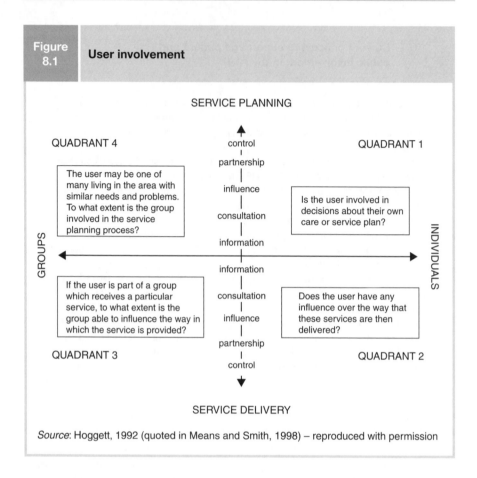

Figure 8.1 User involvement

Source: Hoggett, 1992 (quoted in Means and Smith, 1998) – reproduced with permission

Hirschman's (1970) broader conception of relationships between individuals and organisations involving the three categories of loyalty, voice and exit. Loyalty involves using a service and hoping to exert an influence peripherally. If the organisation has some expectation that it should seek and respond to the views of the individual, then the individual can exercise voice, perhaps through individual advocacy, campaigning or lobbying. If the individual has authority over the way in which the organisation behaves and the right to reject that behaviour and seek support elsewhere, they demonstrate the ability to exit.

In addition, Peck *et al.* (2002b) constructed a schema using the Hirschman, Arnstein and Pilgrim and Rogers formulations that has three distinct conceptions of user involvement as recipients, subjects of consultation or agents in control. At the same time they suggest user involvement within mental health services operates at four levels:

1. In the interaction between service users and the form of self-help.
2. In the interaction between individual users and professionals working with them.

3. In the management of local services.
4. In the planning of overall services.

Peck *et al.* argue that if these two frameworks are combined, it is possible to construct a matrix for user involvement with the conceptions of user involvement forming one axis and the level of user involvement forming the other (see Table 8.1).

Table 8.1	Examples of user involvement

Levels of interaction	Conceptions of user involvement		
	Recipient of communication	Subject of consultation	Agent in control
Interaction between service users	Newsletters Periodicals	Advocacy schemes	Hearing voices Newsletters Periodicals
Interaction between users and professionals	Receiving care plans	Agreeing care plans	Direct payments
Management of local services	Receiving information services	Patient Councils User surveys User-focused monitoring	User-run crisis houses Social firms
Planning of overall services	In receipt of CPA plans	Stakeholder conferences	

Source: Peck *et al.* (2002b) – reproduced with permission

For Peck *et al.* (2002b), the matrix illustrates the sheer diversity of mental health service user-involvement activities in the UK. However, it is also significant that many initiatives are clustered in the consultation category with the 'user control of the overall service' planning box empty.

Although 'user involvement' is the current 'buzz word' and appears regularly in policy documents, in mission statements and in the academic literature, it may be less meaningful in practice. This view is supported by Wallcraft and Bryant's (2003) survey of the mental health service user movement in England which identified 318 user groups and found that 'local service user groups play a very important role in mutual support, combating stigma, helping people to recover and stay out of services and participating in local service planning and development' (p. 1). However, most groups were small, recently formed, poorly funded and non-representative of black and minority ethnic communities, all of which limited their capacity to achieve change. There also appeared to be tensions between centrally determined agendas that failed to acknowledge local needs and choices, perhaps reflecting a wider debate regarding the need for local responsiveness within a system of considerable central government control.

Webb *et al.'s* (2000, p. 281) survey of 503 patients across five NHS Trusts, also found a failure to respond to several prominent and longstanding criticisms from the user movement:

> On the face of it … the results of this study point to the old chestnuts that mental health user campaign groups have raised again and again in the past two decades, and that previous studies have reported on: a lack of information, communication and consultation. It would seem that the National Health Service still has some way to go in meeting these basic principles of good quality care.

So, while it is true that there are now hundreds of user groups where there used to be tens, it appears that their influence may be limited, with an emphasis on information sharing rather than partnership or user-led services.

Why is user involvement important?

There are a number of often interrelated reasons for believing that mental health service user involvement is more than a politically mandated 'good thing' but is a worthwhile activity with a range of practical and ethical benefits (see Box 8.5).

Box 8.5	The benefits of user involvement

1. Users are experts about their own illness and need for care.
2. Users may have different but equally important perspectives about their illness and care.
3. User involvement may increase the existing limited understanding of mental distress.
4. Users are able to develop alternative approaches to mental health and illness.
5. User involvement may of itself be therapeutic.
6. User involvement may encourage greater social inclusion.

First, there is growing recognition that service users are experts, with an in-depth knowledge of mental health services and of living with a mental health problem. By definition, no one else, no matter how well trained or qualified, can possibly have had the same experience of the onset of mental illness, the same initial contact with services or the same journey through the mental health system. These experiences are an important resource that can help to improve individual packages of care as well as services more generally. Borrill (2000), for example, emphasises the way in which users can predict when they are about to become unwell and formulate appropriate responses at an early stage. If mental health professionals can tap into this expertise, they make their own jobs much easier and more productive by focusing on users' considerable strengths.

In addition, service users and mental health professionals often have very different perspectives. Lindow (1999, p. 154), for example, highlights the way in which users and service providers may have very different priorities:

> Our discussions are seldom about new styles of management, or changes in service organisations: I have heard little interest [among users] in the idea of a GP-led National Health Service. There is, rather, much discussion of poverty, employment, housing; about services that control and rob our experiences of meaning and about dangerous treatment.

Involving users can therefore provide insights that prompt practitioners to re-evaluate their work, challenge traditional assumptions and highlight key priorities that users would like to see addressed. May (2001) suggests that the inclusion of users' experiences and knowledge through service user involvement will elaborate the existing limited understanding of mental distress. User involvement in this sense may also lead to a new way of thinking about the nature of evidence itself, with what was sometimes seen as anecdotal experience given new validity through viewing it as 'human testimony' (Glasby and Beresford, 2006).

At the same time, users have been able to develop alternative approaches to mental health that can complement existing services. The Strategies for Living group, for example, have highlighted the importance of alternative and complementary therapies (Faulkner and Layzell, 2000; Mental Health Foundation, 2003) while the Hearing Voices Network encourages positive working practices with people who hear voices and works to promote greater tolerance and understanding of voice hearing (http://www.hearing-voices.org). For some people, moreover, user involvement can be therapeutic. Helping to shape services, particularly when users work together collectively, can help users increase their confidence, raise self-esteem and develop new skills (Clark et al., 2004; Mental Health Foundation, 2003).

Finally, user involvement may encourage greater social inclusion (Sayce and Morris, 1999). As discussed in Chapter 4, on almost any indicator, people with mental health problems are among the most excluded within society, particularly in terms of employment opportunities. Some users are excluded geographically from their community by 'nimbyism' and from communities of identity through negative stereotypes of irrationality and violence. Wilkinson (1996) has suggested that it is relative rather than absolute poverty within societies that creates health inequalities through mediating factors such as powerlessness and social stress. Encouraging greater user involvement, including paid activity, can be empowering and address issues of poverty and therefore may act as one mechanism to encourage greater social inclusion.

The barriers to user involvement in mental health services

Despite the benefits of user involvement and the significant political encouragement in recent years, levels of user involvement in mental health services remain patchy with an emphasis on consultation rather than influence, partnership or control. There are a number of different though often interlinked barriers to greater user involvement (see Box 8.6).

Box 8.6	Barriers to user involvement in mental health services

1. Lack of information.
2. Financial and time costs.
3. Concerns over representativeness.
4. Resistance to the idea of users as experts.
5. Differences in the balance of power between users and professionals.

First and foremost, accessible information is an essential prerequisite for meaningful involvement, yet there is evidence of a widespread lack of information for service users, including a lack of information about the nature of mental health problems, the side effects of medication, alternative forms of treatment and mental health law (Carpenter and Sbaraini, 1997; Hogman and Sandamas, 2001; Morrissey, 1998; Webb *et al.*, 2000). As an example, the User's Voice project, which included interviews with over 500 users in seven geographical areas across England, found very low levels of involvement in individual care planning and in the planning and delivery of services more generally, and suggested this was often related to a lack of information. As Rose (2001, p. 6) observed:

> Mental health service users need information to make informed choices about their care. Around 50% of users interviewed for this work felt they were not getting enough information on a range of issues and therefore felt themselves to be recipients of rather than involved in their mental health care.

However, user involvement, if done properly, can be expensive and time consuming for the organisation and service users themselves (at least in the short term). A good example is provided by Carpenter and Sbaraini (1997, p. 27), whose account of user involvement in the care management process identified time constraints as a major barrier:

> The main disadvantage [of user involvement] perceived by staff was that the process took more time than previously. The assessment and planning meetings themselves took between 45 minutes and one-and-a-half hours, depending on the amount of preparatory work which had been done, the complexity of the user's needs and their ability to contribute to the discussion. In some cases this was longer than the participants and care manager had allowed. To this must be added the time involved explaining the purpose and procedures to the user, liaising with carers and other professionals, and in setting up the meetings themselves. Following the meetings, the forms had to be written out clearly for typing, typed, checked with the user and distributed. In the event that the user's condition had deteriorated severely, or for some reason the care programme had proved difficult to implement, all the preceding work could sometimes be seen by the care manager as time wasted.

In addition, the results of a survey of policy and practice in payments to mental health service users and carers involved in service development in 46 secondary mental health services organisations in England found that only 12 (26 per cent) made transport available to users and 14 (30 per cent) to carers, while only 15 (33 per cent) paid service users and 12 (26 per cent) paid carers for their time. The authors concluded:

> There is considerable desire to develop practice in this area and the issue of payments is viewed as important in addressing user and carer participation. Significantly, many organisations employed unwritten policies based on custom and practice and were most likely to relate to basic expenses and payments rather than payments for time given. (Ryan and Bamber, 2002, p. 635)

They also noted that some respondents felt that having written policies on financial resources might further reduce future user and carer participation because of the cost implications for organisations. At the same time, professionals wishing to promote user involvement have frequently expressed concerns about the 'representativeness' of individual service users, sometimes suggesting that particular users may be 'too well', 'too articulate' or 'too vocal' to represent the views of users more generally. However, Lindow (1999) suggests that the concept of 'representativeness' may be used as a subconscious method of resisting user involvement (see Box 8.7 for a helpful quote which summarises this argument). This also seems to create something of a 'catch 22' situation, with users either 'too well' to be 'representative' or 'too ill' to be involved.

Box 8.7	**User involvement and representation**

'When workers find what we [users] are saying challenging, the most usual strategy to discredit user voices is to suggest we are not to be listened to because we are too articulate, and not representative. Workers seem to be looking for someone, the 'typical' patient, who is so passive and/or drugged that they comply with their plans. We are developing our own strategies to respond to these challenges in an attempt to reveal to such workers their double standards:

We ask how representative are they, and the others on the committee? We point out that as they are selected for their expertise and experience, so are we. Indeed, we are more likely to have been selected by a group than they are.

We ask, would workers send their least articulate colleague to represent their views, or the least confident nurse to negotiate for a change in conditions?

We ask, if a person's criticisms are valid, what relevance has representativeness?

We point out that it is very rude to suggest that someone is not a 'proper' service user (that is, so disempowered and/or medicated that they cannot speak).

We could ask, but do not, that the challenger produce his or her credentials, their certificates of qualification.'

(Lindow, 1999, p. 166)

Allied to this is Peck *et al.'s* interesting distinction between tokenism and symbolism (2002a). Their evaluation of the integrated mental health trust in Somerset found that the Joint Commissioning Board (see Chapter 7) was felt by the researchers and by a number of Board members to have a predominantly symbolic function – emphasising the importance of mental health and interagency working. Although some Board members recognised and were happy with this, others (predominantly GP, service user and carer representatives) felt frustrated by the Board's seeming inability to 'do something'. However, Peck *et al.* suggest that the presence of users and carers was not tokenistic but symbolic, emphasising the importance of user and carer involvement at all levels of the organisation by making a very clear statement about involvement through the composition of the Board.

Finally, some professionals may find it difficult to view service users as experts and resist moves towards greater user involvement. Although there is some evidence to suggest that professionals are generally supportive of user involvement, there are also dissonances between expressed support and actual practice (Campbell, 2001). This could reflect professionals genuinely perceiving themselves to be more supportive than users do (Peck *et al.*, 2002b), resistance to the notion of sharing and transferring power to users, or a clash of professional 'scientific' and users' more 'social' ways of thinking and working (Summers, 2003). At the same time, however, involvement may be difficult from users' perspectives because of differences in perceived and actual power between users and professionals. As an example, Morgan's work on user involvement in three London boroughs revealed a number of worrying findings in this regard, particularly around the difficulty of feeling empowered (see Box 8.8 for a quote illustrating this issue).

Box 8.8	Power differences in user/professional relationships

'Where they did come into contact with staff ... a worrying feature ... was the extent of the feelings of powerlessness and fear that emerged. The anxieties expressed, and the need for reassurance that speaking up would not put them personally at risk, was too common to be put down merely to individual paranoia. People who have experienced compulsory admission to hospital, ECT and having to take medication that they have neither chosen nor understand, know what it is like to be subject to the power of the system and of another person ... The way that some of those in authority had managed this, and the legacy of fear this had left, was disturbing to us.'

(Morgan, 1998, p. 184)

Examples of positive practice in user involvement

Despite the rhetoric/reality gap and barriers to user involvement, there are emerging examples of positive practice in many areas of user involvement in health and social care (see Box 8.9).

Box 8.9	Examples of positive practice

1. Involvement in prioritising and conducting research.
2. Involvement in staff selection.
3. Employment as paid mental health workers.
4. Involvement in planning and redesign of mental health services.
5. Involvement in education and training.
6. Involvement on governing boards.

Although mental health professionals are perhaps less familiar with the concept of service users as active participants in the research process than those working in the disability field or engaged in emancipatory research (research with the aim of empowerment at its core), user involvement in research is important for a number of different reasons. Service users' priorities for research are often different from those of academics, health and social care professionals or funding bodies. A consultation exercise organised by the South London and Maudsley NHS Trust with service users, for example, found that highly ranked research topics included discrimination and abuse, social welfare issues and arts as therapies (Thornicroft *et al.*, 2002). Unfortunately, user-led research projects are still relatively rare but key contributions in this area include the Strategies for Living projects (Faulkner and Layzell, 2000; Mental Health Foundation, 2003) and Rose's (2001) work on users' experiences of mental health services. These projects highlighted the importance of training service users to undertake research and the added value as participants 'visibly relaxed and opened up once they realised the interviewer had 'been through the system' and understood their own situation' (Rose, 2001, p. 4). More recently, the mental health research network has established the Service Users in Research Group for England (SURGE) to co-ordinate service user-led research in mental health and collaborative initiatives (Telford and Faulkner, 2004). This is helping to raise the profile and more importantly the active participation of users in all aspects of the research process.

Second, some mental health service users are being involved in recruiting staff. This is not only a symbolic statement about the importance of user involvement, but can also improve the appointment process. Newnes *et al.* (2001, p. 12) describe an attempt to involve service users in recruiting a clinical psychologist. An evaluation suggested that some participants felt that questions from the service user were 'wise and thought-provoking'. In particular, the user was seen as being able to offer a human perspective that was well respected: 'she came up with questions none of us professionals would ever have thought of and got a much stronger sense of what the candidate was like as a person'.

Third, proposals for the mental health workforce include the role of STR workers (Department of Health, 2003e; Department of Health, 2008e). STR workers come from different walks of life with different backgrounds including volunteers and existing and former services users who have the ability to listen to people without judging them. They work as part of a team that provides mental health services and focus directly on the needs of service users, working across boundaries, providing support, giving time and promoting their recovery. They can be employed by any agency in the NHS or social care field, including the private and voluntary sector. It was originally envisaged that up to 3000 STR workers would be trained and working by 2006. This proved to be a significant overestimate and in spite of an Accelerated Workforce Programme introduced in 2003, the number of STR workers in post is still far less than 3000.

Fourth, involving users in the planning and delivery of health services has grown considerably over the last decade, with a systematic review (Crawford *et al.*, 2002) identifying 337 relevant studies, including a number in the field of mental health. As an example, Collaboratives, part of the government's modernisation agenda as outlined in *The NHS plan* (Department of Health, 2000a), used an approach based on the principles of continuous quality improvement and service redesign. They involved a network of organisations working together for a fixed time period on a specific clinical area. The government saw Collaboratives as a method of redesigning services so they are responsive to the needs of patients rather than the organisation. Within mental health, 37 organisations across two former northern NHS regions participated in the Mental Health Collaborative on inpatient care from October 2000 to November 2001. An evaluation of the user involvement in the Collaborative (Robert *et al.*, 2003) found a strong involvement ethos across services and evidence of the positive effects of user involvement. Users were invited to join project teams as members, to attend learning sessions and to be closely involved in all aspects of work. Improvements made through service user involvement included changes to process issues such as improved documentation. Some of the improvements suggested by service users were not the changes that staff themselves might have prioritised but were perceived as valuable. Many staff also felt that user involvement had challenged their own assumptions and led to new insights about patient care. However, the evaluation also noted scope for future improvements and the need to increase the level of user involvement.

Fifth, there has been recent policy support for greater involvement of both mental health service users and carers throughout the whole education and training process (Department of Health, 2001f). Involving users in training also has the potential to challenge some of the myths around mental illness, enabling those responsible for delivering mental health services to gain an insight into what it is like to be on the receiving end of such services (Repper and Breeze, 2006).

Finally, there are growing numbers of service users represented on the governing boards of local and national organisations. As an example, a report published by the Social Care Institute for Excellence (SCIE) on the roles and responsibilities of a small number of services users in senior governance positions on governing boards of the bodies set up to regulate service, workforce, education and training standards in social care found that the experience of user members on national boards was overwhelmingly positive. Users reported that 'every effort was made to include them' (SCIE, 2003, p. 6) and interviews with other stakeholders found that 'users were felt to contribute a vital perspective to the work' (SCIE, 2003, p. 7). Overall, organisations were perceived to be listening to and learning from the users on their boards. However, a personal account from a mental health service user on the board of an integrated mental health trust shows how isolating and difficult it can be to be the only service user on a governing board and suggests the need for much more planning and forethought about the need for training, support and clarity of role (Brodie, 2003).

The importance of organisational culture and personal attributes

Meaningful user involvement requires organisations to think about their own cultural environment. Service cultures that encourage involvement share a number of common characteristics, including a commitment to genuine partnerships between users and professionals and to the development of shared objectives. As the National Schizophrenia Fellowship (now Rethink) (1997, p. 10) observes:

> Everyone involved in the delivery of care, including service users and carers, should be treated as equal partners. Occasionally, some professionals may initially feel threatened by the involvement of service users and carers and if this is the case, then it is important that this issue is addressed so that all of the parties involved can work well together. It is essential to remember that every care partner brings something different, but equally valuable, to the relationship and that successful delivery of care depends on effective collaboration between the care partners.

The approach and value base of individual practitioners are also crucial. Thus, for service users in a study by Breeze and Repper (1998, p. 1306), individual attributes were a crucial feature:

> All the informants [in our study] were able to identify 'good' relationships that had developed with 'helpful' nurses. A good nurse–patient relationship included the nurse: treating the patient with respect, essentially as a person, but, more than that, as a valued person (for example, exuding warmth, displaying empathy and holding 'normal' conversations with the patients); enabling the patient to have some meaningful control over their own care, for example, working with the patients to develop an appropriate and realistic care plan directed towards achieving the patient's own goals; and listening to and, especially, believing the patient.

Future directions in user involvement: from patient to citizen?

In late 1997, a former British Prime Minister announced measures aimed at improving life for an estimated 5 million citizens affected by crime, unemployment, low educational attainment and poor housing: 'we are passionately committed to making Britain one nation, giving every single person a stake in the future and tackling chronic poverty and social division' (Tony Blair, quoted in *The Independent*, 7th December 1997). It is against this political background that mental health service users have increasingly campaigned for more generalised reform on the grounds that every individual is a citizen with a series of political, civil and social rights. As Campbell (1996, p. 224) eloquently suggests: 'Madpersons as empowered customers of services and madpersons as equal citizens are two quite different propositions.'

Campbell also points out (2001, p. 81):

> The great irony about service user action in the past 15 years is that, while the position of service users within services has undoubtedly improved, the position of service users in society has deteriorated. As a result, it is at least

arguable that the focus of service user involvement needs adjustment. Service users and service providers should accept that the quality of life of people with a mental illness diagnosis in society, indeed their proper inclusion as citizens, depends on education and campaigning. Although the quality of mental health services will continue to be a dominant issue for service providers, it might no longer have such a place in the agendas of service user organisations. The climate may be changing – the Disability Rights Commission, the Human Rights Act, bioethics etc. We should not expect service user involvement not to change.

This agenda will almost certainly require partnerships with other groups who face similar challenges to their citizenship status, including people with physical impairments within the wider disability movement. The former Disability Rights Commission, which started work in 2000, brought over 150 legal actions under the *Disability Discrimination Act* in its first two years, as well as campaigning for strengthening of the Act to make it harder for employers to justify discrimination and to improve access to business premises and transport. This legislation has provided mental health service users with opportunities to pursue their rights. The first legal case backed by the new Disability Rights Commission was that of Pravin Kapadia, a man with severe depression who had been compulsory retired by his employers. The ruling that Kapadia was disabled under the terms of the *Disability Discrimination Act* enabled him to bring a case under the Act for discrimination and unfair dismissal (Valios, 2000) (see Chapter 9 for further discussion of discrimination issues and links between mental health and a social model of disability).

Conclusion

Meaningful user involvement should not be a one-off intervention or a discrete programme of work, but a much broader and more empowering way of working which affects every aspect of mental health provision. As Hutchinson (2000, p. 26) explains:

> If users are to regain some control over their lives there needs to be a shift in the balance of power between themselves and mental health professionals ... The key element to achieving this shift is to involve service users at all levels of the mental health system: in the planning of their own support; in the design and running of statutory and independent services; in the recruitment of staff; in the training of mental health professionals; in monitoring the effectiveness of services; in researching and evaluating services; and finally, in the establishment of user-run or user-led services.

However, despite a plethora of policy reforms and pockets of good practice, it appears that a fundamental shift in the balance of power between users and professionals still remains to be achieved.

Reflection exercises

1. User involvement within your own organisation

Exercise for all workers

Your organisation has asked you to organise a service user reference group. You have a budget to pay for travel costs and a small honorarium. Think through the issues that you will need to address before and during the first meeting.

For example:

- How and where are you going to advertise for members?
- What size should the group be?
- What is the most appropriate location for the first meeting?
- What could the remit of the group be and who should decide this?
- What issues will need to be thought through to ensure that the first meeting is structured, paced and chaired in an appropriate manner?
- Devise an agenda for the meeting
- How will you judge the success of the meeting?

2. The role of LINks in your area

Exercise for all workers

LINks aim to give citizens a stronger voice in how their health and social care services are delivered. Each local authority (that provides social services) has been given funding and is under a legal duty to make contractual arrangements that enable LINk activities to take place and LINks should now be established in most areas of England. Find out about your local LINk and then make contact with the group to explore how they run and what issues they are focusing on.

Suggestions for further reading

1. Sayce, L. (2000) *From psychiatric patient to citizen: overcoming discrimination and social exclusion.* Basingstoke, Palgrave

   This book proposes new theoretical models and practical strategies for tackling the widespread social exclusion faced by people with mental illness. Based on research in the US and UK, it analyses evidence of discrimination and the effectiveness of different responses including disability discrimination law, work to reframe media and cultural images, grass roots inclusion programmes, and challenges to the 'nimby' factor. The book also includes an introduction to the ideas of the social model of disability (explored in more detail in Chapter 9).

2. Sainsbury Centre for Mental Health (2005) *Beyond the water towers: the unfinished revolution in mental health services 1985–2005.* London, Sainsbury Centre for Mental Health

   This edited collection examines the key issues facing mental health services and has a particularly insightful chapter from Peter Campbell on the mental health service user movement.

3. Thornicroft, G. (2006) *Shunned: discrimination against people with mental illness.* Oxford, Oxford University Press

   This book, which includes numerous personal accounts of stigma and discrimination, clearly describes the nature and severity of discrimination against people with mental illness and, importantly, what we can do to help reduce this.

4. Crossley, N. (2006) *Contesting psychiatry: UK mental health movements 1950–2000.* London, Routledge

   This book critically examines the history of resistance to psychiatry between 1950 and 2000 and also provides an empirical account and exploration of theories of power in psychiatry.

It's also worth taking a look at www.shapingourlives.org.uk/ourpubs.html. Shaping Our Lives National User Network is an independent user-controlled organisation. On this website you can find out about publications on user involvement, some produced by Shaping Our Lives and some by other organisations.

9 Anti-Discriminatory Practice

In this chapter we discuss:

- The concept of anti-discriminatory practice
- The current policy context
- Discrimination in mental health services
- The experience of various marginalised groups
- Policy responses and prospects for the future

Introduction

Traditionally, the British welfare state has ignored issues of discrimination, seeing its role as providing a range of standard services to those in need, irrespective of who these recipients are (Dominelli, 1988). For minority ethnic communities, for example, this is sometimes described as a welfare state which is 'colour blind', failing to recognise the different needs of different groups of people due to a commitment to treating everyone the same. In many ways, this is particularly true of the NHS, which has prided itself on offering health care to everyone on the basis of clinical need alone. Unfortunately, we know that different groups of people do not always start from a level playing field. By treating everyone in the same way, therefore, there is a danger that we perpetuate existing inequalities and fail to challenge a divided and unequal society. If, on the other hand, we acknowledge that we all start from a different level within society, then it is possible for us to do things differently for different people to help us all achieve the same outcomes and quality of life. By treating people differently, therefore, we could argue that we are providing more support for those who need it most in order to pursue true equality.

However, current UK society is a long way away from achieving this aim. While our welfare services aspire to treating everyone the same, we nevertheless live in a society that likes to categorise people according to a range of social divisions: whether or not they are male or female, what colour their skin is, how old they are, their sexuality, whether or not they are disabled. How we categorise people can then help to shape how we respond to them, treating some groups more or less favourably than others. As Payne explains (2000, p. 1):

> It is impossible even to begin to think about people without immediately encountering 'social divisions'. We automatically perceive other human beings as being male or female, black or white, older or younger, richer or poorer, sick or well, or friend or foe. In forming a perception of them, we place them in pigeon-holes, adapting our behaviour and attitude to them in terms of the slots into which we have placed them.

As a result, it is naive to assume that we can respond in the same way to all people:

■ As a result of our tendency to make assumptions about people based on their gender, ethnicity, age and other characteristics, we will often find ourselves treating different groups of people differently (either consciously or subconsciously)

■ The services which the welfare state provides have often been designed from the point of view of dominant groups of people within society (typically white males). As an example, many day centres for older people have served very traditional English meals and have produced all their information in English, without recognising that people from particular minority ethnic communities may have particular dietary needs (such as Halal meat for Muslims) and may not necessarily speak English. Thus, a service which was probably designed to meet the needs of all local older people has perhaps inadvertently discriminated against people from certain minority groups

■ Discrimination does not only exist in health and social care, but is also widespread throughout society. Thus, an older woman who has been widowed may find herself financially penalised due to discrimination in the workplace and the social security system, while an Asian disabled person may find himself living in poor housing due to discriminatory employment practices and a failure by local housing services to provide accessible information in community languages. As a result, it is not appropriate to provide a standard level of service to everyone as different groups may well have a much greater need for support due to the discrimination they have faced

One of the earliest disciplines to recognise and respond to issues of discrimination was social work (see, for example, Dominelli, 1988; Thompson, 2006). Building on the civil rights movement of the 1960s, the school of radical social work has emphasised the importance of political, economic and social factors in shaping the lives of social care service users. While this analysis often tended to focus on social class, the debate has since expanded to include issues such as race, gender, sexuality and disability (see Thompson,

2006, for a more detailed description). More recently, issues of discrimination have begun to be taken on board by other disciplines and are now a key feature of a number of government policies (see later in this chapter).

While debate has typically focused on the experiences of different groups of people, there is a danger that each can see itself in isolation and vie for position as the group that is most discriminated against. As a result, this approach is increasingly being replaced with a more inclusive focus on *anti-discriminatory practice* (see Thompson, 2006, for an overview). Instead of focusing on one particular aspect of discrimination (such as racism or sexism), it is important to emphasise the concept of 'multiple oppressions' (a recognition that some groups face a range of different forms of discrimination at once and that the target should not only be sexism or racism by themselves, but discrimination itself in whatever form this takes). The main advantage of this approach is that it has the potential to unite the activities of different civil rights campaigners, creating a greater momentum for a more equal, inclusive society. In addition, it also helps to acknowledge the way in which different aspects of people's lives and identities interact. Thus, a 'black' woman will have potentially very different experiences to a 'black' man, while a disabled 'black' woman may have different needs again. This is sometimes expressed in terms of 'jeopardy' – the 'single jeopardy' that a member of a disadvantaged group (for example, a 'black' person) faces, the 'double jeopardy' that a 'black' woman may experience and the 'triple jeopardy' (Norman, 1985) that a 'black' older person with a low socio-economic status may face.★

For Thompson, discrimination operates at a number of different levels, each reinforcing and being reinforced by other levels. Thus, discrimination can exist at the personal (P) level (of individual thoughts, actions, feelings and attitudes). However, this aspect of discrimination takes place within a cultural context (the C level of common values and shared ways of seeing, thinking and doing). This in turn is embedded in a structural (S) level (the established social order and accepted social divisions). As a result, action is needed at all three levels if discrimination is to be tackled – focusing on the individual alone will not be enough (see Dalrymple and Burke, 1995; Dominelli, 1997, for further discussion and models).

The policy context

In response, there have been a series of official attempts to promote greater equality (see Box 9.1 for a summary of current rights in health and social care). While the different statutes and regulations have traditionally been overseen by separate bodies, these have now been amalgamated into a single

---

★We use this term use to describe the common experiences of those who encounter racism as a result of the colour of their skin. While this term is useful in emphasising the shared experience of racism, it should not distract from the fact that 'black people' are an extremely diverse group and should not overlook the fact that many white minority ethnic groups may also experience racism – such as Irish people.

Equality and Human Rights Commission (www.equalityhumanrights.com). Although this should help to link the struggles of different marginalised groups and emphasise the cross-cutting nature of discrimination, it also runs the risk of diluting existing campaigns with regard to race, gender and disability, and opinion is divided on the best way forward.

Box 9.1	**Your rights in health and social care**

'Most of us need to visit a doctor … from time to time, and may need hospital treatment on occasion. Some of us rely on public health services for help with long-term health conditions or disabilities. Social care services, which are provided by public authorities as well as the independent sector, come in many forms. These include providing support for people with mental health problems, supporting elderly and disabled people in their homes, care in day centres, residential and nursing homes, and caring for children who can't live with their parents.

In most cases, whenever you need health care, medical treatment or social care, you have the right not to be discriminated against because of your race, gender, disability, religion or belief or sexual orientation.

At the moment, it is unlawful to discriminate in employment on grounds of age. There is, however, no statutory prohibition of age discrimination in providing health or social care.

You also have various rights under the 1950 European Convention on Human Rights (enacted through the Human Rights Act 1998 in the UK), which are relevant to health and social care. These include the right to life, the right not to be subjected to torture or to inhuman or degrading treatment or punishment, the right to liberty and security of person, and the right to respect for private and family life.

While certain human rights are absolute, most are subject to some degree of limitation. This means that interference with an individual's human rights may be lawful in some circumstances, such as to protect the rights of others.'

Source: Equality and Human Rights Commission website: www.equalityhumanrights. com/en/yourrights/rightsindifferentsettings/Healthandsocialcare/Pages/healthand socialcare.aspx (accessed 28 October 2008)

Discrimination in mental health services

If discrimination exists in health and social care and in wider society more generally, it should come as no surprise to find that similar issues also exist in mental health services. As Chapters 1 and 2 of this book argue, people with mental health problems remain one of the most excluded groups in society – when this chapter explores the experiences of various marginalised groups, therefore, it is important to remember that even 'non-marginalised' groups are starting from a low base when it comes to mental health services.

In particular, there is a significant literature on the experience of people from lower social classes and the impact of poverty, with poorer people more likely to receive biological and/or coercive rather than psychological/

voluntary forms of treatment (see Pilgrim and Rogers, 2005; see also Box 9.2 for a quote summarising this issue). There has been a range of explanations put forward for this, including social stresses that may contribute to mental ill health (such as poverty, poor housing and unemployment) and the 'cultural gap' that may exist between some mental health workers and their service users (who may sometimes come from very different class backgrounds). However, while still acknowledging this longstanding link between class and mental health (see, for example, Ferguson, 2000), more recent research has criticised this emphasis on class because of its association with traditional Marxist politics (which were felt to have focused on class at the expense of other social divisions such as race or gender) (Day, 1992; Thompson, 2006).

In response, there is now greater recognition of the needs of other groups, such as women, people from minority ethnic communities, people with physical impairments, people with learning difficulties, older people, and gay men, lesbians and bisexuals. Against this background, the remainder of this chapter focuses on each of these groups in turn, before exploring the overall track record of mental health services in tackling discrimination. Perhaps inevitably, this overview is very broad brush, but further reading at the end of the chapter signposts readers to more detailed sources where they may wish to follow up particular issues. Moreover, any account of anti-discriminatory practice has to make some choices about which groups to include – and the subsections in this chapter should be seen as series of case studies to illuminate the way in which different forms of discrimination permeate the provision of mental health services, not as a definitive list (see Thompson, 2006, and Rogers and Pilgrim, 2003, for further discussion).

Box 9.2	**Class and health**

'Generally, in health care there is an "inverse care law", that is, access to health care increases with increasing class status. However, the reverse appears to be the case in mental health care systems. Psychiatric services are dominated by patients from low social class backgrounds. Superficially this might suggest that those with the greatest need are being responded to ... However, there is a problem with this logic. While most health care interventions are voluntary and ameliorative in intent in their response to the needs of sick people, in psychiatric services, involuntary detention and treatment are never far away ... In light of these peculiar features about psychiatry, it might be more accurate to conceptualise mental health work as part of a wider state apparatus which controls the social problems associated with poverty ... Once conceived in this way, it lowers our expectations that service contact should necessarily be about aiming for, or achieving, a gain in the mental health status of service recipients, given that the latent, and sometimes the explicit, function of psychiatry is that of successful coercive social control. The latter entails mental health services serving the interests of parties (such as relatives and strangers in the street) other than the patients they contain and treat.'

(Pilgrim and Rogers, 2005, p. 32)

Women

Many commentators suggest that some women are likely to have extremely negative experiences of various aspects of mental health care (see Box 9.3 for a summary). Above all, a recurring theme is the risk of abuse or harassment while staying on mixed psychiatric wards. A substantial proportion of women using mental health services are thought to have experienced physical or sexual abuse as children and/or as adults (see, for example, Fleischmann, 2000; Killaspy et al., 2000b; Payne, 1998; Warner and Ford, 1998) and there is a clear danger that such abuse may be replicated in hospital after women have been admitted to mixed wards. This has been a crucial issue for some time – in the late 1980s, one commentator claimed that acts of sexual harassment, rape and abduction were an 'everyday occurrence' on some wards (Feinman, 1988, p. 16) and accusations of sexual assault have continued to emerge.

Box 9.3	Women and mental health

'Traditionally, women are more likely than men to be treated for a mental health problem and to be admitted to hospital ... Gender bias and stereotyping in the treatment of female patients and in the diagnosis of psychological disorders has been reported since the 1970s ... Researchers have found that doctors are more likely to diagnose depression in women compared to men even when they have similar scores on standardized measures of depression or present with identical symptoms ...

The dominance of medical discourse in women's lives as a whole has been mirrored in the response to women's mental health. Women report that medication is often the only option made available to them ... Women are 48 per cent more likely than men to be prescribed psychotropic drugs ... Women (particularly older women) are also more likely to receive ECT ... Women have traditionally been more likely than men to both be assessed for compulsory detention under mental health legislation and sectioned followed assessment ... This clearly raises important issues regarding the civil liberties of female service users.'

(Coppock, 2008, p. 100)

'There has been recent recognition that women in acute mental distress may be poorly served by existing mental health facilities where there is a lack of privacy, assaults are common and the atmosphere highly aroused. Female patients' vulnerability to sexual harassment and assault has been highlighted by [a number of commentators] ... Many women admitted to psychiatric wards have experienced childhood sexual abuse or domestic violence and their vulnerability on the ward is especially worrying.'

(Killaspy et al., 2000b, p. 102)

That sexual harassment is a key concern is demonstrated by the 1996 national visit of 118 mental health trusts carried out by the Mental Health Act Commission and the Sainsbury Centre for Mental Health (Warner and Ford, 1998). Here, the researchers found that 162 out of 291 mixed wards

(56 per cent) reported problems of sexual harassment of women patients, ranging from sexual assault in a small number of cases to exploitation, inappropriate touching, exposure and sexually disinhibited behaviour (see Table 9.1). While ward staff identified a range of policies and practices designed to protect women, only 34 wards had written procedures and only 26 of these were able to supply a copy to the researchers. Some policies were out of date and others were not always enforced due to pressures on hospital wards. Thus, there was sometimes insufficient female staff to have a female worker on duty each shift, male patients who had persistently harassed women patients could not always be transferred to another ward and male patients were placed in women-only areas if no beds were available elsewhere. Also of concern was the layout of some wards, which made it difficult to observe patients at all times and which did not always allow sufficient space to defuse potential tensions. That concerns persist is demonstrated by more recent analysis of patient safety issues in mental health services (see Box 9.4).

Table 9.1	Sexual harassment of women patients in mixed-sex wards (n = 162)	
Type of problem		**Number of wards reporting**
Sexual assault		6 (4 per cent)
Exploitation of vulnerable women		60 (37 per cent)
Touching female patients		12 (7 per cent)
Exposure/nudity of male patients		21 (13 per cent)
Watching or following female patients		31 (19 per cent)
Verbal harassment		43 (26 per cent)
Disinhibited behaviour and remarks		67 (43 per cent)

Source: Warner and Ford (1998), p. 226

While much of the literature has tended to focus on the issue of single- versus mixed-sex hospital wards, it is clear that there are other equally significant issues at stake concerning the way in which mental health services respond to the needs of women:

■ Women's mental distress has tended be labelled using purely medical models, when a range of commentators would emphasise the importance of underlying contributory factors such as gendered roles and poverty, seeing much mental illness as a form of social construction in a patriarchal society (see, for example, Halliday, 2005)
■ Some mental health workers may lack awareness of gender issues, with Black and Shillitoe (1997) citing examples of male workers entering women's rooms unannounced

Box 9.4	Ongoing concerns about sexual safety

A national analysis of patient safety issues in mental health services focused in more detail on concerns about sexual safety. This found 122 incidents, including allegations of:

- Rape (19 cases)
- Consensual sex (20 cases)
- Exposure (13 cases)
- Sexual advances (18 cases)
- Touching (26 cases)
- Other incidents (26 cases)

Of the nineteen allegations of rape, the alleged perpetrator was another patient in eight cases and a member of staff in eleven cases.

Unfortunately, 'it is not possible to make firm judgements on the veracity of the reported allegations' (as incidents are often sent to the NPSA soon after the event before an investigation has reported).

In addition, the NPSA noted that 'NHS Litigation Authority data ... include 13 clinical negligence claims between 1995 and August 2005 that involve allegations of harm to patients resulting from sexual activities with other patients, including three cases of unwanted pregnancies.'

(NPSA, 2006, p. 38)

- Women with children admitted to hospital may need to make alternative child care arrangements, often at short notice and sometimes involving the placement of their children in the care of the local authority (Killaspy et al., 2000b)
- The needs of men with mental health problems may take precedence over those of women as men are believed to engage in more problematic behaviours (such as failing to comply with medication or becoming violent) (Mallon, 2001)
- Women often feel that they have insufficient privacy in hospital. During two national visits carried out by the Mental Health Act Commission and the Sainsbury Centre for Mental Health, for example, only 3 per cent of wards were women-only and many women did not have access to self-contained facilities for washing, sleeping or going to the toilet (Ford et al., 1998; Warner and Ford, 1998)
- Where women complain of sexual harassment, there may be insufficient attempts to prevent it happening again. This was a key finding to emerge from a survey of hospital patients conducted by Mind, which found that almost one in six patients had experienced sexual harassment, but that 72 per cent of those who complained felt that no action was taken (Baker, 2000)
- Amongst younger people, boys and girls may have different levels of knowledge about mental health and different sources of stress – suggesting

the need for gender specific educational interventions rather than whole school approaches (Williams and Pow, 2007)

■ There is a potential tension between the need to support families at risk and to protect children from harm, and more arguably needs to be done to recognise the impact that mental health problems can have on family life and on women as mothers (Parrott *et al.*, 2008)

Box 9.5	Case study

Drayton Park is cited as a good practice example by a range of commentators (see, for example, Killaspy *et al.*, 2000b; McMillan, 1997b; Payne, 1998). According to a Camden and Islington Mental Health NHS Trust (2001) leaflet:

'Drayton Park is an alternative to hospital admission for women .... It has been open since December 1995. The service recognises the need for women to have a safe place in which they can recover from crises and it focuses on issues that cause mental health problems for women. It was inspired and supported nationally by government recommendations and work such as the [1994 Mind] Stress on Women campaign. In 1999, it became a Beacon Service as part of the NHS Learning Network ...

A management advisory group consisting of women who have used services and women who work in mental health organisations within Camden and Islington guided [Drayton Park] in its first few years. This group maintained an alternative focus and supported the project in its development stages. In 1999, users of the service, in partnership with staff developed a Women's User Forum. This group has taken over some aspects of the advisory group along with other responsibilities.'

See Johnson *et al.* (2004) for an evaluation.

In response, commentators propose a number of possible solutions. Most prominent has been the call for more women-only spaces within mental health services, for segregated accommodation in hospital and for specialist women-only services (see Box 9.5 for a good practice example). Certainly, this is the direction of current policy, with a pledge to eliminate mixed-sex accommodation (Department of Health, 1999a, p. 2002). However, whether or not this is a sufficient response is open to question in a number of key areas:

■ The debate about the relative merits of single- and mixed-sex provision has existed for some years and thinking has changed over time. Traditionally, hospital services were strictly segregated, with mixed wards only developing in the 1970s in response to suggestions that this might promote a more normal atmosphere which is a more accurate reflection of life outside hospital (Fleischmann, 2000; McMillan, 1997a; Warner and Ford, 1998). Now, the emphasis is on developing segregated services once more. Throughout, the rationale behind such changes has rarely been clearly articulated and there has been insufficient research into the outcomes of different types of service provision for men and women (Kohen, 1999). There also seems to be little recognition that the 'normal' nature of mixed-sex settings is based on a white UK view of the world and may not apply to some minority ethnic communities

■ Some people (male and female) may prefer mixed provision and are hostile to the idea of single-sex services (Batcup, 1997; Black and Shillitoe, 1997)

Above all, however, it seems that the difficulties women experience when accessing and using mental health services are much more fundamental than simply introducing women-only areas. While the debate about single- versus mixed-sex services will continue, it seems likely that the issues at stake are so significant and so engrained that they will require much concerted action (see later in chapter for further discussion). In particular, guidance from the Royal College of Nursing and CSIP calls for a fundamental shift in thinking away from asking 'What is wrong with this woman?' to 'What has happened to this woman?' (RCN/CSIP/NIMHE, 2008, p. 5). While this might only seem like a minor change, the shift in mindset that it entails is potentially revolutionary.

People from minority ethnic communities

There is overwhelming evidence to suggest that 'black' people experience mental health services in a very different way to white people. In particular, 'black' people are over-represented in mental health services, tend to receive more coercive forms of treatment and suggest that existing services are too culturally insensitive to meet their needs (see Box 9.6 for a summary). This may be the result of a number of different factors, and it can be difficult to isolate individual causal explanations (see Box 9.7 for a summary).

As a result of the experiences set out in Boxes 9.6 and 9.7, there have been a number of attempts to promote more culturally sensitive mental health services (see later in this chapter). Despite this, there is widespread evidence to suggest that many 'black' people continue to have very negative experiences of mental health services. Thus, in 1999, a national visit conducted by the Mental Health Act Commission and the Sainsbury Centre for Mental Health found that many patients from minority ethnic communities were not receiving care sensitive to their cultural backgrounds (Warner et al., 2000b). Despite several examples of good practice, three-quarters of the 119 wards had no policy on dealing with racial harassment, two-thirds had no policy on race equality training and a similar number had used patients' relatives or friends to interpret for them. While half the units had a policy on the provision and use of interpreters, only three-quarters used interpreters who were trained in interpreting and some unit managers did not know if the interpreters they worked with were trained or not. Although the vast majority of units recorded the ethnicity of patients, this information was seldom put to great use.

Box 9.6	'Black' people's experiences of mental health services

In 2008, a national census of mental health inpatients found that (Healthcare Commission, 2008b, pp. 3–4):

- Rates of admission to hospital were three to five times higher than the average for various black groups (and almost ten times higher for the 'other black' group)
- Rates of referral for some black groups were lower than average from GPs and community health teams, but higher than average from the criminal justice system
- Rates of detention under the Mental Health Act were between 20 per cent and 36 per cent higher than the average for various black groups
- Detention rates under section 37/41 (imposed by the courts) were also higher in these groups
- Rates of seclusion were higher than average for various black groups
- The rate of hands-on restraint was higher than average in the 'other white' and 'white/black Caribbean mixed' groups

See also Sainsbury Centre for Mental Health (2006d) for further discussion.

Box 9.7	'Black' people and schizophrenia

Sharpely *et al.*'s (2001) review of the literature on the increased rate of schizophrenia among African-Caribbean people in England highlights a wide range of potential hypotheses:

- African-Caribbean people may be misdiagnosed as having schizophrenia
- Biological factors such as genetic predisposition, prenatal and perinatal complications, certain risk factors in childhood and use of cannabis may play a role
- Social factors such as social disadvantage, concentration in inner-city areas, a reluctance to seek GP support, patients' and relatives' opinions and the experience of racism may all be significant
- Psychological factors such as the experience of adverse life events or low self-esteem brought about by racism, unemployment and deprivation may also be a contributing factor

The National Schizophrenia Fellowship (2000) has carried out a survey of 450 people with mental health problems from a range of different ethnic backgrounds. This found that people from minority ethnic communities, particularly African–Caribbean people, had more negative experiences of mental health services than other groups. In particular, 'black' service users were more dissatisfied with the care they received than white respondents, were more likely to feel that their cultural needs had not been met, were more likely to disagree with the diagnosis they had been given, experienced far more detentions under the Mental Health Act and had been forcibly restrained more often. As one participant observed (National Schizophrenia Fellowship. 2000, p. 1), 'I am treated unfairly because of the colour of my skin, although I was born in London. This is not fair.'

Wilson and Francis' (1997, p. 33) survey of 100 African and African-Caribbean users across England and Wales found that 'a significant proportion of [respondents] feel they are largely misunderstood within the mental health system – either because they are feared, stereotyped or ignored. The stereotypes interact in complex ways and appear to have a powerful impact, as people are seen as black, as mad, as dangerous, as inadequate. This can reduce people's trust in the services on offer, and potentially damage their sense of identity and thus their mental health.' A more in-depth qualitative study conducted by Pierre (1999) paints a similar picture of disputed diagnoses, lack of consultation and information, physical and verbal abuse from hospital staff and a failure by staff to challenge racism from other patients.

In addition to these studies, other key issues have been found to include:

- Discriminatory attitudes among mental health workers. As Webbe (1998, p. 12) observes, many practitioners have preconceptions of 'black' people as 'big, black and dangerous'. Whereas mental illness is often equated with 'danger', 'black' mental illness is equated with 'danger x 2' (see also Browne, 1997)
- A frequent complaint from 'black' service users is the lack of accessible information about the services available, the nature of their mental health problem and their legal rights (see, for example, Arshad and Johal, 1999; Grant-Pearce and Deane, 1999; Li et al., 1999)
- The importance of primary care as an arena in which mental health problems can be identified at an early stage before a crisis has occurred. Unfortunately, this opportunity is often lost as a result of the failure of some GPs to diagnose mental health problems in some of their 'black' patients and to over-diagnose in the case of other 'black' groups (see, for example, Bahl, 1999; Browne, 1997; Koffman et al., 1997; Thornicroft et al., 1999)
- A failure to appreciate the importance of religious beliefs in shaping people's attitudes to mental health and their willingness to seek help from western services (Copsey, 1997a, 1997b)
- A lack of understanding of or knowledge about mental health issues in particular minority ethnic communities (see, for example, Li et al., 1999; Tabassum et al., 2000)
- A lack of 'black' staff in mental health services (Pierre, 1999). Often, the small numbers of 'black' staff that do exist can experience just as much discrimination as 'black' service users (Webbe, 1998)
- Often, ethnicity can interact with gender. Thus, Asian women may have different needs than white women and than Asian men (see, for example, Arshad and Johal, 1999; Tabassum et al., 2000).

Above all, however, there is evidence to suggest that all of these factors combine to create a 'vicious circle' (Parkman *et al.*, 1997, p. 264), whereby 'black' people have negative experiences of mental health services and are therefore less inclined to seek help at early stage in the future or to comply with medication. This can then lead to relapse and readmission to hospital, where existing negative expectations are reinforced. This has been described by the Sainsbury Centre for Mental Health (2002e) in terms of a downward spiral or a 'circle of fear' (see Box 9.8 for a quote summarising this argument).

Box 9.8	*Circles of fear*

'Stereotypical views of Black people, racism, cultural ignorance, and the stigma and anxiety associated with mental illness often combine to undermine the way in which mental health services assess and respond to the needs of Black and African Caribbean communities. When prejudice and the fear of violence influence risk assessments and decisions on treatment, responses are likely to be dominated by a heavy reliance on medication and restriction.

Service users and carers become reluctant to ask for help or to comply with treatment, increasing the likelihood of a personal crisis, leading in some cases to self-harm or harm to others. In turn, prejudices are reinforced and provoke even more coercive responses, resulting in a downward spiral, which we call 'circles of fear', in which staff see service users as potentially dangerous and service users perceive services as harmful.

Black people see using mental health services as a degrading and alienating experience: the last resort.'

(Sainsbury Centre for Mental Health, 2002e, p. 8; see also Keating and Robertson, 2004)

In many ways, issues such as these reached a head in late 2003 with the publication of the Independent Inquiry into the death of David Bennett (Norfolk, Suffolk and Cambridgeshire Strategic Health Authority, 2003). A 38-year-old African-Caribbean man, David Bennett died in a medium secure unit in 1998 after being forcibly restrained by staff face down on the floor for some 25 minutes. According to some commentators, Bennett may have been one of at least 27 'black' people since 1980 to die while in psychiatric services and this case is 'typical of the poor care' received by 'black' people (Leason, 2003a, 2003b, p. 12). As part of the subsequent inquiry, evidence was taken from a range of national experts, and one of the key recommendations of the final report was for 'Ministerial acknowledgement of the presence of institutional racism in the mental health services and a commitment to eliminate it' (p. 67). This concept is particularly associated with the 1999 Macpherson Inquiry into the murder of a 'black' young man, Stephen Lawrence. Macpherson's definition of institutional racism was directly quoted by the Bennett Inquiry (see Box 9.9 for a summary of key concepts), which also included a statement from the then Chief Executive of the National

Institute for Mental Health in England that the NHS is racist in parts and that 'institutional racism was a true accusation that should be levelled at the NHS who should have no tolerance of it' (p. 43).

Box 9.9	Institutional racism

'Institutional racism is the collective failure of an organisation to provide an appropriate and professional service to people because of their colour, culture, or ethnic origin. It can be seen or detected in processes, attitudes and behaviour which amount to discrimination through unwitting prejudice, ignorance, thoughtlessness and racist stereotyping, which disadvantage minority ethnic people.'

(Norfolk, Suffolk and Cambridgeshire Strategic Health Authority, 2003, p. 43)

While many commentators have found the concept of institutional racism a helpful way of stressing the need for a concerted whole system approach (see, for example, McKenzie and Bhui, 2007a, 2007b), some have described this analysis as 'a vague, meaningless, yet insulting accusation' (Singh and Burns, 2006, p. 650). In particular, McKenzie and Bhui (2007b, p. 650) identify four tactics that can be used to deny the painful feelings which this issue raises:

- Shooting the messenger (i.e. that the problem is being overstated by people with 'a chip on their shoulder': p. 650)
- Misunderstanding the message (taking offence as if this was a personal accusation rather than a focus on systems)
- Focusing on whether racism is intentional (and vindicating inequity if no proof of intent can be found)
- Ignoring the urgency of the problem (and asking for more research)

For many commentators, the way forward may require a dual approach – working *inside* mental health services to make them more appropriate for people from minority ethnic communities, while at the same time working *outside* mental health to build capacity within black and minority communities and the voluntary sector for dealing with mental ill health. This has been usefully summarised in a NIMHE (2003a) report which highlights these concepts in its title: *Inside outside*. At a very basic level, however, the provision of effective interpretation services with workers trained in mental health issues could help to make services more accessible (Tabassum *et al.*, 2000; Warner *et al.*, 2000a). In addition, a key contribution has been made by the voluntary sector, which has traditionally been able to provide more flexible, responsive and culturally sensitive services (La Grenade, 1999; Sashidharan, 1999; Bhui *et al.*, 2000). However, developing specialist culturally sensitive services is only part of the solution, and several commentators emphasise the mixed messages that this can create. Rather than promoting the needs of 'black' service users, there is a danger that specialist services can marginalise people from minority ethnic communities even further, suggesting to workers that ethnicity is a fringe rather than a mainstream issue. Often, moreover, there is a tendency for workers to assume that ethnicity will be addressed by 'black' staff – an approach which many 'black' workers feel can deskill them and fails to recognise the importance of ethnicity for all workers irrespective of their own skin colour (La Grenade, 1999).

To ensure that culturally sensitive services become a mainstream feature of mental health services rather than an 'optional extra', the majority of commentators emphasise the central importance of training. For some, this would enable staff to explore their own attitudes to people from minority ethnic communities, understand the health beliefs and lifestyles of different communities and provide more culturally sensitive services (see, for example, Bahl, 1999; Koffman et al., 1997; Webbe, 1998). Another key issue is the need for meaningful two-way communication between service providers and minority ethnic communities to ensure that minority ethnic users are involved in the planning and provision of services (Pierre, 1999; see also Bhui and Bhugra, 1999; Copsey, 1997a, 1997b). Above all, however, a number of commentators emphasise that good quality, responsive mental health services will benefit all service users, irrespective of their ethnicity. Thus, for Bhui and Bhugra (1999, p. 231) 'all services need to be local, accessible, comprehensive, flexible and consumer-orientated, empowering those using the services'. For La Grenade (1999, p. 188), moreover, good services should be 'available, affordable, accessible, adaptable and acceptable' – principles that may well apply to 'black' people and white people alike.

Unfortunately, our knowledge of 'black' people's experiences of mental health – although extremely well documented – is limited by two key shortcomings in the current literature. First, the majority of documents focus on the African-Caribbean community, with fewer attempts to consider groups such as South-East Asian people and very few attempts to explore the needs of refugees and asylum seekers, Irish people and smaller minority ethnic communities such as Chinese or Vietnamese people (for exceptions, see Bracken et al., 1998; Li et al., 1999; Rethink, 2007; Bowl, 2007; Bradby et al., 2007). Second, is the tendency for the majority of documents focusing on ethnicity and mental health to *describe* ethnic differences in service provision, without necessarily considering the experiences and views of service users from different minority ethnic communities. As Thornicroft et al. (1999, p. 163) explain:

> Substantial differences have been demonstrated in the pattern of contacts
> with psychiatric services of patients from different ethnic groups,
> especially between those who are White and Black Caribbean … So far,
> these are largely expert-reported differences, or are aggregated data
> from inpatient service contacts. It is striking that information is largely
> absent in the psychiatric literature from the perspective of the patients
> themselves, of whatever ethnic group. Since types of contact with
> services vary so much, it is reasonable to hypothesise that service users'

views of services prior to, during and after such contact may also differ substantially by ethnic group. These views may then affect how such people use services in the future. In this way the experiences that patients accumulate from using services progress in ways which reflect their expectations, satisfaction, perception of illness and 'harder' aspects such as the number of admissions, particularly those which are compulsory. The ways in which such psychiatric 'careers' develop in relation to ethnic group, and their implications for how services can be sensitised to ethnic issues, are yet to be properly understood.

People with physical impairments, people with learning difficulties and older people

In contrast to the extensive body of literature on women and people from minority ethnic communities, the experiences of people with physical impairments, people with learning difficulties and older people have often been neglected. Despite this, more recent research and campaigning has suggested that each of these user groups may face particular difficulties when seeking to access mental health services:

1. While some *people with physical impairments* may also develop mental health problems, attention has tended to focus primarily on sensory impairments. For example, the mental health charity, Mind (2003a), has drawn attention to the emotional and mental health problems which can develop as a result of difficulties coming to terms with loss of sight and feelings of anxiety, depression, isolation and uncertainty. Also significant are the barriers faced by many deaf people who have mental health problems, including the failure of staff to communicate effectively with deaf people, a subsequent risk of misdiagnosis and a lack of specialist service provision (Clark, 2003; Evans, 2003; Mind, 2003b; Sign, n.d.). In addition, Morris's (2004a) study of 25 people with physical impairments and mental health problems reveals a range of difficulties with physical access and with workers not recognising the 'whole person', with both physical and mental health needs (see Box 9.10).

2. *People with learning difficulties* have more mental health problems than the general population (NHS Executive, 1998), yet may experience difficulties accessing services. This may be to do with communication barriers and a lack of accessible information produced by mental health services. However, also significant is a lack of clarity about who should take the lead in meeting the needs of people with mental health problems and learning difficulties. In the past, some mental health services have been reluctant to work with people with learning difficulties, while learning disability services sometimes lack the expertise to work with mental health problems in their service users. In response, the government's learning disability White Paper, *Valuing people*, argues that people with learning difficulties should have full access to general psychiatric services like everyone else in society, but that specialist learning disability workers could

Box 9.10	People with physical impairments and mental health problems

- The majority of respondents said they had difficulty accessing mental health services because of their physical impairments. The majority also had difficulty using physical disability services because of inadequate recognition of mental health needs and negative attitudes among staff towards mental health issues
- Inpatient experiences were often characterised by inaccessible physical environments and a lack of assistance for even simple things
- Medication required for a physical condition was commonly withdrawn on admission to a psychiatric ward and was not always available when needed
- Community mental health staff were often unfamiliar with needs relating to physical impairment and this could be associated with unhelpful attitudes
- There was commonly poor or no communication between mental health and physical disability services
- Medication given for mental health needs often had an impact on physical impairment, but most people said they had not been warned about these potential effects
- 'Talking treatments' received the highest rating of any service, but it was often difficult to find an accessible and, within the private sector, affordable therapist or counsellor
- When people were asked about what they wanted from services, they said they wanted to be seen as 'a whole person', with attention paid to both mental health needs and those relating to physical impairment. They wanted services and professionals to communicate and work together, and easy access to flexible services which could address individual needs. Above all, they wanted to be listened to and treated with respect

(Summarised from Morris, 2004b, p. 1)

help to facilitate and support this process (Department of Health, 2001h). This may require substantial changes before mainstream mental health services are able to work as effectively with people with learning difficulties as they do with members of the general population. In addition to this, the former Disability Rights Commission (2006) has produced a challenging study into the physical health inequalities experienced by people with learning difficulties and/or mental health problems which highlights a range of more general barriers to accessing the same quality health care as other members of the population.

3. *Older people* (often defined as people aged 65 and over) with mental health problems are sometimes considered to be the 'Cinderella' of mental health and often nobody's priority at all. This is despite the fact that older people with mental health problems form a significant user group (and that current numbers are set to rise dramatically as a result of demographic changes). According to the National Inquiry into Mental Health and Well-being in Later Life, this is both morally wrong and a poor use of scarce resources, with a massive negative impact on society and the economy (Age Concern, 2007; see also Box 9.11 for a quote summarising this issue).

However, responding to these needs of older people with mental health problems can be particularly difficult, as social services department tend to include this user group as part of their generic older people's services, while NHS provision tends to include this group as part of its mental health services, making interagency working all the more complex (Glasby and Littlechild, 2004).

Box 9.11	**Older people with mental health problems – nobody's priority?**

'Older people's mental health is an increasingly important area of public policy that does not get the attention it deserves. Three million older people in the UK experience symptoms of mental health problems that significantly impact on quality of life, and this number is set to grow by a third over the next 15 years. This represents an enormous cost to society and the economy, in direct costs to public services and indirect costs in lost contributions from older people who boost the UK economy by over £250 billion each year as workers, volunteers, unpaid carers and grandparents. At a time when the Government wants to make the most of older people's contributions to society, the neglect of older people's mental health needs represents a waste of human potential that we cannot afford.'

(Age Concern, 2007, p. 4)

Uniting all these groups is the concept of a social model of disability (see also Chapter 2). In contrast to traditional medical approaches (which see disability in terms of individual physiological and biological conditions), the social model acknowledges that disabled people have *impairments*. However, rather than focus on individual medical factors, many disabled people define disability in terms of the discrimination and exclusion they face as a result of the way in which society is organised. As UPIAS (1976) has argued (quoted in Oliver and Sapey, 2006, p. 30):

In our view, it is society which disables physically impaired people. Disability is something imposed on top of our impairments by the way we are unnecessarily isolated and excluded from full participation in society. To understand this it is necessary to grasp the distinction between the physical impairment and the social situation, called 'disability', of people with such an impairment. Thus we define impairment as lacking part or all of a limb, or having a defective limb, organism or mechanism of the body; and disability as the disadvantage or restriction of activity caused by a contemporary social organisation which takes no account of people who have physical impairments and thus excludes them in the mainstream of social activities. Physical disability is therefore a particular form of social oppression.

Using this approach, the emphasis shifts from medical intervention and cure for the individual to tackling the way society discriminates against disabled people. As an example, a person who uses a wheelchair may be unable to use public transport – however, depending on the model of disability we adopt, we could attribute this to the person's impairment (they need to use a wheelchair) or to social causes (buses are not always designed for people in wheelchairs). With the current state of medical technology, intervening at a social level can be more effective – thus, it would probably be easier to raise the curb of a bus stop so that a wheelchair user can get on than it would be to intervene individually (working with the individual to try to 'heal' their impairment). Such an approach is also more cost efficient – by altering the bus stop, planners and policy makers could make the bus accessible for all wheelchair users as well as for other groups.

In theory, a social model also has the potential to develop a common cause between people with mental health problems, people with physical impairments, older people, people with learning difficulties and others. While the disability movement has not always been as inclusive of some of these groups as it perhaps could have been, a social model emphasises the way in which all these people are disabled not by their impairment, frailty, learning difficulty or mental distress, but by the way in which society responds to such people and issues. While much more work is required to develop these links, there is at least scope for a much broader and potentially very powerful coalition of groups whose focus is not on individual impairments, but on the way society is organised and the way in which discrimination operates.

Gay men, lesbians and bisexuals

Prohibited since legislation in 1885, homosexuality was only legalised in 1967 when men over 21 were permitted to have sexual relationships with each other (although it was not until 1992 when the Isle of Man came into line). In contrast, lesbianism has never been included in legislation and has therefore never been illegal (see Mind, 1996, for all dates quoted in this paragraph). Despite this, homosexuality has traditionally been seen as a form of mental illness, and was not declassified as such by the American Psychiatric Association until 1973 and, by the World Health Organization, until 1992. Even as late as 1989, the *Oxford Textbook of Psychiatry* could include homosexuality under 'problems of sexuality and gender' and discuss ways of 'curing' homosexual people. While such overt discrimination no longer exists, much of the misunderstanding and prejudice behind these statutes and practices remain. As Mind (1996) emphasises:

> Although blatant examples of bigoted, misinformed theory are
> no longer common in psychiatric writing, evidence shows that
> homosexuality continues to be referred to as a mental disorder in some
> psychiatric texts, and anecdotal evidence shows that homosexuality
> continues to be thought of as a mental illness per se by society in
> general and by some mental health professionals.

That gay men, lesbians and bisexual people continue to have negative experiences of mental health services is demonstrated by a small number of key research studies (see Box 9.12).

Box 9.12	The experiences of lesbian, gay and bisexual service users

Golding's (1997) interviews with 55 gay, lesbian and bisexual service users identified some positive experiences of mental health care, but also found that 73 per cent said they had experienced some sort of prejudice or discrimination in connection with their sexuality:

- 88 per cent of people experiencing discrimination felt unable to challenge it, largely because of feelings of fear or vulnerability
- 22 per cent said they had experienced direct victimisation in connection with their sexuality in the form of violence (including instances of rape or sexual assault)
- 38 per cent experienced additional discrimination due to their religious beliefs, race, physical ability or age
- 16 per cent had partners at the time when they were using mental health services. Two-thirds of these people felt that their partners had not been treated on an equal par with the partners of heterosexual service users
- 51 per cent said that their sexuality had been inappropriately used to explain the cause of their mental distress
- 7 per cent of participants said that they felt they were forced to have a blood test for HIV

Price's (1997) review and in-depth interviews emphasise:

- The prevalence of suicide and self-harm within the gay/lesbian community
- The discriminatory nature of the 'nearest' relative regulations, which discriminate against gay or lesbian partners
- The distress caused by homophobia and harassment
- Professionals seeking to blame or cure people's sexuality
- The value which gay/lesbian users place on 'out' workers
- The tendency for gay or lesbian workers to be seen as 'the gay expert'
- Workers ignoring or responding inappropriately to people's sexuality

McFarlane's (1998) research with 35 service users and 35 mental health workers concluded that (p. 117): 'lesbian, gay and bisexual mental health services users are discriminated against and oppressed, not only by the attitudes and behaviour of society at large, but also from within mental health services. Judgement is made on the basis of their sexual identity and their identity as service users. Not only that, they are also discriminated against from within lesbian, gay and bisexual communities, again on the basis of their use of mental health services.'

King *et al.* (2003) conclude that gay men, lesbians and bisexual people are more likely than heterosexuals to: experience psychological distress; harm themselves; experience harassment or bullying because of their sexuality; have contact with the mental health system; and experience negative reactions from professionals. A subsequent systematic review (King *et al.*, 2007) concluded that lesbian, gay and bisexual people are 'at significantly higher risk of mental disorder, suicidal ideation, substance misuse and DSH [deliberate self-harm] than heterosexual people' (p. 3).

Policy responses

Over time, the research findings set out above point to a poor track record with regard to tackling discrimination in mental health services. However, in the early twenty-first century, there are signs that issues of discrimination and equality are beginning to become more of a mainstream feature of the policy agenda, with a series of key policy documents and initiatives. Examples include:

- Official guidance on women's mental health (Department of Health, 2002h, 2003i; see also RCN/CSIP/NIMHE, 2008; CSIP, 2006)
- Official policy documents on the experience of minority ethnic communities and on race equality in mental health (Department of Health, 2003j, 2004a–c, 2005c, 2005d; NIMHE, 2003a, 2003b, 2004a)
- A consultation on a national strategy for dementia (Department of Health, 2008f)
- An increased focus on tackling stigma and discrimination (see, for example, NIMHE, 2004b)
- The creation of a new Equality and Human Rights Commission

While these policies all place a welcome focus on tackling discrimination, many of the issues highlighted in this chapter are longstanding, complex and seem unlikely to be resolved easily. Moreover, some accounts appear to cast doubt on the extent of official commitment to the radical action required to promote anti-discriminatory practice. Thus, progress in creating women-only hospital settings has sometimes been slow (Copperman and Knowles, 2006), and current approaches to race equality training have been described as 'inappropriate and inadequate in addressing racial inequality in mental health services' (Bennett *et al.*, 2007, p. 7). The social work and medical press have also criticised the government for apparently rejecting some of the Bennett Inquiry recommendations, refusing to acknowledge the existence of institutional racism (Community Care, 2004; Gillen, 2005; McKenzie and Bhui, 2007a). In addition, there have been claims that the Department of Health watered down a critical report into mental health services for people from minority ethnic communities (see also findings by the former Commission for Racial Equality, 2007, for broader discussion of the Department and its approach to equality). According to the report author (quoted in Leason, 2003c, p. 8):

> They [the Department of Health] tried to dilute it as much as they could. We had to fight all the way ... The experience of working with the DH around this document, and subsequently, has reinforced my view that this is an example of institutionally racist attitudes and behaviours on its part.

As a result, it may well be that discrimination in mental health services persists and that the negative experiences of some of the groups set out above continue.

Conclusion

Overall, the particular forms of discrimination addressed in this chapter have a number of themes and issues in common. For example, individual forms of discrimination can interact. Thus, 'black' women may have very different experiences to white women, while gay, lesbian or bisexual service users may face additional discrimination due to their age, physical ability, religion or ethnicity. While specialist services that are sensitive to the needs of a particular marginalised group of people may be welcome, this may actually hinder change in more mainstream services. There is also an additional danger that staff from a particular group may be perceived as the 'expert' on a particular issue (e.g. 'black' staff members as 'experts' on ethnicity and gay staff as 'the gay expert'). This not only deskills and exploits these staff members, but also takes the responsibility away from other workers for making services more responsive to the needs of service users from particular backgrounds.

Above all, many of the negative experiences cited above are longstanding issues which policy makers and practitioners have known about, but have so far been unable to resolve. This suggests either a lack of political will or that the issues concerned are so complex and deep-seated that they are extremely difficult to put right (or both). As we discussed at the beginning of this chapter, discrimination not only exists within mental health services, but also in health and social care as a whole and in wider society. Also, discrimination cannot be tackled simply by changing the way individuals behave. Instead, attempts to root out discrimination in mental health services need to be accompanied by efforts to root out discrimination in wider society at a personal, cultural and structural level. Discrimination, in short, is pervasive and multifaceted, and only an equally multifaceted response will suffice. Of course, this is not to deny that mental health services can do a range of things to tackle discrimination. However, it may mean that changes within mental health should take place alongside more widespread and fundamental action to ensure that services and wider society function in a non-discriminatory manner.

Reflection exercises

1. Experiencing discrimination

Exercise for all workers

Think of a situation where someone made an assumption about you and where you felt unable to challenge it:

■ How did this make you feel?
■ How did you respond to the person concerned?
■ Why did you feel unable to challenge it?
■ Did it affect how you approached other people?
■ What sources of support were available?
■ With hindsight how might you approach such an issue in future?

2. Experiencing discrimination in mental health services

Exercise for all workers

Talk to service users from some of the groups discussed in this chapter – how did they feel using services as:

■ A woman?
■ A person from a minority ethnic community?
■ A person with a physical impairment?
■ A person with a learning difficulty?
■ An older person?
■ A gay man, lesbian or bisexual person?

What can you do differently in future to prevent negative experiences and build on positive examples of good practice?

What training and support exists within your organisation or area to help you?

Share these answers with colleagues from different professional backgrounds – do they agree with you?

3. Tackling discrimination

Exercise for all workers

Using Thompson's PCS framework, talk to a service user from a marginalised group and list the factors that have contributed to their contact with and experience of mental health services. What can you or your organisation do to challenge some of these?

4. Institutional racism

Exercise for all workers

Using Macpherson's definition of institutional racism, discuss this concept with colleagues from different professional backgrounds. To what extent do you and they find this a helpful concept when seeking to work with people from minority ethnic communities? Do some of your views or those of colleagues reflect the defensive tactics identified by McKenzie and Bhui (2007b) above?

Suggestions for further reading

For an overview of the issues presented in this chapter, Pilgrim and Rogers' (2005) *A sociology of mental health and illness* is an essential starting point. However, more detailed reading is listed below for specific topics:

1. Women

   In addition to official policy documents on mental health and gender (Department of Health, 2002h, 2003i), the national visit carried out by the Sainsbury Centre for Mental Health and the Mental Health Act Commission provides an accessible overview (Warner and Ford, 1998), as does Coppock (2008). Also helpful is a guide to *Informed gender practice* produced by the Royal College of Nursing and NIMHE (RCN/ CSIP/NIMHE, 2008) and a guide to *The mental health of women in contact with the criminal justice system* (CSIP, 2006). The Parental Mental Health Network (www.pmhcwn.org.uk) is also a useful source of information, as is SCIE's research briefing on *Stress and resilience factors in parents with mental health problems and their children* (Parrott *et al.*, 2008).

2. People from minority ethnic communities

   Key introductions to the experiences of people from minority ethnic communities include the Sainsbury Centre for Mental Health's (2002e) *Breaking the circles of fear*, the inquiry into the death of David Bennett (Norfolk, Suffolk and Cambridgeshire Strategic Health Authority, 2003) and NIMHE's (2003a) *Inside outside*. Mind also publish a number of factsheets on mental health and the African Caribbean, Chinese and Vietnamese, Irish and South Asian communities (www.mind.org.uk/Information/Factsheets/ Diversity), while the Department of Health (2004e–g) produces a series of guides to mental health promotion and particular minority ethnic communities. The Mental Health Foundation's *Black spaces project* (2003) reviews the learning from a series of innovative black voluntary sector projects working with mental health issues, while a second report on *Keeping the faith* (Mental Health Foundation, 2007) explores issues of spirituality within mental health services.

3. People with physical impairments, people with learning difficulties and older people

   Key sources for people with physical impairments and mental health problems include factsheets by Mind (www.mind.org.uk) on visual impairments and deafness, and research by Sign (n.d.) into mental health services for deaf people (see also www.signcharity.org.uk). Debates about the relationship between disability rights and mental health are explored in more detail by leading commentators such as Peter Beresford (Beresford *et al.*, 2002). Morris's (2004a) study into the experiences of people who have physical impairments and mental health problems is also a ground-breaking and powerful account.

For older people, the Audit Commission (2000a, 2000b, 2002) has produced a number of key reports, while the *National service framework for older people* includes a specific standard about older people with mental health problems (Department of Health, 2001i). More recently, national overviews have been provided by the UK Inquiry into Mental Health and Well-being in Later Life (Age Concern, 2007), while the Department of Health (2008) has consulted on a national strategy for dementia.

The government's learning disability strategy, *Valuing people*, summarises official policy and introduces the concept of health facilitation to support people with learning difficulties to access mainstream community services (Department of Health, 2001h). This was subsequently updated with the publication of *Valuing people now* (Department of Health, 2007f). Although dated, *Signposts for success* provides a good practice guide to commissioning and providing health services (including mental health services) for people with learning difficulties (NHS Executive, 1998), while the Valuing People Support Team (2004) have produced a toolkit for improving mental health services for people with learning difficulties. More generally, a review of abusive practice in a local mental health and learning disability service shows what can still happen in closed, isolated hospital settings (see, for example, Healthcare Commission/Commission for Social Care Inspection, 2006). In addition, *Equal treatment: closing the gap* is a powerful review of the physical health inequalities experienced by people with learning difficulties and/or mental health problems produced by the former Disability Rights Commission (2006).

Additional information about the social model of disability is available from introductory disability studies textbooks such as those by Oliver (1990; Oliver and Sapey, 2006) and Swain *et al.* (2004).

4. Sexuality

In addition to the studies cited in the main body of the chapter, good practice guidance is available via the website of PACE, a London-based counselling and mental health project working to promote lesbian and gay health and well-being (www.pacehealth.org.uk).

5. Outside mental health services, more general sources include:

- Thompson's (2006) introductory textbook on anti-discriminatory practice (which remains a standard text)
- The Equality and Human Rights Commission (www.equalityhumanrights. com) – see also a paper by the former Disability Rights Commission (2007), which sets out some priorities around mental health, equality and human rights for the new Commission

10 Carers

In this chapter we discuss:

- The importance of carers
- Definitions of 'the carer'
- The policy context
- The neglect of carers of people with mental health problems
- Marginalised groups
- The needs of carers

The importance of carers

When working in health and social care, it is tempting to assume that the people workers meet are somehow representative of society as a whole. When all you see on a daily basis are people facing considerable difficulties or changes in their lives, and who need input from formal services, it is easy to get a distorted view of the world. In fact, most people make little or no use of formal health or social care, and manage by themselves or with help from friends and family. As an example, around 60 per cent of adults with a learning difficulty live with their families, and up to 25 per cent of people with a learning difficulty do not become known to formal services until their parents become too frail to continue caring for them (Department of Health, 2001j, pp. 56–7).

Even when they do need help from statutory welfare services, most people do not rely solely on this form of provision. On the contrary, the vast majority of care is (and always has been) provided by carers: family members, friends and neighbours who support someone else as a result of a personal relationship with that person, not as a paid job or as part of a statutory service. In the UK, it has been estimated that there are 5.2 million carers, with over 1 million people caring for more than 50 hours per week (HM Government, 2008, p. 33). This support saves public services an estimated £87 billion per year (House of Commons Work and Pensions Committee, 2008, p. 5). Without this support – often unseen and unheard – statutory services would be unable to function. As former Prime Minister, Tony Blair, has stated (Department of Health, 2000c, p. 3):

> When I talk about the importance to Britain of strong communities and of people having responsibilities towards each other, I'm not speaking of abstract ideas, but of real people and real events: the things many people do to make things better for those around them. The extraordinary work which carers do may well be the best example of what I mean. Extraordinary not in ways which make headlines, but in ways which really matter and which really make a difference to those they are caring for. Carers devote large parts of their own lives to the lives of others – not as part of a job, but voluntarily … For the sick, the frail, the vulnerable and the elderly, carers provide help and support in ways which might otherwise not be available. By their effort, their patience, their knowledge, their understanding, their companionship, their determination and their compassion, carers very often transform the lives of the people they're caring for … Carers are among the unsung heroes of British life.

In many respects, therefore, this chapter is in the wrong place in this book – it should not be last after primary, community and hospital services, but should come first, because carers provide the bulk of support. However, as explained below, it is only in the last twenty years or so that we have come to recognise the needs and contribution of carers, and, until relatively recently, this has often been a neglected area – with the needs of carers under-researched and undervalued.

Definitions of 'the carer'

Part of the difficulty in discussing the needs of carers revolves around terminological and conceptual problems. This is true in four main areas:

1. There is a tendency within health and social care to refer to 'informal carers'. This term is usually adopted to distinguish between paid carers in statutory services and those family members and friends who provide care on a non-statutory, voluntary basis. However, many carers suggest that they find this phrase highly patronising and demeaning, implying that they are not 'proper' carers – they are merely 'informal' with the 'real' care provided by professionals. As we have already seen, exactly the opposite is often true and we have adopted the term 'carer' in this book to reflect the central importance of carers within health and social services.
2. Much of the generic literature on carers portrays the caring task in a negative light and as 'a burden'. While there are many difficulties associated with caring (see below), it can also be very hard for the person being cared for, who may feel frustrated and angry as a result of their perceived

dependence on someone else. In addition, caring can be a very positive experience. At its best, caring *for* someone arises out of caring *about* someone, and the word itself implies warm and loving relationships. Of course, as noted below, carers can be spouses, parents, children or siblings, and caring has the potential to cement relationships and bring people closer together. At the same time, service users can contribute positively to the lives of carers. As an example, an American study by Greenberg *et al.* (1994) highlighted the contribution made by people with mental health problems in terms of providing family members with companionship, helping with meal preparation and household chores, listening to problems and providing advice, helping with shopping and providing care for others during periods of illness.

3. For some people, the term 'service user' and 'carer' are artificial constructs which do not reflect the reality of people's lives and relationships. For example, an older married couple may both have needs that the other can help meet, while a child or young person can be a carer for a parent with a learning difficulty or a mental health problem. In many ways, this is true of all of us: in practice, no one is completely independent of family or friends and we all rely on other people to meet some of our needs, whether it be practical or financial support from parents to young people, emotional support, neighbours babysitting or communities getting together to tackle a particular issue locally. While it is true that some people have greater support needs than others as a result of a physical impairment, mental health problem or learning difficulty, we are all interdependent.

4. There is an ongoing debate about the usefulness of the term 'carer'. While it is helpful to distinguish users' family and social networks, many people do not see themselves as 'carers' and do not respond to official policies or sources of support badged in this way. As Sayce (2000, p. 11) observes:

> A further personal dimension was added when I became involved with a partner who has a diagnosis of manic depression. I do not, however, think that this makes me a 'carer', because this is a mutual relationship, not one in which 'care' goes one way, and not one involving 'burden' (an offensive term that should be dropped).

This may be particularly true for young carers, older people, people from minority ethnic communities and the carers of people with mental health problems (Department of Health/Social Services Inspectorate 1997, 1998a, 1998b; Heron, 1998; Rogers, 2000), who may see themselves as children, spouses and family members rather than as 'carers'. This is a significant issue and one which defies an easy answer. Our own personal preference is to adopt a generic term such as 'carer' as a useful shorthand for a group of people who offer support to someone close to them; however, we are equally aware that others would argue that if a term does not make sense to carers themselves then it has little meaning.

The policy context

In the late twentieth century, the needs of carers slowly began to acquire increasing recognition and significance. Much of this began in the 1980s, with a series of research studies, often influenced by feminism and the gendered nature of caring, which began to highlight the substantial caring tasks which family members and friends (often women) were undertaking on behalf of older people, people with physical impairments, people with learning difficulties and others (see, for example, Baldwin and Twigg, 1990; Finch and Groves, 1983; Ungerson, 1987). In 1989, the *Caring for people* White Paper provided one of the first official acknowledgements of the substantial role played by carers, and made support for carers a key priority (Department of Health, 1989a, p. 4):

> The government acknowledges that the great bulk of community care
> is provided by friends, family and neighbours. The decision to take
> on a caring role is never an easy one. However, many people make
> that choice and it is right that they should be able to play their part in
> looking after those close to them. But it must be recognised that carers
> need help and support if they are to continue to carry out their role.

While this commitment to meeting the needs of carers was an important statement of government intent, the White Paper and 1990 Act did little to deliver substantial change for carers. The disputed and shifting nature of the concept of community was simply ignored and huge assumptions were made therefore about the ability, desire and capacity of the community to care.

In 1995, the *Carers (Services and Recognition) Act* gave people providing care on a regular basis to someone eligible for community care services the right to an assessment of their needs, but with a number of limitations (Mandelstam, 1998, p. 45; see also Department of Health, 1996b):

- Entitlement to an assessment depended on the carer either providing or intending to provide a substantial amount of care on a regular basis
- Entitlement depended on the carer requesting an assessment
- Carers' assessments could only take place if the person being cared for was themselves being assessed under the *Community Care Act* – carers had no independent right to an assessment
- Any services provided would be offered to the 'service user', and carers were not entitled to any services to meet their own assessed needs
- Social services were not given any additional funding to implement the Act

As a result, the *Carers (Recognition and Services) Act* 1995 attracted a degree of criticism from the field – while it certainly focused on *carers*, it offered little *recognition* and very little by way of *services* (personal communications, frontline workers). In addition, while the emphasis on assessing carers' needs may, in time, help to raise them up the policy agenda of health and social care, it also suggests that carers carry problems that need to be assessed and managed. Viewed in this way, it may be difficult for carers to develop equal and constructive relationships with services, or to be treated, along with the service user, as experts in their own right.

In recognition of some of these previous shortcomings, the *National strategy for carers* underlined the government's commitment to improving information, support and care for carers (Department of Health, 2000c). This was followed in 1999 by the *National service framework for mental health* (Department of Health, 1999a), which included a specific standard about the needs of carers (see Box 10.1). In 2000, *The Carers and Disabled Children Act* strengthened the entitlement to an assessment by giving carers aged sixteen or over the right to an assessment (even where the person they care for has refused an assessment by social services or has refused services following an assessment). Policy guidance also emphasised that workers should give carers verbal and written information about their right to an assessment. In addition, local authorities were given the power to supply certain services direct to carers (such as short-term break voucher schemes or direct payments) (Department of Health, 2001j). In 2004, the *Carers (Equal Opportunities) Act* sought to ensure that all carers are informed of their right to an assessment, that councils take account of carers' outside interests (such as wishes to work, undertake education or training and leisure activities), and that the NHS and social services work together more effectively to provide support for carers. More recently, these measures have been boosted by a range of additional policies and initiatives, including greater rights to flexible working and a new carers strategy to update the previous 1998 version (see Box 10.2).

Box 10.1	*The NSF for mental health*

Standard six: Caring about carers

Aim: To ensure health and social services assess the needs of carers who provide regular and substantial care for those with severe mental illness, and provide care to meet their needs.

Standard six – all individuals who provide regular and substantial care for a person on CPA should:

■ Have an assessment of their caring, physical and mental health needs, repeated on at least an annual basis
■ Have their own written care plan which is given to them and implemented in discussion with them

Rationale: Carers play a vital role in helping to look after service users of mental health services, particularly those with severe mental illness. Providing help, advice and services to carers can be one of the best ways of helping people with mental health problems. While caring can be rewarding, the strains and responsibilities of caring can also have an impact on carers' own mental and physical health, and these needs must be addressed by health and social services.

(Department of Health, 1999a, p. 69)

Box 10.2	The 2008 carers strategy

In 2008, the government's updated carers strategy set out a new vision for carers: 'by 2018, carers will be universally recognised and valued as being fundamental to strong families and stable communities. Support will be tailored to meet individuals' needs, enabling carers to maintain a balance between their caring responsibilities and a life outside caring, whilst enabling the person they support to be a full and equal citizen' (p. 9).
  Key commitments included:

- Providing every carer with access to comprehensive information
- £150 million to increase breaks for carers from caring
- Pilots to enable the NHS to better support carers (including pilots to improve GP support and pilot annual health checks for carers)
- Up to £38 million to support carers to combine employment and caring and to re-enter the job market after their caring role has finished
- Improving the emotional support offered to carers
- Over £6 million to improve support for young carers
- Training carers to strengthen their caring role and empower them in their dealings with professionals
- Additional training for welfare professionals
- Extension of third-sector support for carers
- Providing data to help commissioners and policy makers provide better support for carers
- Establishing a standard definition of carers across government

This is claimed to represent a total of £255 million additional investment (2008–11) above and beyond £22 million previously committed (HM Government, 2008, pp.10–12).

Despite this emphasis on the needs of carers, there is evidence from the wider literature to suggest that such policy measures have not always been translated fully into practice. In particular, a large body of research demonstrates that carers may be unaware of their rights to an assessment, that they may feel unsupported in their role as carers and that some public services may not always perceive support for carers as a high priority (see, for example, Carers UK, 2003, 2004, 2006). That this is the case in mental health services is demonstrated below.

The neglect of carers of people with mental health problems

In 2001, the case of James Lawson provided a powerful example of the lack of support which some carers of people with mental health problems receive and the sense of helplessness which they may experience (see Box 10.3).

  Shortly after the Lawson case, the Department of Health and the National Schizophrenia Fellowship (since renamed as Rethink) launched their Commitment to Carers campaign to coincide with National Carers Week (Department of

Box 10.3	The pressures facing carers

'The assisted suicide of Sarah Lawson brought the plight of people caring for those with mental health problems sharply into focus. The reality of looking after people with such severe problems means they often live under unimaginable pressures with very little support.

When Sarah Lawson committed suicide in April last year, it was a desperate act by a severely depressed young woman. The fact that her father, James Lawson, assisted in her suicide by placing a bag over her head as she lay dying from an overdose is shocking – even appalling.

But few of the estimated 1.26 million people caring for a friend or relative with some form of mental illness are going to be appalled by the actions of this man – an exhausted, distraught and desperate parent. Caring for someone in these circumstances can be tough, unremitting and lonely. Every year, a few people are inevitably pushed beyond the limit of their endurance (Winchester, 2001).'

James Lawson later received a two-year suspended sentence (Community Care, 2001).

Health/National Schizophrenia Fellowship, 2001). Figures published by the National Schizophrenia Fellowship (n.d.) suggest that almost one in four of Britain's carers (22 per cent or 1.26 million people) are caring for someone with a mental health problem, often with only limited support from statutory services. Traditionally, the needs of carers of people with mental health problems have received even less attention than carers of people from other user groups. This was initially highlighted in a ground-breaking study of *Families caring for people diagnosed as mentally ill* (Perring *et al.*, 1990) funded by the Department of Health and conducted by the Social Policy Research Unit at the University of York. In particular, Perring *et al.* argued that the carers of people with mental health problems had been neglected for two main reasons:

1. The literature on caring tends to focus on physical caring tasks (i.e. of people with physical impairments and frail older people).
2. Mental health services have tended to focus on the person with mental health problems, without necessarily recognising the needs and contributions of the user's family and friends. This may be partly because of the strong medical influence within mental health practice and research which had tended to focus on definitions and theories of mental illness and neglected 'the more general non-medical, societal and familial aspects' of living with a mental health problem (Perring *et al.*, 1990, p. 3). Even where families have been considered, this is often only as an adjunct to helping 'the patient'. On other occasions, families have been seen as 'part of the problem' rather than 'part of the solution' – either contributing to the mental health problem in the first place or exacerbating it (personal communications, mental health workers).

Despite these limitations in the literature, Perring *et al.* were able to identify a number of key issues for the carers of people with mental health problems, including the considerable stresses and strains of the caring role and a lack of support from formal services (see Box 10.4).

Box 10.4   **The carers of people with mental health problems**

Perring *et al.*'s (1990) review of the literature suggests that:

- Carers of people with mental health problems face 'difficult' behaviour, including social withdrawal, uncontrollable restlessness, threatened or actual suicide or hypochondriacal preoccupations. Often carers are uncertain how to respond, wanting to be sympathetic, but feeling baffled and frustrated
- Carers often take on unexpected new roles, from personal care to household and financial responsibilities
- There can be a substantial impact on every aspect of family life (marital and parental relationships, domestic routine, social life, leisure activities, employment and financial circumstances)
- Caring can provoke a range of emotions (including negative feelings such as fear, anger, resentment and a sense of being overloaded, as well as positive emotions such as warmth and love)
- Caring can have a negative effect on health and mental health
- Carers are concerned about the low quality and quantity of their contact with formal services. Key issues include frequent staff changes and a lack of continuity, family concerns being ignored until a crisis is reached, unsympathetic workers and poor communication between workers and families
- There are high levels of unmet need

Overall:

'The ability of families to cope against a background of inadequate formal support does not mean that services to families need no improvement. The issues of unreported need, the continuing evidence that care by the family is associated with various indicators of stress, and criticisms that families make of their experience with professional workers all underline the fact that some effective intervention for families with a mentally ill member is essential, for the benefit of the family and identified patient alike' (Perring *et al.*, 1990, p. 44).

Many of these themes have since been supported and developed in more recent studies. For example, in 1995 the National Schizophrenia Fellowship published a national survey of carers' needs on behalf of the Department of Health's Mental Health Taskforce (Hogman and Pearson, 1995). For the research authors, the carers of people with mental health problems had become 'silent partners' in community care: so used to the difficulties associated with caring and with lack of support from formal services that they see this way of life as the norm and do not ask for help (see Box 10.5 for a summary). As a result, the study began with 'four facts you need to know about carers' (p. 4):

1. Every carer has individual caring responsibilities and individual needs. Carers cannot be classified as one group with a shared set of needs.
2. Carers are experts in severe mental illness.
3. Carers do not always want to care.
4. Carers have a low ceiling in terms of demands for services. They are not a group that make unrealistic demands.

Box 10.5	*'The silent partners'*

- 71 per cent said that caring had resulted in health problems such as stress, depression, heart trouble, sleep problems and anxiety: 'Don't you know anyone it hasn't affected? You live on a knife edge all the time.'
- 58 per cent said that caring led to significant extra expense: 'We are doing the government's job for them for free without it being acknowledged.'
- 42 per cent said that time spent caring had prevented them from working as much as they would have liked: 'As a carer I had to go part-time and also had to have time off ... Therefore I did not reach my full potential in work, and therefore could not demand a higher salary, thus affecting my pension on retirement.'
- Many carers wanted more services than they were receiving to help them continue in their role: 'The problem is that there are not enough facilities within the community, and many people do not know how to gain access to what little there is.'
- Information is crucial for carers, yet is often neglected: 'I have had to search for all the information regarding services, sections and care management, nothing has been offered.'
- Many carers had experienced a crisis and felt that there was insufficient support: 'I found it very frustrating that nothing was being done to help when she was ill.'

Overall, many people found caring without adequate support extremely difficult:

'It has been a nightmare which I wouldn't wish on any living soul. It has broken a part of my heart, which I feel will never heal.'

'The carer is almost as much a victim of the illness as the patient.'

'I know how to care – but I have had enough. I want to be able to live whatever life I have left – my way – and know my daughter is safe and will be helped.'

(Summarised from Hogman and Pearson, 1995: assorted quotes; sample: 400 carers)

Of course, both these studies took place prior to more recent carers' legislation, and considerable progress might have been expected given the policy initiatives set out earlier in this chapter. Despite this, Wright *et al.*'s (2000) thematic review of NHS-funded research suggests that there are significant variations in terms of the amount of support available to carers, with many not receiving the services they need to continue in a caring role or to maintain their own health. Research by the Mental Health Foundation (2001) also highlights the emotional difficulties and the lack of support which respondents experienced when trying to support a friend with mental health problems. Similar themes are also echoed by a number of other commentators, who suggest that the contribution of carers is often undervalued and their needs unrecognised. As Allen (1997, p. 34) suggests: 'Carers are the invisible corner-stone of community care. For the relatives and friends of someone with a severe and enduring mental health problem, community care represents a 24-hour burden with serious, often unacknowledged consequences.'

More recently, the needs of the carers of people with mental health problems have received renewed attention from the national voluntary organisation Rethink (2003b, 2003c). According to a survey of 1451 users and carers, around half of carers felt that improvements were taking place in mental health services, but that there was still a long way to go, with many people not receiving a proper break from caring, not sufficiently involved with health and social care professionals and concerned about the availability of relevant services. Many carers also felt that caring had adverse affects on their health, their social life and their family relationships, and that access to and take-up of carers assessments was low (see Box 10.6). Similar issues have also been raised by monitoring undertaken on behalf of the Department of Health, which emphasises the adverse effect which caring can have on carers' own mental health (Singleton *et al.*, 2002). As the Rethink Chair and Chief Executive suggested in their introduction to one of these reports (Rethink, 2003c, p. 2):

> Mental health carers ... are recognised now in a way that they were
> not 20 years ago. More carers than ever before are involved not
> just in one-to-one care but also in the planning of mental health
> services. On paper, carers have never had it so good. And yet the
> reality of caring today is to see a deterioration in your own mental
> and physical health, reduced finances and career prospects, strained
> family relationships and lost leisure. There are regional variations in
> the availability of information, help and support. Too many carers find
> the present legal right to an assessment of their needs a sham because
> identified needs go unmet. Pockets of good practice for supporting
> carers are emerging but the challenge is to see these vital supports and
> services extended to all.

However, one of the most substantial contributions to date has been the work of Arksey *et al.* (2002) at the University of York. Commissioned by the NHS Service Delivery and Organisation Research and Development programme (SDO), Arksey *et al.*'s review of the literature and consultation with key stakeholders suggests that services should be underpinned by four key principles:

1. Positive and inclusive: mental health professionals should have a positive approach to carers, involve them in decision making and recognise them as partners or 'co-experts'.
2. Flexible and individualised: services should be person-centred, reflecting the diversity of carers.
3. Accessible and responsive: services should be available at all times, including outside 'office hours', and offer a rapid response.
4. Integrated and co-ordinated: services should be 'joined up'; carers' services should be embedded within mainstream mental health services.

Box 10.6	Rethink survey 2003

- 92 per cent of carers want contact with a professional, but only 49 per cent say they are in regular contact all or most of the time. A key barrier was concerns about 'patient confidentiality', which many carers felt was used by professionals in an unhelpful way to block the sharing of information (see also Pinfold *et al.*, 2004; Rapaport *et al.*, 2006; Gray *et al.*, 2008, for further discussion)
- One in four carers said they had been denied access to help during the past three years. For one person, a 'lack of beds and resources locally means my son doesn't get help until a crisis', while for another carer 'no one ever phones back when I make a call requesting help. [It] usually takes seven or eight calls to get hold of anyone'
- Key frustrations for carers include shortage of adequate service provision locally (30 per cent), difficulty accessing crisis services (16 per cent), difficulty getting access to mental health professionals (14 per cent), concerns about the quality of mental health staffing (11 per cent) and a feeling of not being listened to or valued by professionals (10 per cent)
- One in four carers feel that they don't have any information to help them
- 41 per cent of carers said that caring had moderately or significantly affected their physical or mental health
- 60 per cent of carers say that their ability to have a social life outside the home is significantly or moderately affected
- 50 per cent of carers feel that they never have any choice about whether they continue to provide help and support
- Only one in four carers had received a carers assessment

(Summarised from Rethink, 2003b, 2003c)

Overall (Arksey *et al.*, 2002, p. 40):

Support for carers of people with mental health problems needs to be offered in the form of a flexible package of services that is tailored to suit the individual carer–care recipient dyad; that is underpinned by key principles of service delivery such as inclusiveness, responsiveness and co-ordination; and that takes account of local contexts. The content of these packages will vary, and will reflect the diversity of carer experience in terms of geography, socioeconomic variables, patient diagnosis and stage of illness, as well as differing delivery methods provided by both the statutory, private and voluntary sectors.

A consensual view emerged ... that ... interventions should be tailored to the needs of both individual carers and care recipients; disregarding care recipients can lead to unanticipated outcomes, as well as hindering the full realisation of benefits ... On this basis, we feel that it is important to identify and examine what carers, and care recipients, believe is effective in terms of the range of services available and explore how best these can be delivered in order to lead to improved outcomes for both carers and care recipients.

Marginalised groups

A key criticism of some of the existing literature is the implicit assumption that carers are a single category of people, each with similar needs. As the quote from Arksey *et al.* above suggests, this is an oversimplistic view that runs the risk of neglecting the needs of individual carers. In particular, we know relatively little about (Arksey *et al.*, 2002, p. 11):

- Black and minority ethnic community carers
- Carers of people with dual diagnosis
- Carers supporting more than one person
- Less-common caring situations (for instance, caring in gay and lesbian relationships or caring at a distance)

An additional group traditionally neglected in the literature are young carers – children and young people caring for a parent with a mental illness. This issue has been particularly highlighted in recent years as a result of a general growth in our awareness of the needs of young carers (through research and campaigning carried out by academic bodies such as the Young Carers Research Group at Loughborough University) and by a specific research study into young carers and mental health by Aldridge and Becker (2003; see also Barnado's, n.d.). Although estimates vary, there may be some 68,000 young carers in Britain, with anywhere between 6000 and 17,000 young carers looking after mentally ill parents. Overall (Aldridge and Becker, 2003, p. 137):

The findings [of this study] suggest that, where professionals engage in effective intervention procedures (recognising children's caring roles, acknowledging needs, making appropriate assessments and referrals), these can be crucial in preventing crises and allowing children (and parents) some degree of choice in undertaking informal care responsibilities. Furthermore, when professionals offer sensitive and non-demeaning assistance, this help is also highly valued by families. However, in most cases it seems that professionals fail to engage in these effective intervention procedures and to offer needs-led assistance.

The needs of carers

From the growing literature, it is clear that caring for someone with a mental health problem can have significant implications for almost every aspect of daily life. While some people describe positive aspects of caring (such as increasing self-confidence and putting other issues into perspective), negative aspects of caring include the potential impact on the carer's family and social life, work and health (see Box 10.7). Such difficulties can also be exacerbated if the person being supported is placed in a service out of the local area (see, for example, Rethink/CSIP, 2007). More generally, there is significant evidence to suggest that caring can have a significant impact on the physical and mental health of carers (see Box 10.8 for a summary).

In response to these issues, carers have expressed a desire for a range of support services to enable them to carry on in their caring role. In Leeds, for example, a carers' support service identified the importance of emotional support, respite, advocacy, 24-hour crisis support and good quality information (Allen, 1997). Also in the north of England, an evaluation of voluntary sector family support workers found that carers valued the workers as a counselling, information, listening and advocacy resource, providing both emotional and practical support (Weinberg and Huxley, 2000). Similar findings have also emerged from Hill et al.'s (1998) study of the carers of people with manic depression. When asked to rate the importance of seventeen areas of need and whether they had experienced any difficulties in accessing services in these areas, the carers concerned gave a very clear indication not only of the support they wanted, but also of the significant unmet need which continues to exist. In particular, carers said they saw as a high priority:

- 24-hour professional support seven days per week (valued by 67 per cent but with 67 per cent reporting difficulties accessing such support)
- Information about the illness of the person they cared for (valued by 61 per cent but with 55 per cent finding it difficult to obtain this)
- Opportunities to learn personal coping strategies (valued by 41 per cent but with 70 per cent finding this difficult to access)
- Regular updates from professionals (valued by 35 per cent but with 60 per cent finding this difficult to access)
- More education about manic depression (valued by 31 per cent but with 53 per cent finding it difficult to access)

Crucially, many of the priorities expressed by carers are also highly valued by service users – information, being involved by professionals (see Chapter 8) – and it may well be that a good quality service for users is also a good quality service for carers. Similar issues have also been raised by Huang and Slevin (1999, pp. 91–2) in their review of the literature on the carers of people with schizophrenia. According to this review, carers particularly value:

- Advice and guidance on the use of medication
- Education in the use of cognitive and behavioural strategies

- Education of the total family regarding the need for family support
- Contact information for external support groups
- Family and individual counselling if required
- Education about schizophrenia to improve family knowledge
- Practical advice and guidance, including financial advice

Box 10.7	The impact of caring

Hill *et al.*'s (1998) survey of 1113 carers of people with manic depression found that many participants saw caring as having a negative effect on their friends and social life, with some also reporting a negative impact on their self-esteem, their family relationships and their work/work prospects.

Huang and Slevin's (1999) review of the literature on carers who live with someone who has schizophrenia suggests that many carers may experience:

- Physical problems (such as sleeping problems, headaches and chest tightness)
- Social difficulties (such as economic problems, stigma, social alienation and loss of leisure time/employment)
- Relationship difficulties (such as the disruption of family life, marriage problems or loss of friends)
- Psychological or emotional difficulties (such as anxiety about the future, grief reactions, mental health problems such as depression, loneliness and loss of motivation)

Leavey *et al.*'s (1998) study of 50 carers in north London found that 56 per cent saw caring as moderately stressful and 36 per cent considered it very stressful. Fifty-six per cent sometimes felt unable to cope with the person being cared for and 20 per cent often felt unable to cope.

In one evaluation of voluntary family support workers, interviews with 62 carers revealed the stressful nature of caring (Weinberg and Huxley, 2000, pp. 500–1). Of the 62 people, 21 had consulted their GP for help with an emotional problem in recent months and a further 20 had received treatment for a potentially stress-related illness (such as high blood pressure, chest pains and palpitations). Carers also reported significant restrictions on their social and leisure activities, hidden expenses, a lack of understanding from family or friends and difficulties engaging in paid employment.

'Black' carers may have particular unmet needs as a result of culturally insensitive services and the difficulty of obtaining information in languages other than English (Arshad and Johal, 1999).

Carers in Gloucester said that they had given up various things to be a carer, including careers, independence, finances, holidays, health, social life and, for two people, 'everything'. Problems included tiredness, the unpredictability of the person cared for, emotional stress, physical and mental strain, isolation, relationship difficulties, financial pressure, boredom and worry about the future (Gregory *et al.*, 2006).

Although the focus is often on the risk that people with mental health problems may or may not pose to wider society (see Chapter 6), carers also face potential risk and little is known about the risk management strategies that they adopt (see Ryan, 2002, for an exception).

- Education on the use of stress–management techniques
- Access to adequate respite services
- 24-hour access to professionals in emergencies
- Carer and client involvement in care planning
- Access to multidisciplinary services via a keyworker
- Access to specialist mental health services when required

Focus groups with users and carers carried out by Rethink (2005) suggest a similar list, with carers wanting to feel valued and respected by professionals, to be seen as a full and equal partner, to get better access to short breaks and to have their own personal support needs recognised more fully. As with user involvement, discussed in Chapter 8 of this book, ensuring that services

---

Box 10.8	**The physical and mental health needs of carers**

Results from the General Household Survey (ONS, 2000) suggest that:

- Over a third (35 per cent) of carers reported that their physical or mental health had been affected as a result of their caring responsibilities
- Among carers devoting at least 20 hours per week to caring, half reported having a longstanding illness and over a third (35 per cent) stated that their illness limited their activities
- One fifth of this group reported that their health over the past twelve months was 'not good'. Older carers spending twenty hours or over per week caring reported still higher levels of health problems; just under half (47 per cent) reported a limiting long-term illness (compared with 41 per cent in the general population)
- A fifth of carers (20 per cent) reported feeling tired and the same number reported that they had a general feeling of stress
- 17 per cent reported being short tempered
- 14 per cent reported feeling depressed
- 14 per cent reported having disturbed sleep

Further ONS analysis of the mental health of carers (Singleton *et al.*, 2002) found that:

- 53 per cent of carers said their caring responsibilities caused them to worry a little or a lot of the time
- 33 per cent said that caring made them depressed at least a little of the time
- 48 per cent said that caring made them tired
- The prevalence of mental health problems was highest among those caring for a spouse or partner, while carers who spent the least time caring had the best levels of mental health
- Carers who were able to take a break from caring had lower levels of neurotic symptoms than those who had not
- 13 per cent of carers reported having consulted a GP about being anxious or depressed or about a mental, nervous or emotional problem – 1 per cent had done so in the last two weeks

are responsive to the needs of carers is likely to require an explicit commitment to carer involvement, both in designing individual care packages and in shaping services more generally. As an example of the importance of carer involvement, Allen (1997) describes the development of a carers' service in south Leeds, emphasising the following guiding principles:

- The participation of carers in service provision, service development and service evaluation
- Involvement that gives carers the power to influence policy and practice
- Carer-led rather than service-led provision
- Commitment to a continuing process rather than a one-off activity
- Flexibility in the face of the diverse and potentially conflicting needs of users and carers
- The strategic development of carer involvement in all aspects of the agency's work

As in other chapters, by far the most powerful evidence comes from carers themselves, and Box 10.9 cites examples of carers talking directly about their experiences. Above and beyond the issues discussed in this chapter (definitions, legislation, services etc.), these quotes capture just some of the practical and emotional struggles that being a 'carer' for someone with a mental health problem involves, as well as the many positives, hopes and loving relationships.

Box 10.9	Carers' stories

'My husband suffers from bipolar disorder. I suffer from him suffering from bipolar disorder. We have been married nearly 17 years and he was only diagnosed 18 months ago. It explained a lot of his bizarre behaviour over the years and how we grew apart and slept in separate bedrooms for years. After a particular horrendous episode where he kept disappearing, spending lots of money and having an affair, he eventually started to receive the help he needs. By God's grace we were getting along fine and he was so much better, but now he has disappeared again. Too much pressure from me to restore the marriage I think. Too much of me checking up on him and him wanting to control his own life. My pain is horrendous and I am not the sufferer. The problem is it's not just me he's left again it's his grandsons too, who adore him. He believes that so much damage has been done by his bipolar that we can't be fixed. But I haven't given up hope yet, although I am pretty close. I still love him. People who don't understand simply expect me to accept that I am better off without him but I made a covenant with him, for richer for poorer, better or worse, in sickness and in health.'

'Oh my god, I think Mum is ill again. She seems really happy and full of energy. She seemed to have laughed a little too long at that joke. Oh my god ... Mum is singing! This means there is going to be a massive drop. This means more medication, more watching and waiting for Mum to get better!

Box 10.9	Carers' stories (*continued*)

Hang on a minute, I seem to have forgotten that Mum is human too. She has the right to feel happy just as I do. Wanting to laugh uncontrollably about something that is not so funny happens to all us 'normal' people so why do I find it so hard to deal with Mum's laughter? I am getting paranoid. I'm waiting for the bad time to come again. I am watching her every mood, her every feeling and her every action. I am waiting for the depressed stage to kick in. This is just five minutes in my mind. My mum suffers from bipolar.

It is a common mistake for the relative to make. When you are always waiting for your loved one to 'crash' it can drive *you* insane. It can make you paranoid. Your mum stops being your mum and instead is an episode waiting to happen. Forgetting to see the person instead of the illness is something carers and suffers fight against everyday in our society. Yet, how can we blame society, when it's also happening in our own homes? I wanted to highlight how difficult it can be to keep an open mind when you are trying to protect one of the closest people to you. All you want to do is protect them and keep them safe ... safe and away from that miserable place that consumes them when they are not well. After a while I got tired, no actually, I got exhausted of being on edge. After all, it would be no good with both of us ill, so I changed. I started to laugh and sing with mum, I started to sit with her in silence when she was down and then it hit me as hard as a baseball bat to the face. *This is my mum and I am her daughter!* Slowly the illness and the carer status melted away.'

'My sister has a severe mood disorder [bipolar disorder]. Like a little boat on heavy seas she bobs about on the crests and troughs of her moods. Of course I love her, she's my sister. But it's hard to be close to someone who is so changeable. Hard to know how to make her happy, even harder to know what will offend her. But that doesn't mean I won't try. People with mental health problems are involved in the hardest battle any person can fight, against the unimaginable horrors and personalised fear that your own brain can conjure up when it turns on you. And why did this happen to her? She's not a druggie [drug taker], not a criminal, not a bad person. She's just a lonely little girl who didn't get the same chances in life as me. And so I need to love her harder. And I don't hate the illness. It's a symptom of the tumult in her little head. I only see the tumult when it knocks against my own life. She lives with it. She is the real hero. I admire her. I salute her. I send her my love and thank the gods that it isn't me on those heavy seas.'

(www.mentalhealthcare.org.uk/carersstories/?id=115). With permission.

Conclusion

Despite much greater official recognition of the needs of carers, much remains to be done if carers generally (and the carers of people with mental health problems in particular) are to receive sufficient support to be able to continue in their role. Caring has a substantial impact on the lives of many people in the UK and, although we have only begun to acknowledge it relatively recently, it is the contribution of carers that makes the work of statutory health and social services possible. While caring can be a positive experience, it can also bring a series of negative consequences (both for the carer and for the person being cared for). As a result, statutory services have a duty to provide much better and more responsive support than they currently do in order to give carers the help they deserve and need. While there has been relatively little research in this area (compared to other chapters in this book), it seems clear that the way forward must lie in providing a range of support (from accessible information and practical advice to specialist and crisis support). However, also significant seems to be the value base and interpersonal skills of individual workers, with a much greater need for human skills such as empathy and the ability to listen, and a much greater willingness to acknowledge the expertise of carers and value them as people with a key contribution to make. Hopefully, if we could achieve this, then the 'silent partners' of Hogman and Pearson's (1995) study could one day become genuine partners – valued, listened to and supported to continue in their role as the key providers of community care.

Reflection exercises

1. The impact of caring

Exercise for all staff

Imagine that someone you care about (a family member or friend) develops a mental health problem:

- Would this change how you felt about them?
- If so, in what way? If not, what is it about them that you most like and value?
- What would your priorities as a family be and how might these change?
- How could services either make things better or make things worse?

2. Services for carers

Exercise for all staff

Reflect on someone you have worked with recently who the system would define as a 'carer':

- Would the person themselves identify themselves as a 'carer' too?
- If not, how would they see themselves and their relationship with the 'service user'?
- What services are available to support carers in your area?
- What role does your organisation and your profession have in identifying and supporting carers?
- What can you do as an individual to find out more about carers' experiences and about the support available?

If you work in a team setting, try to raise the issues identified in this chapter in a team meeting to explore as a group.

3. Working with carers

Exercise for NHS staff

In initial carers' legislation, the responsibility for identifying and responding to the needs of carers was given to social services. More recently, there have been a number of attempts to broaden this out to ensure that health care professionals play a key role too:

- How well does your agency/profession identify and support carers?
- What could you do to ensure that the needs of carers are seen as more central to your role in future?

Suggestions for further reading

1. Arksey *et al.'s* (2002) report on *Services to support carers of people with mental health problems* summarises a review of the literature (1985–2001) and consultation with national statutory and voluntary agencies, local managers and practitioners and carers. A second report by the same funder (the Department of Health's SDO programme) on sharing information with carers offers a helpful guide to good practice (see Pinfold *et al.*, 2004, for the full report or SDO, 2006, for a short summary).

2. Directgov (www.direct.gov.uk/en/CaringForSomeone/DG_071391) provides access to government information about caring for someone, as well as a link to the Department of Health's carers website (www.dh.gov.uk/en/SocialCare/Deliveringadultsocialcare/Carers/index.htm).

3. Carers UK is a national voluntary organisation which campaigns for the rights of carers, conducts research, produces policy briefings and develops good practice guides based on the experiences of carers. For further information, visit www.carersonline.org.uk. Additional information is also available from the Princess Royal Trust for Carers, who have worked with the Royal College of Psychiatrists to campaign for the carers of people with mental health problems and people with learning disabilities (see www.partnersincare.co.uk).

4. The Mental Health Care website (www.mentalhealthcare.org.uk) contains information for carers about mental health, research from the Institute of Psychiatry and the South London and Maudsley NHS Foundation Trust, and personal stories from carers (see Box 10.9 for some examples).

5. For young carers, Aldridge and Becker's (2003) *Children caring for parents with mental illness* is the first in-depth study of its kind, drawing on detailed research with 40 families. After exploring prevalence and previous research, the book examines the views of children, their parents and professionals, before making a series of recommendations for future policy and practice. In addition, the book contains an invaluable chronology and guide to policy which has an impact on young carers looking after a parent with a mental illness, stretching from the *National Health Service Act* of 1946 to debates around the review of the Mental Health Act. A briefing paper by Barnado's (n.d.) is also available on young carers whose parents have mental health problems.

6. For overall policy, see the government's 2008 carers' strategy (HM Government, 2008). The Department of Health (2002i) has also published guidance on *Developing services for carers and families of people with mental illness*.

7. In terms of more general background reading, useful textbooks include:

   - Heron's (1998) *Working with carers*
   - Nolan *et al.'s* (2003) *Partnerships in family care*
   - Stalker's (2003) *Reconceptualising work with 'carers'*

11 Conclusion

Despite all the attention and funding they have received over the last ten years or so, mental health services still seem some way away from a clear and consistent vision for the way forward. While there have been positive developments in some services and greater recognition of the importance of partnership working, user involvement and tackling discrimination, a series of longstanding and complex problems remain. Underfunded compared to other parts of the NHS, mental health too often seems to be seen as a standalone and poorly understood area of policy and practice. While mental health practitioners too often seem to fail to take part in broader debates about health and social care, non-mental health workers too often fail to appreciate the importance of tackling mental illness.

For us, one of the key dilemmas is reflected in the subtitle of the 1998 White Paper, *Modernising mental health services: safe, sound and supportive* (Department of Health, 1998a) – even over ten years after it first came out. When all is said and done, can services that are perceived as 'supportive' by mental health service users be seen as 'safe' and 'sound' by the public and the media? While these different phrases have a nice, alliterative ring to them, what happens when safety is perceived as coming into conflict with being supportive (and who decides)? In many ways, it was these tensions that came to the fore during the heated debates which surrounded the passage of the *2007 Mental Health Act*. Although many people agreed about the need for further reform, it proved a lot easier to critique the previous approach than it did to find a practical way forward. Indeed, the coalition of different groups that formed to protest against the proposed Act was almost unprecedented – rarely have such uneasy bedfellows been able to rise above so many of their individual differences in order to develop a common voice. Viewed from this angle, the ability of the proposed Act to unite previously divided groups was a major achievement – albeit not one that the architects of the changes had intended.

Taking a step back from the detailed discussions in specific chapters, it seems amazing that something as central to health care as mental health services remain the subject of such significantly different perspectives. Probably more than any other area of health and social care, this is an area where we have constantly failed to agree a general way forward and where it is difficult even to be clear about what we mean by 'mental illness' in the first place. For all that these debates have been rehearsed over the years, the early twenty-first century system seems no closer to developing shared answers to some of the key questions. For example:

- What is mental illness and what causes it?
- What is the best way of responding?
- How should society deal with behaviour or acts that it finds virtually impossible to comprehend?
- How do we balance individual rights and well-being with the safety of other people?

Although the technical debates in this book are important (for example, the best way of providing community mental health services), the broader issues seem to be moral and political ones. What kind of life do we want to have as a community and society, how do we best achieve this and how do we support people experiencing mental distress to live a full and satisfying life? No matter how difficult these questions are to answer, it is our contention that a solution will never be forthcoming unless the voices of mental health service users, their families and mental health workers are heard more fully than has been the case in the past.

Appendix: Mental Health Policy Chronology, 1975– and Key Legislation

1975	*Better services for the mentally ill* published
1986	*Making a reality of community care* published
1988	*Griffiths report* published
1989	*Caring for people* published
1990	*NHS and Community Care Act* passed
1991	CPA introduced
1994	*Ritchie report* published
1994	Supervision registers introduced
1995	*Disability Discrimination Act* passed
1995	*Mental Health (Patients in the Community Act)* passed
December 1997	*The new NHS: modern, dependable* published
November 1998	*Modernising social services* published
December 1998	*Modernising mental health services: safe, sound and supportive* published
April 1999	481 PCGs go live
April 1999	*The Health Act* passed
October 1999	*NSF for mental health* published
November 1999	*Richardson report* and *Green paper on reforming the MHA* published
April 2000	17 first-wave PCTs go live
July 2000	*The NHS plan* published
October 2000	*Human Rights Act 1998* came into effect
March 2001	First *Mental health policy implementation guidance* published
July 2001	*Shifting the balance of power* published
August 2001	The *Health and Social Care Act* passed
January 2002	*Shifting the balance of power: the next steps* published
April 2002	*New deal for disabled people* goes national
April 2002	*Adult acute in-patient care provision* published
April 2002	PCTs go live across England
June 2002	*NHS Reform and Health Care Professionals Act* passed
June 2002	Draft *Mental Health Bill* published

June 2002	Launch of NIMHE
September 2003	*Mainstreaming gender and women's mental health* published
September 2003	*Building on the best: choice, responsiveness and equity in the NHS* published
June 2004	*Mental health and social exclusion* report published
June 2004	*The NHS improvement plan* published
June 2004	*Choosing health: making healthier choices easier* published
November 2004	*The national service framework for mental health – five years on* published
January 2005	*Delivering race equality in mental health care* published
March 2005	*Independence, well-being and choice* published
March 2005	*Commissioning a patient-led NHS* published
January 2006	*Our health, our care, our say* published
June 2008	*High quality care for all: NHS next stage review final report* published
October 2008	Reform of the Incapacity Benefit system came into force
November 2008	*Mental Health Act 2007* came into force

Key legislation (selected)

Carers (Equal Opportunities) Act 2004
Carers (Recognition and Services Act) 1995
Carers and Disabled Children Act 2000
Community Care (Direct Payments) Act 1996
Community Health and Standards Act 2003
Disability Discrimination Act 1995
Equal Pay Act 1970
Health Act 1999
Health and Social Care Act 2001
Human Rights Act 1998
Local Government and Public Involvement in Health Act 2007
Mental Capacity Act 2005
Mental Health Act 1983
Mental Health Act 2007
NHS and Community Care Act 1990
NHS Reform and Health Care Professionals Act 2002
Primary Care Act 1997
Race Relations Act 1976
Race Relations (Amendment) Act 2000
Sex Discrimination Act 1970

Bibliography

Abel-Smith, B. (1964) *The hospitals 1800–1948: a study in social administration in England and Wales.* London, Heinemann

Age Concern (2007) *Improving services and support for older people with mental health problems.* London, Age Concern

Album, D. and Westin, S. (2008) Do diseases have a prestige hierarchy? A survey among physicians and medical students, *Social Science and Medicine*, 66(1), 182–8

Aldridge, J. and Becker, S. (2003) *Children caring for parents with mental illness: perspectives of young carers, parents and professionals.* Bristol, Policy Press

Allebeck, P. (1989) Schizophrenia: a life-shortening disease, *Psychiatric Bulletin*, 15(1), 81–9

Allen, C. (1997) Somebody cares, *Health Service Journal*, 107(5558), 34–5

Anthony, W.A. (1993) Recovery from mental illness: the guiding vision of the mental health service system in the 1990s, *Psychological Rehabilitation Journal*, 16, 11–24

Appleby, J. (2006) *Where's the money going?*, London, King's Fund

Appleby, J., Harrison, A. and Devlin, N. (2003) *What is the real cost of more patient choice?* London, King's Fund

Appleby, L. (2008) *Policies and practice for Europe*, DH / WHO Europe, 10 October

Arksey, H. *et al.* (2002) *Services to support carers of people with mental health problems: overview report.* York, Social Policy Research Unit, University of York

Armstrong, E. (2002) *The guide to mental health for nurses in primary care.* Abingdon, Radcliffe Medical Press

Armstrong, L. (1997) Do practice nurses want to learn about depression?, *Practice Nursing*, 8, 21–6

Arnstein, S.R. (1969) A ladder of citizen participation, *American Institute of Planning Journal*, July, 216–24

Arshad, J. and Johal, B. (1999) Culture club, *Nursing Times*, 95(9), 66–7

Association of Directors of Adult Social Services (ADASS) (2008) *Mental health into the mainstream.* Available online via www.adass.org.uk (accessed 29 August 2008)

Auckland, G., Bontoft, C. and Feaviour, P. (2000) Resource management: making a difference in mental health, *Nursing Standard*, 14(24), 42–6

Audini, B. *et al.* (1999) Over-occupancy in London's acute psychiatric units: fact or fiction?, *Psychiatric Bulletin*, 23(10), 590–4

Audit Commission (1986) *Making a reality of community care.* London, HMSO

Audit Commission (1997) *The coming of age: improving care services for older people.* London, Audit Commission

Audit Commission (2000a) *The way to go home: rehabilitation and remedial services for older people.* London, Audit Commission

Audit Commission (2000b) *Forget me not: mental health services for older people*. London, Audit Commission

Audit Commission (2002) *Integrated services for older people: building a whole systems approach in England*. London, Audit Commission

Audit Commission (2004) *Transforming primary care*. London, Audit Commission

Badger, D. *et al*. (1999) Planning to meet the needs of offenders with mental disorders in the United Kingdom, *Psychiatric Services,* 50(12), 1624–7

Baguley, C., Rushforth, D. and Whyte, M. (2006) *The graduate primary care mental health worker programme: a view form higher education training providers.* HEA Psychology Network, University of York

Bahl, V. (1999) Mental illness: a national perspective, in D. Bhugra and V. Bahl (eds) *Ethnicity: an agenda for mental health*. London, Gaskell

Baker, S. (2000) *Environmentally friendly? Patients' views of conditions on psychiatric wards*. London, Mind

Baldwin, S. and Twigg, J. (1990) Women and community care: reflections on a debate, in M. Maclean and D. Groves (eds) *Women's issues in social policy*. London, Routledge

Balloch, S. and Taylor, M. (eds) (2001) *Partnership working: policy and practice*. Bristol, Policy Press

Barnado's (n.d.) *Keeping the family in mind: a briefing on young carers whose parents have mental health problems*. Ilford, Barnado's

Barnes, C. (1998) Review of the rejected body by Susan Wendall, *Disability and Society*, 13(1), 145–6

Barnes, D. (1997) *Older people with mental health problems living alone: anybody's priority?* London, Department of Health

Barnes, M. (1997) *Care, communities and citizens*. London, Longman

Barnes, M. and Bowl, R. (2001) *Taking over the asylum: empowerment and mental health*. Basingstoke, Palgrave

Barnes, M. and Walker, A. (1996) Consumerism versus empowerment: a principled approach to the involvement of older service users, *Policy and Politics*, 24(4), 375–93

Barnes, M., Davis, A. and Tew, J. (2000) Valuing experience: users' experiences of compulsion under the Mental Health Act 1983, *Mental Health Review*, 5(3), 11–14

Barrett, G., Sellman, D. and Thomas, J. (eds) (2005) *Interprofessional working in health and social care*. Basingstoke, Palgrave Macmillan

Bartlett, C. *et al*. (1999) Projection of alternatives to acute psychiatric beds: review of an emerging service assessment method, *Journal of Mental Health*, 8(6), 555–68

Batcup, D. (1997) The problems of researching mixed sex wards, *Journal of Advanced Nursing*, 25, 1018–24

Bean, P. and Mounser, P. (1993) *Discharged from mental hospitals*. Basingstoke, Macmillan

Beck, A. *et al*. (1997) The Nottingham Acute Bed Study: alternatives to acute psychiatric care, *British Journal of Psychiatry*, 170, 247–52

Beer, D. *et al*. (2005) Low secure units: factors predicting delayed discharge, *Journal of Forensic Psychiatry and Psychology*, 16(4), 621–37

Bennett, J., Kalathil, J. and Keating, F. (2007) *Race equality training in mental health services in England: does one size fit all?* London, Sainsbury Centre for Mental Health

Bentall, R. (2003) *Madness explained: psychosis and human nature*. London, Allen Lane

Beresford, P. (2000) What have madness and psychiatric system survivors got to do with disability studies?, *Disability and Society*, 15(1), 167–72

Beresford, P. (2002) Thinking about mental health: towards a social model, *Journal of Mental Health*, 11(6), 581–84

Beresford, P., Harrison, C. and Wilson, A. (2002) Mental health service users and disability: implications for future strategies, *Policy and Politics*, 30(3), 387–96

Bevan, A. (1948) A message to the medical profession, *British Medical Journal*, ii, 1

Beveridge, W. (1942) *Social insurance and allied services*. London, HMSO

Bhui, K. and Bhugra, D. (1999) Service provision for ethnic minorities, in D. Bhugra and V. Bahl (eds) *Ethnicity: an agenda for mental health*. London, Gaskell

Bhui, K. and Olajide, D. (eds) (1999) *Mental health service provision for a multi-cultural society*. London, W.B. Saunders

Bhui, K., Bhugra, D. and McKenzie, K. (2000) *Specialist services for minority ethnic groups?* (Maudsley discussion paper no.8). London, Institute of Psychiatry

Bierer, J. (1951) *The day hospital*. London, H & K Lewis

Bindman, J. *et al.* (2000) Psychiatric patients at greatest risk and in greatest need: impact of the supervision register policy, *British Journal of Psychiatry*, 177, 33–7

Birchwood, M., Todd, P. and Jackson, C. (1998) Early intervention in psychosis: the critical period hypothesis, *British Journal of Psychiatry*, Supplementrum, 172, 53–9

Bird, L. (1999) *Fundamental facts of mental illness*. London, Mental Health Foundation

Birmingham, L.*et al.* (2006) The mental health of women in prison mother and baby units, *Journal of Forensic Psychiatry and Psychology*, 17(3), 393–404

Black, K. and Shillitoe, R. (1997) Developing mental health services sensitive to women's needs, *British Journal of Health Care Management*, 3(1), 27–9

Blashfield, R.K. (1996) Predicting DSM V, *Journal of Nervous and Mental Disease*, 184, 4–7

Blinkhorn, M. (2004) *Social worker: leading roles in mental health – adjustment to change, new ways of working and other potential solutions*. Durham, Northern Centre for Mental Health

Bloor, K. and Maynard, A. (1994) An outsider's view of the NHS reforms, *British Medical Journal*, 309, 352–3

Blount, A. (1998) *Integrated primary care: the future of medical and mental health collaboration*. London, Norton and Co.

Blumenthal, S. and Lavender, T. (2000) *Violence and mental disorder: a critical aid to the assessment and management of risk*. London, Jessica Kingsley (published for the Zito Trust)

Boardman, R.E. and Hodgson, A.P. (2000) Community in-patient units and halfway hospitals, *Advances in Psychiatric Treatment*, 6, 120–7

Borrill, J. (2000) *Developments in treatment for people with psychotic experiences* (Updates, volume 2, issue 9). London, Mental Health Foundation

Bower, P. and Sibbald, B. (2003) On-site mental health workers in primary care: effects on professional practice (Cochrane Review), *The Cochrane Library*, 1, Oxford, Update Software

Bower, P., Jerrim, S. and Gask, L. (2004) Primary care mental health workers: role expectations, conflict and ambiguity, *Health and Social Care in the Community*, 12, 4, 336–45

Bowl, R. (2007) The need for change in UK mental health services: South Asian service users' views, *Ethnicity and Health*, 12(1), 1–19

Bracken, P.J. *et al.* (1998) Mental health and ethnicity: an Irish dimension, *British Journal of Psychiatry*, 172, 103–5

Bradby, H. *et al.* (2007) British Asian families and the use of child and adolescent mental health services: a qualitative study of a hard to reach group, *Social Science and Medicine*, 65, 2413–24

Braye, S. (2000) Participation and involvement in social care: an overview, in H. Kemshall and R. Littlechild (eds) *User involvement and participation in social care: research informing practice*. London, Jessica Kingsley

Breeze, J. and Repper, J. (1998) Struggling for control: the care experiences of 'difficult' patients in mental health services, *Journal of Advanced Nursing*, 28(6), 1301–11

Bristol Royal Infirmary Inquiry (2001) *Learning from Bristol: the report of the public inquiry into children's heart surgery at the Bristol Royal infirmary 1984–1995*. CM5207 (11), London, TSO

British Medical Association (BMA) (1992) *Priorities for community care*. London, British Medical Association

British Medical Association/NHS Confederation (2003) *Investing in general practice: the new general medical services contract*. London, BMA

British Medical Association/NHS Employers (2009) *Quality and outcomes framework guidance for GMS contract 2009/10: delivering investment in general practice*. London, BMA/NHS Employers

Brodie, D. (2003) Partnership working: a service user perspective, in J. Glasby and E. Peck (eds) *Care trusts: partnership working in action*. Abingdon, Radcliffe Medical Press

Brooker, C. and Repper, J. (2009) *Mental health: from policy to practice*. Edinburgh, Elsevier

Brown, G.W. and Harris, T. (1978) *The social origins of depression*. London, Tavistock Press

Browne, D. (1997) *Black people and sectioning: the black experience of detention under the civil sections of the Mental Health Act*. London, Little Rock

Burchadt, T. (2003) *Employment retention and the onset of sickness or disability: evidence from the Labour Force Survey longitudinal datasets*. Department of Workforce and Pensions in-house report no. 109

Burns, T. (2004) *Community mental health teams: a guide to current practices*. Oxford, Oxford University Press

Burns, T. *et al.* (2007) Use of intensive case management to reduce time in hospital in people with severe mental illness: systematic review and meta-regression, *British Medical Journal*, 335, 336–40

Busfield, J. (1996) *Men, women and madness: understanding gender and mental disorder*. Basingstoke, Macmillan

Butterfield, W.J.A.H. (1964) *New frontiers in health*. London, Office of Health Economics

Byng, R. and Single, H. (1999) *Developing primary care for patients with long term mental illness: your guide to improving services*. London, King's Fund

Byng, R. *et al.* (2004) Exploratory cluster randomised controlled trial of shared care development for long term mental illness, *British Journal of General Practice*, 54, 259–66

Cabinet Office (1999) *Modernising government*. London, TSO

Calnan, M. and Gabe, J. (1991) Recent developments in general practice: asociological analysis, in J. Gabe, M. Calnan and M. Bury (eds) *Sociology of the health service*. London, Routledge

Camden and Islington Mental Health NHS Trust (2001) *Drayton Park crisis project for women: an alternative to hospital admission for women in mental health crisis*. Unpublished leaflet, London, Camden and Islington Mental Health NHS Trust

Campbell, J. and Oliver, M. (1996) *Disability politics in Britain: understanding our past, changing our future*. London, Routledge

Campbell, P. (1996) The history of the user movement in the United Kingdom, in T. Heller (eds) *Mental health matters*. Basingstoke, Macmillan

Campbell, P. (2001) The role of users in psychiatric services in service development – influence not power, *Psychiatric Bulletin*, 25, 87–8

Campbell, S. *et al.* (2007) Quality of primary care in England with the introduction of pay for performance, *New England Journal of Medicine*, 357, 181–90

Care Services Improvement Partnership (CSIP) (2006) *Women at risk: the mental health of women in contact with the criminal justice system*. London, CSIP

CSIP (2007) *A positive outlook: a good practice toolkit to improve discharge from inpatient mental health care*. London, CSIP

CSIP (2008) *Mental health digest*. London, CSIP

CSIP/National Mental Health Partnership/DH (2006) *National acute inpatient project position statement (December 2006)*. London, CSIP/National Mental Health Partnership/DH

CSIP/NIMHE/Changing Workforce Programme/Royal College of Psychiatrists (2005) *New ways of working for psychiatrists: enhancing effective, person-centred services through new ways of working in multidisciplinary and multi-agency contexts*. London, Department of Health

Carers UK (2003) *Missed opportunities: the impact of new rights for carers*. London, Carers UK

Carers UK (2004) *In poor health: the impact of caring on health*. London, Carers UK

Carers UK (2006) *In the know: the importance of information for carers*. London, Carers UK

Carpenter, J. and Sbaraini, S. (1997) *Choice, information and dignity: involving users and carers in care management in mental health*. Bristol, Policy Press

Carpenter, J. *et al.* (2003) Working in multidisciplinary community mental health teams: the impact on social workers and health professionals of integrated mental health care, *British Journal of Social Work*, 33, 1081–1103

Cawley, S., Praveen, S. and Salib, E. (1997) Brief psychiatric admissions: a review, *Nursing Standard*, 12(10), 34–5

Centre for Economic Performance's Mental Health Policy Group (2006) *The depression report: a new deal for depression and anxiety disorders*. London, London School of Economics

Centre for Mental Health Services (1995) *Additions and resident patients at end of year, state and county resident mental hospitals by age and diagnosis*. Rockville, Maryland (US), Centre for Mental Health Services

Centre for Public Mental Health (2006) *Adult mental health service mapping: report autumn 2004 and spring 2006*. Durham, University of Durham

Chamberlain, L. (1998) Murdered worker's family win apology from Kingston, *Community Care*, 9–15 July, 2

Chambers R., Boath, E. and Wakley, G. (2001) *Mental healthcare matters in primary care*. Abingdon, Radcliffe Medical Press

Chesler, P. (1974) *Women and madness*. London, Allen Lane

Chisholm, A. and Ford, R. (2004) *Transforming mental health care: assertive outreach and crisis resolution in practice*. London, Sainsbury Centre for Mental Health

Churchill, R. *et al.* (2007) *International experiences of using community treatment orders*. London, Department of Health

Clark, M. (2003) First of the few, *Community Care*, 2–8 October, 30–1

Clark, M., Glasby, J. and Lester, H.E. (2004) Cases for change: user involvement in mental health services and research, *Research Policy and Planning*, 22(2), 31–8

Clarke, S. (2004) *Acute inpatient mental health care: education, training and continuing professional development for all.* Leeds, NIMHE

Coast, J. *et al.* (2005) Economic evaluation of a general practitioner with special interests led dermatology service in primary care, *British Medical Journal*, 33, 1444–9

Cohen, A. (2008) *Delivering mental health in primary care.* London, Royal College of General Practitioners

Cohen, A., Bishop, N. and Hegarty, M. (1999) Working in partnership with probation: the first two years of a mental health worker scheme in a probation service in Wandsworth, *Psychiatric Bulletin*, 23(7), 405–8

Cohen, P. (1992) High risk mix, *Social Work Today*, 23(31), 10

Coid, J. (1994) Failure in community care: psychiatry's dilemma, *British Medical Journal*, 308, 965–6

Coid, J. and Dunn, W. (2004) Forensic psychiatry assessments and admissions from East London, 1987–1994, *Journal of Forensic Psychiatry and Psychology*, 15(1), 76–95

Coid, J. and Kahtan, N. (2000) Are special hospitals needed?, *Journal of Forensic Psychiatry*, 11(1), 17–35

Coid, J. *et al.* (2001) Medium secure forensic psychiatry services: comparison of seven English health regions, *British Journal of Psychiatry*, 178, 55–61

Commander, M.J. *et al.* (1999) Mental health care for Asian, black and white patients with non-effective psychoses: pathways to the psychiatric hospital, in-patient and after-care, *Social Psychiatry and Psychiatric Epidemiology*, 34(9), 484–91

Commission for Health Improvement (2003) *Investigation into matters arising from care on Rowan ward, Manchester Mental Health and Social Care Trust.* London, TSO

Commission for Racial Equality (2007) *Report of formal investigation into the Department of Health.* London, CRE

Community Care (2001) Father given suspended sentence for killing depressed daughter, *Community Care*, 11 June. Available online via www.communitycare.co.uk (accessed 8th April 2004)

Community Care (2004) Government rejects Bennett proposals, *Community Care*, 19 February. Available online via www.communitycare.co.uk (accessed 28 May 2004)

Connolly, M.A. and Ritchie, S. (1997) An audit of in-patients aged 18–65 in acute psychiatric wards who are inappropriately placed three months after admission, *Health Bulletin*, 55(3), 156–61

Cook, G., Gerrish, K. and Clarke, C. (2001) Decision-making in teams: issues arising from two UK evaluations, *Journal of Interprofessional Care*, 15(2), 141–51

Copperman, J. and Burrows, F. (1992) Reducing the risk of assault, *Nursing Times*, 88(26), 64–5

Copperman, J. and Knowles, K. (2006) Developing women-only and gender sensitive practices in inpatient wards – current issues and challenges, *Journal of Adult Protection*, 8(2), 15–30

Coppock, V. (2008) Gender, in R. Tummey and T. Turner (eds) *Critical issues in mental health.* Basingstoke, Palgrave Macmillan

Coppock, V. and Hopton, J. (2000) *Critical perspectives on mental health.* London, Routledge

Copsey, N. (1997a) *Keeping faith: the provision of community mental health services within a multi-faith context.* London, Sainsbury Centre for Mental Health

Copsey, N. (1997b) *Forward in faith: an experiment in building bridges between ethnic communities and mental health services in East London.* London, Sainsbury Centre for Mental Health

Corney, R. (1999) Mental health services in primary care: the overlap in professional roles, *Journal of Mental Health*, 8, 187–94

Craddock, N. *et al.* (2008) Wake-up call for British psychiatry, *British Journal of Psychiatry*, 193, 6–9

Craig, T.K.J. *et al.* (2004) The Lambeth Early Onset Community Team: a randomised controlled trial of assertive outreach for psychosis, *British Medical Journal*, 329, 1067–73

Crawford, M.J. *et al.* (2002) Systematic review of involving patients in the planning and development of health care, *British Medical Journal*, 325, 1263–5

Creed, F. *et al.* (1990) Randomised controlled trial of day patients versus in-patient psychiatric treatment, *British Medical Journal*, 300, 1033–7

Creed, F. *et al.* (1997) Cost effectiveness of day and inpatient psychiatric treatment, *British Medical Journal*, 314, 1381–5

Crosland, A. and Kai, J. (1998) They think they can talk to nurses: practice nurses' views of their roles in caring for mental health problems, *British Journal of General Practice*, 48, 1383–6

Crossley, N. (2006) *Contesting psychiatry: UK mental health movements 1950–2000.* London, Routledge

Crowther, R. *et al.* (2001) Helping people with severe mental illness to obtain work: systematic review, *British Medical Journal*, 322, 204–8

Curry, N. and Thorlby, R. (2007) *Practice-based commissioning.* London, King's Fund

Dabbs, H. and Isherwood, J. (2000) Bridging the gap: service developments in forensic psychiatric rehabilitation at district level, *Journal of Forensic Psychiatry*, 11(1), 198–205

Dalrymple, J. and Burke, B. (1995) *Anti-oppressive practice: social care and the law.* Buckingham, Open University Press

Davidson, L., and Roe, D. (2007) Recovery from and recovery in serious mental illness: one strategy for lessening confusion plaguing recovery, *Journal of Mental Health*, 16, 459–70

Davies, S. *et al.* (2007) Long-term outcomes after discharge from medium secure care: a cause for concern, *British Journal of Psychiatry*, 191, 70–4

Day, L. (1992) Women and oppression: race, class and gender, in M. Langan and L. day (eds) *Women, oppression and social work: issues in anti-discriminatory practice.* London, Routledge

Department for Constitutional Affairs (2007) *Mental Capacity Act 2005 code of practice.* London, TSO

Department of Employment, Transport and Regions (1998) *Modernising local government.* London, TSO

Department of Health (1989a) *Caring for people: community care in the next decade and beyond.* London, HMSO

Department of Health (1989b) *Working for patients.* London, HMSO

Department of Health (1990a) *The care programme approach for people with a mental illness referred to the specialist psychiatric services.* London, Department of Health

Department of Health (1990b) *Community care in the next decade and beyond: policy guidance.* London, HMSO

Department of Health (1991) *The patient's charter.* London, HMSO

Department of Health (1992) *The health of the nation.* London, TSO

Department of Health (1993) *Attitude to mental illness.* London, Taylor Nelson Sofres

Department of Health (1994) *Working in partnership: a collaborative approach to care – report of the mental health nursing review.* London, HMSO

Department of Health (1995) *Building bridges: a guide to the arrangements for interagency working for the care and protection of severely disabled people.* London, Department of Health

Department of Health (1996a) *The National Health Service: a service with ambitions.* London, TSO

Department of Health (1996b) *Carers (Recognition and Services) Act 1995: policy guidance and practice guidance.* London, Department of Health

Department of Health (1997a) *The new NHS: modern, dependable.* London, TSO

Department of Health (1997b) *Omnibus survey of public attitudes to mental illness.* London, Department of Health

Department of Health (1998a) *Modernising mental health services: safe, sound and supportive.* London, Department of Health

Department of Health (1998b) *Frank Dobson outlines third way for mental health.* Press Release 98/311, 29th July, London, Department of Health

Department of Health (1998c) *Partnership in action: new opportunities for joint working between health and social services – a discussion document.* London, Department of Health

Department of Health (1998d) *Modernising social services: promoting independence, improving protection, raising standards.* London, TSO

Department of Health (1999a) *National service framework for mental health: modern standards and service models.* London, Department of Health

Department of Health (1999b) *Effective care co-ordination in mental health services: modernising the care programme approach – a policy booklet.* London, Department of Health

Department of Health (1999c) *Report of the expert committee: review of the Mental Health Act 1983.* London, Department of Health

Department of Health (1999d) *Reform of the Mental Health Act 1983: proposals for consultation.* London, TSO

Department of Health (2000a) The *NHS plan: a plan for investment, a plan for reform.* London, Department of Health

Department of Health (2000b) *Attitudes to mental illness.* London, Taylor, Nelson and Sofres

Department of Health (2000c) *Caring about carers: a national strategy for carers* (2nd edn, first published in 1998). London, Department of Health

Department of Health (2001a) *Safety first: five-year report of the National Confidential Inquiry into Suicide and Homicide by People with Mental Illness.* London, Department of Health

Department of Health (2001b) *The journey to recovery: the government's vision for mental health care.* London, Department of Health

Department of Health (2001c) *Shifting the balance of power within the NHS: securing delivery.* London, Department of Health

Department of Health (2001d) *Reforming the Mental Health Act – part I: the new legal framework.* London, Department of Health

Department of Health (2001e) *Reforming the Mental Health Act – part II: high risk patients.* London, Department of Health

Department of Health (2001f) *Mental health national service framework (and the NHS plan) workforce planning, education and training underpinning programme: adult mental health services: final report by the Workforce Action Team.* London, Department of Health

Department of Health (2001g) *Mental health policy implementation guidance.* London, Department of Health

Department of Health (2001h) *Valuing people: a new strategy for learning disability for the 21st century.* London, Department of Health

Department of Health (2001i) *National service framework for older people: modern standards and service models.* London, Department of Health

Department of Health (2001j) *Carers and Disabled Children's Act 2000: carers and people with parental responsibility for disabled children – policy guidance.* London, Department of Health

Department of Health (2002a) *Adult acute in-patient care provision.* London, Department of Health

Department of Health (2002b) *National suicide prevention strategy for England.* London, Department of Health

Department of Health (2002c) *Improvement, expansion and reform – the next 3 years: priorities and planning framework, 2003–2006.* London, Department of Health

Department of Health (2002d) *Shifting the balance of power: the next steps.* London, Department of Health

Department of Health (2002e) *Primary Care Trust revenue resource limits, 2003/4, 2004/5, 2005/6 and exposition tables 2003–6.* London, Department of Health

Department of Health (2002f) *Mental health policy implementation guidance: community mental health teams.* London, Department of Health

Department of Health (2002g) *A guide to NHS foundation trusts.* London, Department of Health

Department of Health (2002h) *Women's mental health: into the mainstream.* London, Department of Health

Department of Health (2002i) *Developing services for carers and families of people with mental illness.* London, Department of Health

Department of Health (2003a) *Practitioners with special interests in primary care: implementing a scheme for nurses with special interests in primary care - liberating the talents.* London, Department of Health

Department of Health (2003b) *Fast-forwarding primary care mental health: graduate primary care mental health workers – best practice guidance.* London, Department of Health

Department of Health (2003c) *Guidelines for the appointment of general practitioners with special interests in the delivery of clinical services: mental health.* London, Department of Health

Department of Health (2003d) *National statistics on adults' attitudes to mental illness in Great Britain.* London, Department of Health

Department of Health (2003e) *Mental health policy implementation guide: support, time and recovery workers.* London, Department of Health

Department of Health (2003f) *Change Agent Team.* Available online via www.doh. gov.uk/changeagentteam/index.htm (accessed 25 April 2003)

Department of Health (2003g) *Building on the best: choice, responsiveness and equity in the NHS.* London, TSO

Department of Health (2003h) *Strengthening accountability: involving patients and the public – policy guidance, Section 11 of the Health and Social Care Act 2001.* London, Department of Health

Department of Health (2003i) *Mainstreaming gender and women's mental health.* London, Department of Health

Department of Health (2003j) *Delivering race equality: a framework for action – mental health services – consultation document.* London, Department of Health

Department of Health (2004a) *The national service framework for mental health – five years on.* London, Department of Health

Department of Health (2004b) *The NHS improvement plan.* London, Department of Health

Department of Health (2004c) *Practice-based commissioning: engaging practices in commissioning.* London, Department of Health

Department of Health (2004d) *Choosing health: making healthier choices easier.* London, Department of Health

Department of Health (2004e) *Celebrating our cultures: mental health promotion with the South Asian community.* London, Department of Health

Department of Health (2004f) *Celebrating our cultures: mental health promotion with the African Caribbean community*. London, Department of Health

Department of Health (2004g) *Celebrating our cultures: mental health promotion with refugees and asylum seekers*. London, Department of Health

Department of Health (2005a) *Commissioning a patient-led NHS: delivering the NHS improvement plan*. London, Department of Health

Department of Health (2005b) *Independence, well-being and choice*. London, Department of Health

Department of Health (2005c) *Community development workers for black and minority ethnic communities*. London, Department of Health

Department of Health (2005d) *Delivering race equality in mental health care: an action plan for reform inside and outside services and the government's response to the independent inquiry into the death of David Bennett*. London, Department of Health

Department of Health (2005e) *New ways of working for psychiatrists: enhancing effective, person-centred services through new ways of working in multidisciplinary and multi-agency contexts*. London, Department of Health

Department of Health (2006a) *Our health, our care, our say: a new direction for community services*. London, TSO

Department of Health (2006b) *Mental Health Bill: regulatory impact assessment*. London, Department of Health

Department of Health (2006c) *Practice-based commissioning: practical implementation – what does it mean for practices?* London, TSO

Department of Health (2006d) *Crisis resolution and home treatment guidance statement*. London, Department of Health

Department of Health (2006e) *Direct payments for people with mental health problems: a guide to action*. London, Department of Health

Department of Health (2006f) *A stronger local voice: a framework for creating a stronger local voice in the development of health and social care services*. London, Department of Health

Department of Health (2006g) *From value to actions: the Chief Nursing Officer's review of mental health nursing*. London, Department of Health

Department of Health (2007a) *The NHS in England: the operating framework for 2008/9*. London, Department of Health

Department of Health (2007b) *Our NHS, our future: NHS next stage review – interim report*. London, Department of Health

Department of Health (2007c) *Our NHS: practice-based commissioning: implementation monitoring – progress towards universal coverage and practical take up*. London, TSO

Department of Health (2007d) *Improving access to psychological therapies programme: computerised cognitive behavioural therapy implementation guidance*. London, Department of Health

Department of Health (2007e) *Breaking down barriers: clinical case for change – report by Louis Appleby, National Director for Mental Health*. London, Department of Health

Department of Health (2007f) *Valuing people now: from progress to transformation*. London, Department of Health

Department of Health (2007g) *Mental health: new ways of working for everyone – developing and sustaining a capable and flexible workforce*. London, Department of Health

Department of Health (2007h) *Commissioning framework for health and well-being*. London, HMSO

Department of Health (2008a) *High quality care for all: NHS next stage review – final report*. London, Department of Health

Department of Health (2008b) *The NHS in England: the operating framework for 2009/10.* London, Department of Health

Department of Health (2008c) *Practice-based commissioning GP practice survey: December 2008.* London, Department of Health

Department of Health (2008d) *Refocusing the care programme approach: policy and positive practice guidance.* London, Department of Health

Department of Health (2008e) *Support, time and recovery workers: a competence framework.* London, Department of Health

Department of Health (2008f) *Transforming the quality of dementia care: consultation on a national dementia strategy.* London, Department of Health

Department of Health and Social Security (DHSS) (1975) *Better services for the mentally ill.* London, HMSO

DHSS (1983) *NHS management inquiry.* London, Department of Health and Social Security

Department of Health/HM Prison Service/National Assembly for Wales (2001) *Changing the outlook: a strategy for developing and modernising mental health services in prisons.* London, Department of Health

Department of Health/HM Prison Service/National Assembly for Wales (2002) *Mental health in-reach collaborative: launch document.* London, Department of Health

Department of Health/Home Office (1992) *Review of services for mentally disordered offenders and others requiring similar services: final summary report* (the Reed Report). London, HMSO

Department of Health/NIMHE (2005) *Offender mental health care pathway.* London, Department of Health

Department of Health/National Schizophrenia Fellowship (2001) *A commitment to carers.* London, National Schizophrenia Fellowship

Department of Health/Social Services Inspectorate (1997) *Young carers: something to think about.* London, Department of Health

Department of Health/Social Services Inspectorate (1998a) *Young carers: making a start.* London, Department of Health

Department of Health/Social Services Inspectorate (1998b) *A matter of chance for carers? Inspection of local authority support for carers.* London, Department of Health

Department of Health/Social Services Inspectorate (1999) *Review of social work service in the high security hospitals.* London, Department of Health

Department of Health/Social Services Inspectorate (2001) *National standards for the provision of social care services in the high security hospitals.* London, Department of Health

Department of Health/Welsh Office (1999) *Mental Health Act 1983: code of practice.* London, TSO

Department of Trade and Industry (2004) *Fairness for all: a new Commission for Equality and Human Rights.* London, TSO

Dickinson, H., Peck, E. and Smith, J. (2006) *Leadership in organisational transition – what can we learn from research evidence?* (summary report). Birmingham, Health Services Management Centre

Disability Rights Commission (DRC) (2006) *Equal treatment: closing the gap. A formal investigation into physical health inequalities experienced by people with learning disabilities/ and or mental health problems.* London, DRC

DRC (2007) *Coming together: mental health, equality and human rights.* London, DRC

Docherty, J. D. (1997) Barriers to the diagnosis of depression in primary care, *Journal of Clinical Psychology*, 58, 5–10

Dolan, M. and Lawson, A. (2001) Characteristics and outcomes of patients admitted to a psychiatric intensive care unit in a medium secure unit, *Psychiatric Bulletin*, 25(8), 296–9

Dominelli, L. (1988) *Anti-racist social work*. Basingstoke, Macmillan

Dominelli, L. (1997) *Sociology for social work*. Basingstoke, Macmillan

Doran, T. *et al.* (2008) Effect of financial incentives on inequalities in the delivery of primary clinical care in England: analysis of clinical activity indicators for the quality and outcomes framework, *The Lancet*, 372, 728–36

Durcan, G. (2008) *From the inside: experiences of prison mental health care*. London, Sainsbury Centre for Mental Health

Durkheim, E. (1897) *Le suicide*. Paris, Alcan

Elder, A. and Holmes J. (2002) *Mental health in primary care*. Oxford, Oxford University Press

11 Million (Office of the Children's Commissioner for England) (2007) *Pushed into the shadows: young people's experiences of adult mental health facilities*. London, 11 Million

Engel, G. (1980) The clinical application of the biopsychosocial model, *American Journal of Psychiatry*, 137, 535–44

England, E. and Lester, H.E. (2007) Implementing the role of the graduate primary care mental health worker: a qualitative study, *British Journal of General Practice*, 57, 204–11

Enthoven, A. (1985) *Reflections in the management of the NHS*. London, Nuffield Provincial Hospitals Trust

Etzioni, A. (1995) *The spirit of community: rights, responsibilities and the communitarian agenda*. London, Fontana

Etzioni, A. (1998) *The essential communitarian reader*. Maryland, Rowman & Littlefield

Evans, P. (2003) Silent fight, *The Guardian*, 20 August. Available online via www.society.guardian.co.uk (accessed 20th August 2003)

Faulkner, A. and Layzell, S. (2000) *Strategies for living: a report of user-led research into people's strategies for living with mental distress*. London, Mental Health Foundation

Faulkner, A. and Morris, B. (2003) *User involvement in forensic mental health research and development*. Liverpool, National R&D Programme on Forensic Mental Health

Feinmann, J. (1988) Corridors of fear, *Nursing Times*, 84(39), 16–17

Ferguson, I. (2000) Identity politics or class struggle? The case of the mental health users' movement, in M. Lavalette and G. Mooney (eds) *Class struggle and social welfare*. London, Routledge

Finch, J. and Groves, D. (eds) (1983) *A labour of love: women, work and caring*. London, Routledge

Fleischmann, P. (2000) Separating the sexes, *Nursing Standard*, 14(25), 20–1

Fletcher, J. *et al.* (2008) A collaborative approach to embedding graduate primary care mental health workers in the UK National Health Service, *Health and Social Care in the Community*, 16, 5, 451–9

Ford, R. *et al.* (1993) Developing case management for the long-term mentally ill, *Psychiatric Bulletin*, 17(7), 409–11

Ford, R. *et al.* (1998) One day survey by the Mental Health Act Commission of acute adult psychiatric inpatient wards in England and Wales, *British Medical Journal*, 317(168), 1279–83

Foucault, M. (1961) *Madness and civilization: a history of insanity in the age of reason*. New York, Vintage

Freeman, G. *et al.* (2002) *Promoting continuity of care for people with severe mental illness whose needs span primary, secondary and social care*. London, SDO

Freeman, T. and Peck, E. (2006) Evaluating partnerships: a case study of integrated specialist mental health services, *Health and Social Care in the Community*, 14(5), 408–17

French, S. (1993) Can you see the rainbow, in J. Swain *et al.* (eds) *Disabling barriers – enabling environments*. London, Sage

Friedli, L. and Parsonage, M. (2007) *Mental health promotion: building an economic case*. Belfast, Northern Ireland Association for Mental Health

Fryers, T. *et al.* (2002) Social inequalities and the distribution of mental disorders: a systematic literature review. Unpublished paper commissioned by the Department of Health

Fulop, N., Koffman, J. and Hudson, M. (1992) Challenging bed behaviours: the use of acute psychiatric beds in an inner-London District Health Authority, *Journal of Mental Health*, 1, 335–41

Fulop, N.J. *et al.* (1996) Use of psychiatric beds: a point prevalence study in North and South Thames regions, *Journal of Public Health Medicine*, 18(2), 207–16

Gask, L., Sibbald, B. and Creed, F. (1997) Evaluating models of working between mental health and primary care, *British Journal of Psychiatry*, 70, 6–11

Gask, L. *et al.* (2003) Qualitative study of patients' perceptions of the quality of care for depression in general practice, *British Journal of General Practice*, 53, 278–83

Gask, L. *et al.* (eds) (2009) *Primary care mental health*. London, Royal College of Psychiatrists

Gater, R. *et al.* (1997) The care of patients with chronic schizophrenia: a comparison between two services, *Psychological Medicine*, 27(6), 1325–36

Geelan, S. *et al.* (2000) A bail and probation hostel for mentally disordered defendants, *Journal of Forensic Psychiatry*, 11(1), 93–104

Georgiades, N.J. and Phillimore, L. (1975) *The myth of the hero-innovator and alternative strategies for organisational change*. New York, Associated Scientific

Gerada, C., Wright, N. and Keen, J. (2002) The general practitioners with special interest: new opportunities or the end of the generalist practitioner?, *British Journal of General Practice*, 52, 796–8

Gibbons, J. (1988) Residential care for mentally ill adults, in I. Sinclair (ed.) *Residential care: the research reviewed*. London, HMSO

Giddens, A. (1998) *The third way: the renewal of social democracy*. Cambridge, Polity Press

Giddens, A. (2000) *The third way and its critics*. Cambridge, Polity Press

Giles, S. (2003) Care trusts: a positive option for service improvement, in J. Glasby and E. Peck (eds) *Care trusts: partnership working in action*. Abingdon, Radcliffe Medical Press

Gillen, S. (2005) Campaigners furious as government 'ducks' key Bennett inquiry findings, *Community Care*, 13–19 January, 6

Glasby, J. (2003) *Hospital discharge: integrating health and social care*. Abingdon, Radcliffe Medical Press

Glasby, J. and Beresford, P. (2006) Who knows best? Evidence-based practice and the service user contribution, *Critical Social Policy*, 26(1), 268–84

Glasby, J. and Dickinson, H. (eds) (2008a) *Better partnership working* (series of five books on interagency working focusing on partnership working, teamworking, managing and leading in interagency settings, interprofessional education, and evaluating outcomes in health and social care). Bristol, Policy Press

Glasby, J. and Dickinson, H. (2008b) *Partnership working in health and social care*. Bristol, Policy Press

Glasby, J. and Lester, H. (2004) Delayed hospital discharge and mental health: the policy implications of recent research, *Social Policy and Administration*, 38(7), 744–57

, J. and Littlechild, R. (2004) *The health and social care divide: the experiences of older people* (2nd edn). Bristol, Policy Press

Glasby, J. and Littlechild, R. (2009) *Direct payments and personal budgets: putting personalisation into practice* (2nd edn). Bristol, Policy Press

Glasby, J., Littlechild, R. and Pryce, K. (2004) *Show me the way to go home: delayed hospital discharges and older people.* Birmingham, Health Services Management Centre/ Institute of Applied Social Studies

Glasby, J. and Peck, E. (eds) (2003) *Care trusts: partnership working in action.* Abingdon, Radcliffe Medical Press

Glendinning, C. *et al.* (2002a) *National evaluation of notifications for use of the section 31 partnership flexibilities of the Health Act 1999: final project report.* Manchester/Leeds, National Primary Care Research and Development Centre and Nuffield Institute for Health

Glendinning, C., Powell, M. and Rummery, K. (eds) (2002b) *Partnerships, New Labour and the governance of welfare.* Bristol, Policy Press

Glendinning, C. *et al.* (2008) *Evaluation of the individual budgets pilot programme.* York, Social Policy Research Unit

Glover, G., Arts, G. and Babu, K. (2006) Crisis resolution/home treatment teams and psychiatric admission rates in England, *British Journal of Psychiatry*, 189, 441–5

Goffman, E. (1961) *Asylums: essays on the social situation of mental patients and other inmates.* Harmondsworth, Penguin

Goldberg, D. (2008) Improved investment in mental health services: value for money?, *British Journal of Psychiatry*, 192, 88–91

Goldberg, D. and Huxley, P. (1992) *Common mental disorders.* London. Routledge

Golding, J. (1997) *Without prejudice: Mind lesbian, gay, bisexual mental health awareness research.* London, Mind

Goodwin, I. *et al.* (1999) A qualitative analysis of the views of in-patient mental health service users, *Journal of Mental Health*, 8(1), 43–54

Goodwin, S. (1990) *Community care and the future of mental health service provision.* Aldershot, Avebury

Goodwin, S. (1997) *Comparative mental health policy: from institutional to community care.* London, Sage

Gould, M. (2007) Home truths, *Health Service Journal*, 24 May, 24–6

Gournay, K, (2000) Role of the community psychiatric nurse in the management of schizophrenia, *Advances in Psychiatric Treatment*, 6, 243–51

Gournay, K. and Brooking, J. (1994) The CPN in primary care: an outcome study, *British Journal of Psychiatry*, 165, 231–8

Gournay, K. and Brooking, J. (1995) The CPN in primary care: an economic analysis, *Journal of Advanced Nursing*, 22, 769–78

Grant, G., Repper, J. and Nolan, M. (2008) Young people supporting parents with mental health problems: experiences of assessment and support, *Health and Social Care in the Community*, 16(3), 271–81

Grant-Pearce, C.M. and Deane, J. (1999) Joint working between the public and purchasing authorities to determine mental health information needs, in D. Bhugra and V. Bahl (eds) *Ethnicity: an agenda for mental health.* London, Gaskell

Gray, B. *et al.* (2008) 'Confidentiality smokescreens' and carers for people with mental health problems: the perspectives of professionals, *Health and Social Care in the Community*, 16(4), 378–87

Gray, R. *et al.* (1999) A national survey of practice nurse involvement in mental health interventions, *Journal of Advanced Nursing*, 30, 901–6

Greenberg, J.S., Greenley, J.R. and Benedict, P. (1994) Contributions of persons with serious mental illness to their families, *Hospital and Community Psychiatry*, 45(5), 475–9

Greengross, R., Hollander, D. and Stanton, R. (2000) Pressure on adult acute psychiatric beds: results of a national questionnaire survey, *Psychiatric Bulletin*, 24(2), 54–6

Gregory, N. *et al.* (2006) Identifying the needs of carers in mental health services, *Nursing Times*, 102(17), 32–5

Griffiths Report (1988) *Community care: an agenda for action*. London, HSMO

Grounds, A. (2001) Reforming the Mental Health Act, *British Journal of Psychiatry*, 178, 387–9

Grove, B. (1994) Reform of mental health care in Europe, *British Journal of Psychiatry*, 165, 431–3

Grove, B. and Drurie, S. (1999) *Social firms: an instrument for social and economic inclusion*. Redhill, Social Firms UK

Grove, B., Freudenberg G.M. and Harding, A. (1997) *The social firm handbook*. Brighton, Pavilion

Gulliver, P. (1999) Two approaches to the joint commissioning of mental health services, *Mental Health Review*, 4(3), 21–3

Gulliver, P., Peck, E. and Towell, D. (2002) Balancing professional and team boundaries in mental health services: pursuing the holy grail in Somerset, *Journal of Interprofessional Care*, 16(4), 359–70

Gunn, J. (2000) Future directions for treatment in forensic psychiatry, *British Journal of Psychiatry*, 176, 332–8

Gunn, J. and Maden, A. (1998) Bed requirements in high security hospitals, *Health Trends*, 30(3), 86–88

Hacking, S. and Bates, P. (2008) The inclusion web: a tool for person-centred planning and service evaluation, *Mental Health Review Journal*, 13, 4–15

Hall, I. and Ali, A. (2009) Changes to the Mental Health and Mental Capacity Acts: implications for patients and professionals, *Psychiatric Bulletin*, 33, 226–30

Hall, S. (2001) Argument rages over Sarah's law, *The Guardian*, 13 December. Available online via www.guardian.co.uk (accessed 9 February 2004)

Halliday, P. (2005) What sort of mental health problems are experienced by women in contemporary British society? What do different feminist perspectives offer as alleviation?, *Journal of International Women's Studies*, 6(3), 40–9

Ham, C. (2009) *Health policy in Britain: the politics and organisation of the National Health Service* (6th edn). Basingstoke, Palgrave Macmillan

Hancock, M. and Villeneau, L. (1997) *Effective partnerships: developing key indicators for joint working in mental health*. London, Sainsbury Centre for Mental Health

Hancock, M., Villeneau, L. and Hill, R. (1997) *Together we stand: effective partnerships – key indicators for joint working in mental health*. London, Sainsbury Centre for Mental Health

Hannay, D. (1979) *Health and lifestyles*. London, Routledge

Hannigan, B. (2003) The policy and legal context, in B. Hannigan and M. Coffey (eds) *The handbook of community mental health nursing*. London, Routledge

Hannigan, B. and Coffey, M. (eds) (2003) *The handbook of community mental health nursing*. London, Routledge

Hardcastle, M. *et al.* (eds) (2007) *Experiences of mental health in-patient care: narratives from service users, carers and professionals*. London, Routledge

Harding, C.M. and Zahniser, J.H. (1994) Empirical correction of seven myths about schizophrenia with implications for treatment, *Acta Psychiatrica Scandinavica*, 3(1), 140–6

Harrison, G. *et al.* (2001) Recovery from psychotic illness: a 15- and 25-year international follow-up study, *British Journal of Psychiatry*, 178, 506–17

Harrison, P. (1973) Careless community, *New Society*, 28 June

Hatton, C. *et al.* (2008) *A report on in Control's second phase: evaluation and learning 2005–2007*. London, in Control

Hayward, R. (2000) Somerset's development of an integrated information system for mental health services: organisational foundations, *British Journal of Healthcare Computing and Information Management*, 17(1), 18–19

Health Education Authority (1997) *Mental health promotion: quality framework*. London, Health Education Authority

Healthcare Commission (2004) *State of healthcare report, 2004*. London, Healthcare Commission

Healthcare Commission (2005a) *A snapshot of hospital cleanliness in England – findings from the Healthcare Commission's rapid inspection programme, 2005*. London, Healthcare Commission

Healthcare Commission (2005b) *The national audit of violence (2003–2005): final report*. London, Royal College of Psychiatrists' Research Unit/Healthcare Commission

Healthcare Commission (2006) *State of healthcare report, 2006*. London, Healthcare Commission

Healthcare Commission (2008a) *The path to recovery: a review NHS acute inpatient mental health services*. London, Healthcare Commission

Healthcare Commission (2008b) *Count me in 2008: results of the 2008 national census of inpatients in mental health and learning disability services in England and Wales*. London, Healthcare Commission (with CSIP/NIMHE)

Healthcare Commission/Commission for Social Care Inspection (2006) *Joint investigation into the provision of services for people with learning disabilities at Cornwall Partnership NHS Trust*. London, Healthcare Commission

Heater, D. (1990) *Citizenship: the civic ideal in world history, politics and education*. London, Longman

Heath, I. (1999) Uncertain clarity: contradiction, meaning and hope, *British Journal of General Practice*, 49, 651–7

Heath, I., Hippisley-Cox, J. and Smeeth, L. (2007) Measuring performance and missing the point?, *British Medical Journal*, 335, 1075–6

Henwood, M. (1998) *Ignored and invisible? Carers' experience of the NHS*. London, Carers National Association

Heron, C. (1998) *Working with carers*. London, Jessica Kingsley

Higgins, R., Hurst, K. and Wistow, G. (1999) Nursing acute psychiatric patients: a quantitative and qualitative study, *Journal of Advanced Nursing*, 29(1), 52–63

Higgitt, A, and Fonagy, P. (2002) Clinical effectiveness, *British Journal of Psychiatry*, 181, 170–4

Hill, M. and Hupe, P. (2002) *Implementing public policy*. London, Sage

Hill, R.G., Shepherd, G. and Hardy, P. (1998) In sickness and in health: the experiences of friends and relatives caring for people with manic depression, *Journal of Mental Health*, 7(6), 611–20

Hill, S., Mather, G. and Laugharne, R. (2007) Attitudes of psychiatrists towards forensic psychiatry: a survey, *Medicine, Science and the Law*, 47(3), 220–4

Hirschman, A. (1970) *Exit, voice or loyalty*. Cambridge (MA), Harvard University Press

HM Government (2008) *Carers at the heart of 21st-century families and communities*. London, Department of Health

HM Treasury (2007) *Meeting the aspirations of the British people, 2007 – pre-budget report and Comprehensive Spending Review.* London, HM Treasury

Hoggett, P. (1992) The politics of empowerment, *Going Local*, 19, 18–19

Hogman, G. and Pearson, G. (1995) *The silent partners: the needs and experiences of people who provide informal care to people with a severe mental illness.* Kingston upon Thames, National Schizophrenia Fellowship (now Rethink)

Hogman, G. and Sandamas, G. (2001) Mental patients are at last asked about the drugs they are given, *The Health Summary*, January, 8–11

Home Office (1990) *Provision for mentally disordered offenders.* Circular 66/90

Hopper, K. (2007) Rethinking social recovery in schizophrenia: what a capabilities approach might offer, *Social Science and Medicine*, 65, 868–79

Hoult, J. (1986) Community care of the acutely mentally ill, *British Journal of Psychiatry*, 149, 137–44

House of Commons (1948) *Hansard*, volume 447, column 50, 9 February

House of Commons Health Committee (2002) *Delayed discharges.* London, TSO

House of Commons and the House of Lords (2005) *Report of the Joint Scrutiny Committee on the Mental Health Bill.* PP HL (2004–5) 79/HC (2004–5) 95

House of Commons Work and Pensions Committee (2008) *Valuing and supporting carers.* London, TSO

Huang, M.C. and Slevin, E. (1999) The experiences of carers who live with someone who has schizophrenia: a review of the literature, *Mental Health and Learning Disabilities Care*, 3(3), 89–93

Hudson, B. (2002) Integrated care and structural change in England: the case of Care Trusts, *Policy Studies*, 23(2), 77–95

Hudson, B. (2003) Care trusts: a sceptical view, in J. Glasby and E. Peck (eds) *Care trusts: partnership working in action.* Abingdon, Radcliffe Medical Press

Hudson, B. and Henwood, M. (2002) The NHS and social care: the final countdown?, *Policy and Politics*, 30(2), 153–66

Hudson, B. *et al.* (1997) *Inter-agency collaboration: final report.* Leeds, Nuffield Institute for Health

Hunkler, E.M. *et al.* (2000) Efficacy of nurse telehealth care and peer support in augmenting treatment of depression in primary care, *Archives of Family Medicine*, 9, 700–8

Hutchinson, M. (2000) Issues around empowerment, in T. Basset (ed.) *Looking to the future: key issues for contemporary mental health services.* Brighton, Pavilion

Huxley, P. and Thornicroft, G. (2003) Social inclusion, social quality and mental illness, *British Journal of Psychiatry*, 182, 289–90

Independent Police Complaints Commission (2008) *Police custody as a 'place of safety': examining the use of section 136 of the Mental Health Act 1983.* London, IPCC

Information Centre (2007) *General and Personal Medical Services, England, 1996–2006.* Leeds, Information Centre

Information Centre (2008a) *Trends in consultation rates in general practice 1995–2007: analysis of the QRESEARCH database.* Leeds, Information Centre

Information Centre (2008b) *National quality and outcomes framework statistics for England 2007/08.* Leeds, Information Centre

Information Centre (2008c) *General and Personal Medical Services, England, 30 September 2007.* Leeds, Information Centre

Information Centre (2008d) *Community care statistics 2007–08.* London, Information Centre

Ireland, J.L. and Snowden, P. (2002) Bullying in secure hospitals, *Journal of Forensic Psychiatry*, 13(3), 538–54

Jenkins, R., Ustun, T. and Bedhiran, E. (1998) *Preventing mental illness: mental health promotion in primary care*. Chichester, Wiley

Jewesbury, I. (1998) *Risks and rights: mentally disordered offenders and public protection.* London, NACRO

Johnson, S. and Thornicroft, G. (1993) The sectorisation of psychiatric services in England and Wales, *Social Psychiatry and Psychiatric Epidemiology*, 28 (1), 45–7

Johnson, S. *et al.* (2004) Women's experiences of admission to a crisis house and to acute hospital wards: a qualitative study, *Journal of Mental Health*, 13(3), 247–62

Johnson, S. *et al.* (2005) Randomised controlled trial of acute mental health care by crisis resolution teams: the North Islington CRISIS study, *British Medical Journal*, 331, 599–602

Judge, J., Harty, M.A. and Fahy, T. (2004) Survey of community forensic psychiatry services in England and Wales, *Journal of Forensic Psychiatry and Psychology*, 15(2), 244–53

Kai, J. and Crosland, A. (2001) Perspectives of people with enduring mental ill health from a community-based qualitative study, *British Journal of General Practice*, 51, 730–73

Karp, D.A. (1996) *Speaking of sadness: depression, disconnection and the meanings of illness.* Oxford, Oxford University Press

Kates, N. and Mach, M. (2007) Chronic disease management for depression in primary care: summary of the current literature and implications for practice, *Canadian Journal of Psychiatry*, 52(2), 77–85

Katon, W. and Unutzer, J. (2006) Collaborative care models for depression: time to move from evidence to practice, *Archives of Internal Medicine*, 66, 2304–6

Katon, W. *et al.* (1996) A multifaceted intervention to improve treatment of depression in primary care, *Archives of General Psychiatry*, 53, 924–32

Katon, W. *et al.* (1999) Stepped collaborative care for primary care patients with persistent symptoms of depression, *Archives of General Psychiatry*, 56, 1109–15

Katon, W.J. *et al.* (2004) The Pathways Study: a randomised trial of collaborative care in patients with diabetes and depression, *Archives of General Psychiatry*, 61, 1042–9

Keating, F. and Robertson, D. (2004) Fear, black people and mental illness: a vicious cycle, *Health and Social Care in the Community*, 12(5), 439–47

Kendrick, T. *et al.* (1998) Practice nurse involvement in giving depot neuroleptic injections: development of patient assessment and monitoring checklist, *Primary Care Psychiatry*, 4, 149–54

Kendrick, T. *et al.*(2000) Are specialist mental health services being targeted on the most needy patients? – the effects of setting up special services in general practice, *British Journal of General Practice*, 50, 121–6

Kendrick, T. *et al.* (2005) GP treatment decisions for patients with depression: an observational study, *British Journal of General Practice*, 55, 280–6

Kennedy, P. (2008) We need to monitor implementation: commentary on new ways of working, *Psychiatric Bulletin*, 32, 46

Killaspy, H. (2007) Assertive community treatment in psychiatry, *British Medical Journal*, 335, 311–12

Killaspy, H. *et al.* (1999) Non-attendance at psychiatric outpatient clinics: communication and implications for primary care, *British Journal of General Practice*, 49, 880–3

Killaspy, H. *et al.* (2000a) Prospective controlled study of psychiatric outpatient non attendance, *British Journal of Psychiatry*, 176, 160–5

Killaspy, H. *et al.* (2000b) Drayton Park: an alternative to hospital admission for women in acute mental health crisis, *Psychiatric Bulletin*, 24(3), 101–4

Killaspy, H. *et al.* (2006) REACT: a randomised evaluation of assertive community treatment in north London, *British Medical Journal*, 332, 815–19

King, M. *et al.* (2003) *Mental health and social wellbeing of gay men, lesbians and bisexuals in England and Wales: a summary of findings.* London, Mind

King, M. *et al.* (2007) *Mental disorders, suicide, and deliberate self harm in lesbian, gay and bisexual people: a systematic review.* London, NIMHE

Kingdon, D. (1989) Mental health services: results of a survey of English district plans, *Psychiatric Bulletin,* 13, 77–8

Kingdon, J.W. (1995) *Agenda, alternatives and public policies* (2nd edn). New York, HarperCollins

King's Fund Institute (1988) *Health finance: assessing the options.* London, King's Fund Institute

Kingsland, J.P. and Williams, R. (1997) General practice should be central to community mental health services, *British Medical Journal,* 315, 1377

Koffman, J. *et al.* (1996) No way out: the delayed discharge of elderly mentally ill acute and assessment patients in North and South Thames regions, *Age and Ageing,* 25(4), 268–72

Koffman, J. *et al.* (1997) Ethnicity and use of acute psychiatric beds: one-day survey in North and South Thames regions, *British Journal of Psychiatry,* 171, 238–41

Kohen, D. (1999) Specialised in-patient psychiatric service for women, *Psychiatric Bulletin,* 23(1), 31–3

Kosa, J. and Zola, I.K. (1975) (eds) *Poverty and health: a sociological analysis.* Cambridge, MA/London, Harvard University Press

Kumar, S., Guite, H. and Thornicroft, G. (2001) Service users' experience of violence within a mental health system: a study using a grounded theory approach, *Journal of Mental Health,* 10(6), 597–611

Kupshik, G. and Fisher, C. (1999) Assisted bibliotherapy: effective, efficient treatment for moderate anxiety problems, *British Journal of General Practice,* 49, 47–8

La Grenade, J. (1999) The National Health Service and ethnicity: services for black patients, in D. Bhugra and V. Bahl (eds) *Ethnicity: an agenda for mental health.* London, Gaskell

Laing, R.D. (1960) *The divided self.* London, Tavistock Press

Laing, R.D. (1961) *The self and others.* London, Tavistock Press

Laming, H. (2003) *The Victoria Climbié inquiry: summary and recommendations.* London, HSMO

Lart, R. (1997) *Crossing boundaries: accessing community mental health services for prisoners on release.* Bristol, Policy Press

Laurance, J. (2003) *Pure madness: how fear drives the mental health system.* London, Routledge

Lawton-Smith, S., Dawson, J., Burns, T. (2008) Community treatment orders are not a good thing, *British Journal of Psychiatry,* 193, 96–100

Leason, K. (2003a) Mental health 'tsar' admits services suffer from institutional racism, *Community Care,* 17th–23 July, 18–19

Leason, K. (2003b) Bennett case typical of way NHS treats black people, inquiry told, *Community Care,* 7th–13 August, 12

Leason, K. (2003c) Author of mental health report says government diluted racism findings, *Community Care,* 17th–23 July, 8

Leatherman, S. and Sutherland, K. (2003) *The quest for quality on the NHS: a mid term evaluation of the ten-year quality agenda.* London, TSO

Leavey, G., Healy, H. and Brennan, G. (1998) Providing information to carers of people admitted to psychiatric hospital, *Mental Health Care,* 1(86), 260–2

Lee, P. (2002) Shooting for the moon, in C. Barnes, L. Barton and M. Oliver (eds) *Disability Studies Today.* Cambridge, Quality Press

Lee, R. and Bradley, D. (2000) Wrong side of beds, *Health Service Journal*, 110(5726), 30–1

Leff, J. (1997) *Care in the community: illusion or reality?* Chichester, John Wiley and Sons

Leff, J. *et al.* (2000) The TAPS Project: a report on 13 years of research 1985–1998, *Psychiatric Bulletin*, 24,165–8

Lelliott, P. (2008) Time for honest debate and critical friends: commentary on new ways of working, *Psychiatric Bulletin*, 32, 47–8

Lelliott, P. and Wing, J. (1994) A national audit of new long-stay psychiatric patients II: impact on services, *British Journal of Psychiatry*, 165, 170–8

Lelliott, P., Audini, B. and Duffett, R. (2001) Survey of patients from an inner-London health authority in medium secure psychiatric care, *British Journal of Psychiatry*, 179, 62–6

Lesperance, F. *et al.* (2002) Five-year risk of cardiac mortality in relation to initial severity and one year changes in depression symptoms after myocardial infarction, *Circulation*, 105, 1049–53

Lester, H.E. and Tritter, J.Q. (2005) Listen to my madness: exploring the views of people with serious mental illness using a disability framework, *Sociology of Health and Illness*, 27(5), 649–69

Lester, H.E., Tritter, J. and England, E. (2003) Satisfaction with primary care: the perspectives of people with schizophrenia, *Family Practice*, 20, 508–13

Lester, H.E., Tritter, J.Q. and Sorohan, H. (2004) Managing crisis: the role of primary care for people with serious mental illness, *Family Medicine*, 36(1), 28–34

Lester, H.E., Tritter, J.Q. and Sorohan, H. (2005) Providing 'good enough' primary care: a focus group study, *British Medical Journal*, 330, 1122–8

Lester H.E. *et al.* (2007) Cluster randomized controlled trial of the effectiveness of graduate primary care mental health workers, *British Journal of General Practice*, 57, 196–203

Lester, H.E. *et al.* (2009) Development and implementation of early intervention services for young people with psychosis: a case study, *British Journal of Psychiatry*, 194, 446–50

Lewis, R. and Glasby, J. (2006) Delayed discharge from mental health hospitals: results of a postal survey, *Health and Social Care in the Community*, 14(3), 225–30

Lewis, R.L., Curry, N. and Dixon, M. (2007) *Practice-based commissioning: from good idea to effective practice.* London, King's Fund

Li, P.L. *et al.* (1999) Barriers to meeting the mental health needs of the Chinese community, *Journal of Public Health Medicine*, 21(1), 74–80

Lindow, V. (1999) Power, lies and injustice: the exclusion of service users' voices, in M. Parker (eds) *Ethics and community in the health care professions.* London, Routledge

Link, B.J. and Phelan, J.C. (2001) Conceptualising stigma, *Annual Review of Sociology*, 27, 363–85

MacInnes, D. (2000) Interventions in forensic psychiatry: the caregiver's perspective, *British Journal of Nursing*, 9(15), 992–7

Mac Gabhann, L. (2000) Are nurses responding to the needs of patients in acute adult mental health care?, *Mental Health and Learning Disabilities Care*, 4(3), 85–8

Maden, A. *et al.* (1999a) Outcome of admission to a medium secure psychiatric unit 1: short- and long-term outcome, *British Journal of Psychiatry*, 175, 313–16

Maden, A. *et al.* (1999b) Outcome of admission to a medium secure psychiatric unit: 2 – role of ethnic origin, *British Journal of Psychiatry*, 175, 317–21

Maguire, N. (1999) Models of imperfection, *Health Service Journal*, 109(5654), 20–2

Mallon, S. (2001) The therapeutic benefits of a women-only environment, *Nursing Times*, 97(37), 40–1

Malone, D. *et al.* (2000) Community mental health teams (CMHTs) for people with severe mental illnesses and disordered personality (Cochrane Review), *The Cochrane Library*, 3, Oxford, Update Software

Mandelstam, M. (1998) *An A–Z of community care law*. London, Jessica Kingsley

Manning, C. and White, P.D. (1995) Attitudes of employers to the mentally ill, *Psychiatric Bulletin*, 19, 541–3

Mannion, R., Davies, H.T.O. and Marshall, M.N. (2003) *Cultures for performance in health care: evidence on the relationships between organisational culture and organisational performance*. York, Centre for Health Economics

Markham, G. (2000) Policy and service development trends: forensic mental health and social care services, *Tizard Learning Disability Review*, 5(2), 26–31

Marmot, M. (2004) Evidence based policy or policy based evidence?, *British Medical Journal*, 328, 906–7

Marshall, M. and Lockwood, A. (1998) Assertive community treatment for people with severe mental disorders (Cochrane Review), *The Cochrane Library*, 3, Oxford, Update Software

Marshall, M., Lockwood, A, and Green, R. (1998) Case management for people with severe mental disorders. (Cochrane Review), *The Cochrane Library*, 1 Oxford, Update Software

Marshall, M. *et al.* (1999) PRiSM psychosis study: design limitations, questionable conclusions, *British Journal of Psychiatry*, 173, 501–3

Marshall, M. *et al.* (2001) Systematic reviews of the effectiveness of day care for people with severe mental disorders: (1) acute day hospital versus admission; (2) vocational rehabilitation; (3) day hospital versus outpatient care, *Health Technology Assessment*, 5, 1–75

Marshall, R. (1990) The genetics of schizophrenia: axiom or hypothesis?, in R.P. Bentall (ed.) *Reconstructing schizophrenia*. London, Routledge

Marshall, T.H. (1950) *Citizenship and social class and other essays*. Cambridge, Cambridge University Press

Martin, J.P. (1984) *Hospitals in trouble*. Oxford, Basil Blackwell

Mauksch, L.B. and Leahy, D. (1993) Collaboration between primary care medicine and mental health in an HMO, *Family Systems Medicine*, 11, 121–35

Maunder, L., Cameron, L. and Liddon, A. (2001) Targeting services to meet need: a tiered approach to mental health care, *Mental Health and Learning Disabilities Care*, 4(11), 366–9

May, R. (2001) Crossing the 'them and us' barriers: an insider perspective on user involvement in clinical psychology, *Clinical Psychology Forum*, 150, 14–17

Maynard, A. and Tingle, R. (1975) The objectives and performance of the mental health services in England and Wales in the 1960s, *Journal of Social Policy*, 151–68

Mays, N. *et al.* (1998) *Total purchasing: a step towards primary care groups*. London, King's Fund

McCabe, A. and Ford, C. (2001) *Redressing the balance: crime and mental health*. Manchester, UK Public Health Association

McCann, G. (1999) Care of mentally disordered offenders, *Mental Health Care*, 3(2), 65–7

McCormick, A., Fleming, D. and Charlton, J. (1995) *Morbidity statistics from general practice: fourth national morbidity study 1991–1992*. London, HMSO

McCrone, P., Dhanasiri, S. and Patel, A. (2008) *Paying the price: the cost of mental health care in England to 2026*. London, King's Fund

McDermott, G. and Reid, L. (1999) Model for integrated mental health care measures up, *Nursing Times*, 95(13), 46–7

McDonagh, M.S., Smith, D.H. and Goddard, M. (2000) Measuring appropriate use of acute beds: a systematic review of methods and results, *Health Policy*, 157–84

McDougall, T. *et al.* (2009) Young people on adult mental health wards, *Mental Health Practice Today*, 12(8), 16–21

McFadyen, J.A. (1999) Safe, sound and supportive: forensic mental health services, *British Journal of Nursing*, 8(21), 1436–40

McFarlane, L. (1998) *Diagnosis: homophobic – the experiences of lesbians, gay men and bisexuals in mental health services*. London, PACE

McGlynn, P. (2007) *Crisis resolution and home treatment teams: a practical guide*. London, Sainsbury Centre for Mental Health

McIntyre, B. (1999) Placement and community support needs of patients in a medium secure unit, *Mental Health Care*, 2(11), 379–82

McKenna, J. *et al.* (1999) 'Long stay medium secure' patients in special hospital, *Journal of Forensic Psychiatry*, 10(2), 333–42

McKenzie, K. and Bhui, K. (2007a) Better mental healthcare for minority ethnic groups – moving away from the blame-game and putting patients first ..., *Psychiatric Bulletin*, 31, 368–9

McKenzie, K. and Bhui, K. (2007b) Institutional racism in mental health care, *British Medical Journal*, 334, 649–50

McMillan, I. (1997a) Ancient and modern, *Nursing Standard*, 11(34), 28–9

McMillan, I. (1997b) Refuge reaching out, *Nursing Standard*, 11(39), 26–7

McMillan, I. (2000) One-stop service, *Nursing Standard*, 13(33), 16–17

Means, R., Richards, S. and Smith, R. (2008) *Community care: policy and practice* (4th edn). Basingstoke, Palgrave Macmillan

Means, R. and Smith, R. (1998) *Community care: policy and practice* (2nd edn). Basingstoke, Palgrave Macmillan

Medawar, C. *et al.* (2002) Paroxetine, *Panorama* and user reporting of ATDRs: consumer intelligence matters in clinical practice and post-marketing drug surveillance, *International Journal of Risk and Safety in Medicine*, 15, 161–9

Meehan, E. (1993) Citizenship and the European Community, *Political Quarterly*, 64(2), 172–86

Meltzer, H. *et al.* (2002) *The social and economic circumstances of adults with mental disorders*. London, ONS

Melzer, D. *et al.* (2002) Quantifying associations between social position and the common mental disorders in Britain. Unpublished paper commissioned by the Department of Health

Melzer, D. *et al.* (2004) Access to medium secure psychiatric care in England and Wales. 3: the clinical needs of assessed patients, *Journal of Forensic Psychiatry and Psychology*, 15(1), 50–65

Mental Health After Care Association (1999) *First national GP survey of mental health in primary care*. London, MACA

Mental Health Foundation (2001) '*Is anybody there?' A survey of friendship and mental health* (Mental Health Foundation Updates, vol. 2, issue 16). London, Mental Health Foundation

Mental Health Foundation (2003) *Black spaces project*. London, Mental Health Foundation

Mental Health Foundation (2007) *Keeping the faith: spirituality and recovery from mental health problems*. London, Mental Health Foundation

Millar, B. (2000) All in a day's work, *Therapy Weekly*, 27(10), 48

Mind (1996) *Lesbians, gay men, bisexuals and mental health*. Mind factsheet (updated 2002). Available online via www.mind.org.uk (accessed 4 February 2004)

Mind (2003a) *Developing a visual impairment and mental health.* Mind factsheet, available online via www.mind.org.uk (accessed 4 February 2004)

Mind (2003b) *Deafness and mental health.* Mind factsheet, available online via www. mind.org.uk (accessed 4 February 2004)

Mind (n.d.) *Mind: the mental health charity.* Available online via www.mind.org.uk (accessed 4 February 2004)

Mind (2004) *Ward watch.* London, Mind

Minghella, E. and Ford, R. (1997) Focal points?, *Health Service Journal,* 107(5583), 36–7

Minghella, E. *et al.* (1998) *Open all hours: 24-hour response for people with mental health emergencies.* London, Sainsbury Centre for Mental Health

Ministry of Health (1962) *A hospital plan for England and Wales.* London, HMSO

Mohan, R. and Fahy, T. (2006) Is there a need for community forensic mental health services?, *Journal of Forensic Psychiatry and Psychology,* 17(3), 365–71

Mohan, R., Slade, M. and Fahy, T.A. (2004) Clinical characteristics of community forensic mental health services, *Psychiatric Services,* 55(11), 1294–8

Monkley-Poole, S. (1995) The attitudes of British fund holding general practitioners to community psychiatric nursing services, *Journal of Advanced Nursing,* 21, 238–47

Mooney, H. (2004) Mental health changes slammed, *Health Service Journal,* 9th September, 5

Moore, C. and Wolf, J. (1999) Open and shut case, *Health Service Journal,* 109(5660), 20–2

Morgan, C. *et al.* (2007) Social exclusion and mental health: conceptual and methodological review, *British Journal of Psychiatry,* 191, 477–83

Morgan, H. (1998) A potential for partnership? Consulting with users of mental health services, in A. Foster and V.Z. Roberts (eds) *Managing mental health in the community: chaos and containment.* London, Routledge

Morris, J. (2004a) *'One town for my body, another for my mind': services for people with physical impairments and mental health support needs.* York, Joseph Rowntree Foundation

Morris, J. (2004b) *Services for people with physical impairments and mental health support needs* (Joseph Rowntree Foundation Findings 574). York, Joseph Rowntree Foundation

Morrissey, M. (1998) Improving information for clients in mental health care, *Mental Health Nursing,* 18(2), 25–7

Mulvany, J. (2000) Disability, impairment or illness? The relevance of the social model of disability to the study of mental disorder, *Sociology of Health and Illness,* 22(5), 582–681

Murphy, E. (1991) *After the asylums: community care for people with mental illness.* London, Faber and Faber

Murray, S. (1998) Evaluation of shifted out-patient clinics, *Psychiatry Audit Trends,* 6, 64–7

Mynors-Wallis, L.M. *et al.* (2000) Randomised controlled trial of problem solving treatment, antidepressant medication, and combined treatment for depression in primary care, *British Medical Journal,* 320, 26–30

NACRO (2005) *Findings of the 2004 survey of court diversion/criminal justice mental health liaison schemes for mentally disordered offenders in England and Wales.* London, NACRO

Nadkarni, R., Chipchase, B. and Fraser, K. (2000) Partnership with probation hostels: a step forward in community forensic psychiatry, *Psychiatric Bulletin,* 24(6), 222–4

National Association of Psychiatric Intensive Care Units (2006) *Behind closed doors: acute mental health in the UK.* London, NAPICU/Rethink/SANE/Zito Trust

National Audit Office (2007) *Helping people through mental health crisis: the role of crisis resolution and home treatment services.* London, National Audit Office

National Confidential Inquiry into Suicide and Homicide (2006) *Five year report of the National Confidential Inquiry into Suicide and Homicide by People with Mental Illness.* Manchester, University of Manchester

National Institute for Clinical Excellence (NICE) (2003) *Schizophrenia: full national clinic guidelines on core interventions in primary and secondary care.* London, Royal College of Psychiatrists and the British Psychological Society

National Institute for Clinical Excellence (2004a) *Depression: management of depression in primary and secondary care.* London, National Institute for Clinical Excellence

National Institute for Clinical Excellence (2004b) *Anxiety: management of anxiety (panic disorder, with or without agoraphobia, and generalised anxiety disorder) in adults in primary, secondary and community care: clinical guideline 22.* London, National Institute for Clinical Excellence

National Institute for Clinical Excellence (2009) *Depression in adults.* London, National Institute for Clinical Excellence

National Patient Safety Agency (NPSA) (2006) *With safety in mind: mental health services and patient safety.* London, NPSA

National Schizophrenia Fellowship (1997) *How to involve users and carers in planning, running and monitoring care services and curriculum development.* Kingston-upon-Thames, National Schizophrenia Fellowship (now Rethink)

National Schizophrenia Fellowship (2000) *No change?* London, National Schizophrenia Fellowship

National Schizophrenia Fellowship (n.d) *Carers facts and figures.* Available online at www.nsf.org.uk (accessed 26 June 2001)

Neill, J. and Williams, J. (1992) *Leaving hospital: older people and their discharge to community care.* London, HMSO

Newnes, C., Long, N. and MacLachlan, A. (2001) Recruits you, sir, *OpenMind,* 108, 12

NHS Centre for Involvement (2008) *The current state of patient and public involvement in NHS Trusts across England.* Coventry, NHS Centre for Involvement

NHS Confederation (2003) *The role of nurses under the new GMS Contract.* London, NHS Confederation

NHS Executive (1994) *Introduction of supervision registers for mentally ill people from 1 April 1994.* HSG(84)5

NHS Executive (1996) *Workforce planning for general medical services* Leeds, NHS Executive

NHS Executive (1998) *Signposts for success in commissioning and providing health services for people with learning disabilities.* Leeds, NHS Executive

NHS Management Executive (1992) *Local voices: the views of local people in purchasing for health.* Leeds, NHS Management Executive

NHS Service and Delivery Organisation (2003) *SDO News,* 6 (December). London, National Co-ordinating Centre for NHS Service Delivery and Organisation Research and Development

NIMHE (2003a) *Inside outside: improving mental health services for black and minority ethnic communities in England.* Leeds, NIMHE

NIMHE (2003b) *Engaging and changing: developing effective policy for the care and treatment of black and minority ethnic detained patients.* Leeds, NIMHE

NIMHE (2004a) *Celebrating our cultures: guidelines for mental health promotion with black and minority ethnic communities.* Leeds, NIMHE

NIMHE (2004b) *From here to equality: a strategic plan to tackle stigma and discrimination on mental health grounds, 2004–2009.* Leeds, NIMHE

NIMHE (2008) *Mental Health Act 2007 new roles: guidance for approving authorities and employers on Approved Mental Health Professionals and Approved Clinicians.* London, NIMHE

Nocon, A. (1994) *Collaboration in community care in the 1990s.* Sunderland, Business Education Publishers

Nolan, P, and Badger, F. (2002) *Promoting collaboration in primary mental health care.* Cheltenham, Nelson Thornes

Nolan, P., Dunn, L. and Badger, F. (1998) Getting to know you, *Nursing Times,* 94(39), 34–6

Nolan, M. *et al.* (eds) (2003) *Partnerships in family care: understanding the caregiving career.* Maidenhead, Open University Press

Norfolk, Suffolk and Cambridgeshire Strategic Health Authority (2003) *Independent inquiry into the death of David Bennett.* Cambridge, Norfolk, Suffolk and Cambridgeshire Strategic Health Authority

Norman, A. (1985) *Triple jeopardy: growing old in a second homeland.* London, Centre for Policy on Ageing

Norman, I.J. and Peck, E. (1999) Working together in adult community mental health services: an inter-professional dialogue, *Journal of Mental Health,* 8(3), 217–30

Norman, R. and Malla, A. (2001) Duration of untreated psychosis: a critical examination of the concept and its importance, *Psychological Medicine,* 31, 381– 400

Norman, R.M.G. and Townsend, L.A. (1999) Cognitive behavioural therapy for psychosis: a status report, *Canadian Journal of Psychiatry,* 44, 245–52

Office of the Deputy Prime Minister (ODPM) (2004) *Mental health and social exclusion* (Social Exclusion Unit Report). London, ODPM

Office of the Deputy Prime Minister (2006) *Reaching out: an action plan for social inclusion.* London, ODPM

Office for National Statistics (ONS) (2000) *Carers 2000.* London, ONS

Office for National Statistics (ONS) (2002) *Labour Force Survey.* London, ONS

Office for National Statistics (ONS) (2003) *Labour Force Survey, Autumn 2003.* London, ONS

Office for National Statistics (ONS) (2007) *Attitudes to mental illness 2007.* London, ONS

Okai, D. *et al.* (2007) Mental capacity in psychiatric patients: systematic review, *British Journal of Psychiatry,* 191, 291–7

Oliver, M. (1983) *Social work with disabled people.* Basingstoke, Macmillan

Oliver, M. (1990) *The politics of disablement.* Basingstoke, Macmillan

Oliver, M. (1996) Defining impairment and disability: issues at stake, in E. Barnes and G. Mercer (eds) *Exploring the divide: illness and disability.* Leeds, Disability Press

Oliver, M. and Sapey, B. (2006) *Social work with disabled people* (3rd edn). Basingstoke, Palgrave Macmillan

Onyett, S., Standee, R. and Peck, E. (1997) The challenge of managing community mental health teams, *Health and Social Care in the Community,* 5(1), 40–7

Organisation for Economic Co-operation and Development (OECD) (2001) *OECD health data.* Paris, OECD

O'Sea, T. (2004) Take your partners? A local authority perspective on reform, re-organisation and integration of mental health services, *Mental Health Review,* 9(4), 19–24

Owen, A.J., Sashidharan, S.P. and Edwards, L.J. (2000) Availability and acceptability of home treatment for acute psychiatric disorders, *Psychiatric Bulletin*, 24(5), 169–71

Oxford Economics (2007) *Mental health and the UK economy*. Oxford, Oxford Economics

Parker, G. (2002) Evidence based policy in practice: health services, *Managing Community Care*, 10(1), 22–6

Parkman, S. *et al.* (1997) Ethnic differences in satisfaction with mental health services among representative people with psychosis in south London: PRiSM study 4, *British Journal of Psychiatry*, 171, 260–4

Parrott, L., Jacobs, G. and Roberts, D. (2008) *Stress and resilience factors in parents with mental health problems and their children*. London, SCIE

Parsons, T. (1964) *The social system*. London, RKP (first published 1951)

Parsonage, M. (2009) The NSF for mental health: costs of implementation, in C. Brooker. and J. Repper (eds) *Mental health: from policy to practice*. Edinburgh, Elsevier

Patel, V. *et al.* (2007) Treatment and prevention of mental disorders in low-income and middle-income countries, *Lancet*, 370, 991–1005

Patmore, C. and Weaver, T. (1991) *Community mental health teams: lessons for planners and managers*. London, Good Practice in Mental Health

Paton, J.M., Fahy, M.A. and Livingston, G.A. (2004) Delayed discharge – a solvable problem? The place of intermediate care in mental health care of older people, *Aging and Mental Health*, 8(1), 34–9

Payne, G. (ed.) (2000) *Social divisions*. Basingstoke, Macmillan

Payne, S. (1998) 'Hit and miss': the success and failure of psychiatric services for women, in L. Doyal (ed.) *Women and health services*. Buckingham, Open University Press

Payne, S. (1999) Outside the walls of the asylum? Psychiatric treatment in the 1980s and 1990s, in P. Bartlett and D. Wright (eds) *Outside the walls of the asylum: the history of care in the community*, 1750–2000. London, Athlone Press

Peat, L. (1979) Twenty-five yeas of community psychiatric nursing, *Community Psychiatric Nurses Association Journal*, January

Peck, E. (2002) Integrating health and social care, *Managing Community Care*, 10(3), 16–19

Peck, E. and Crawford, A. (2002) 'You say tomato': culture as a signifier of difference between health and social care, *Mental Health Review*, 7(3), 23–6

Peck, E. and Crawford, A. (2004) *'Culture' in partnerships – what do we mean by it and what can we do about it?* Leeds, Integrated Care Network

Peck, E. and Dickinson, H. (2008) Partnership working and organisational culture, in H. Dickinson and J. Glasby (eds) *International perspectives on health and social care*. Oxford, Wiley-Blackwell/CAIPE

Peck, E. and Greatley, A. (1999) Developing the mental health agenda for primary care groups, *Managing Community Care*, 7, 3–6

Peck, E., Gulliver, P. and Towell, D. (2002a) *Modernising partnerships: an evaluation of Somerset's innovations in the commissioning and organisation of mental health services – final report*. London, Institute of Applied Health and Social Policy, King's College

Peck, E., Gulliver, P., Towell, D. (2002b) Information, consultation or control: user involvement in mental health services in England at the turn of the century, *Journal of Mental Health*, 11 (4), 441–51

Peck, E., Gulliver, P. and Towell, D. (2003) The Somerset story: the implications for Care Trusts of the evaluation of the integration of health and social services in

Somerset, in J. Glasby and E. Peck (eds) *Care trusts: partnership working in action.* Abingdon, Radcliffe Medical Press

Peck, E. and Norman, I.J. (1999) Working together in adult community mental health services: exploring inter-professional role relations, *Journal of Mental Health,* 8(3), 231–42

Pelosi, A. and Birchwood, M. (2003) Is early intervention of psychosis a waste of valuable resources?, *British Journal of Psychiatry,* 182, 196–8

Percy Commission (1957) *The Report of the Royal Commission on Mental Illness and Mental Deficiency.* London, HMSO

Perring, C., Twigg, J. and Atkin, K. (1990) *Families caring for people diagnosed as mentally ill: the literature re-examined.* London, HMSO

Peterson, L. *et al.* (2005) A randomised multi-centre trial of integrated versus standard treatment for patients with a first episode of psychotic illness, *British Medical Journal,* 331, 602–9

Peveler, R. *et al.* (1999) Effect of antidepressant drug counselling and information leaflets on adherence to drug treatment in primary care: randomised controlled trial, *British Medical Journal,* 319, 612–15

Phelps, K. and Regen, E. (2008) *To what extent does the use of Health Act flexibilities promote effective partnership working and positive outcomes for older people?* Leicester, Leicester Nuffield Research Unit

Phillips, P. and Johnson, S. (2003) Drug and alcohol misuse among in-patients with psychotic illnesses in three inner-London psychiatric units, *Psychiatric Bulletin,* 27, 217–20

Pierre, S. (1999) The experiences of African and Afro-Caribbean people in acute psychiatric hospital: a qualitative study, *Mental Health Care,* 3(2), 52–6

Pilgrim, D. (2002) The biopsychosocial model in Anglo-American psychiatry: past, present and future?, *Journal of Mental Health,* 11(6), 585–94

Pilgrim, D. (2008) Recovery and current mental health policy, *Chronic Illness,* 4, 295–304

Pilgrim, D. and Rogers, A. (2005) *A sociology of mental health and illness* (3rd edn) Buckingham, Open University Press

Pinfold, V., Smith, J. and Shiers, D. (2007) Audit of early intervention in psychosis service development in England in 2005, *Psychiatric Bulletin,* 31, 7–10

Pinfold, V. *et al.* (2001) Persuading the persuadable: evaluating compulsory treatment in England using Supervised Discharge Orders, *Social Psychiatry & Psychiatric Epidemiology,* 36(5), 260–6

Pinfold, V. *et al.* (2004) *Positive and inclusive? Effective ways for professionals to involve carers in information sharing.* London, Rethink/Institute of Psychiatry/King's College London

Pinnock, H. *et al.* (2005) General practitioners with a special interest in respiratory medicine: national survey of UK primary care organisations, *BMC Health Services Research,* 5(1), 40

Plummer, S.E. *et al.* (2000) Detection of psychological distress by practice nurses in general practice, *Psychological Medicine,* 30, 1233–7

Polczyk-Przybyla, M. and Gournay, K. (1999) Psychiatric nursing in prison: the state of the art?, *Journal of Advanced Nursing,* 30(4), 893–900

Poll, C. *et al.* (2006) A *report on in Control's first phase, 2003–2005.* London, in Control

Pollock, A. *et al.* (2007) The market in primary care, *British Medical Journal,* 335, 475–7

Porter, R. (1987) *Mind forged manacles.* Harmonsworth, Penguin

Porter, R. (1999) *A social history of madness: stories of the insane.* London, Phoenix

Porter, R. (2002) *Madness: a brief history*. Oxford, Oxford University Press

Powell, E. (1961) Speech to the Annual Conference of the National Association of Mental Health (now Mind)

Poxton, R. (1999) Primary and community mental health and social care: making a difference at the interface, *Mental Health Review*, 4(3), 24–7

Poxton, R. (2003) What makes effective partnerships between health and social care?, in J. Glasby and E. Peck (eds) *Care trusts: partnership working in action*. Abingdon, Radcliffe Medical Press

Pressman, J. and Wildavsky, A. (1973) *Implementation*. Berkeley, University of California Press

Preston, C. *et al.* (1999) Left in limbo: patients' views on care across the primary/secondary interface, *Quality in Health Care*, 8(1), 16–21

Price, J. (1997) *Queer in the head: an examination of the response of social work mental health services to the needs and experiences of lesbians and gay men*. Surbiton, Social Care Association

Priebe, S., Sleed, M. and Beecham, J. (2006) Effectiveness and costs of acute day hospital treatment compared with conventional in-patient care, *British Journal of Psychiatry* 188, 243–9

Priebe, S. *et al.* (2005) Reinstitutionalisation in mental health care: comparison in data in service provision from six European countries, *British Medical Journal*, 33, 123–6

Prior, D. (1993) *Social organisation of mental illness*. London, Sage

Quirk, A. and Lelliott, P. (2001) What do we know about life on acute psychiatric wards in the UK? A review of the research evidence, *Social Science and Medicine*, 53(12), 1565–74

Quirk, A., Lelliott, P. and Seale, C. (2004) Service users' strategies for managing risk in the volatile environment of an acute psychiatric ward, *Social Science and Medicine*, 59, 2573–83

Quirk, A., Lelliott, P. and Seale, C. (2006) The permeable institution: an ethnographic study of three acute psychiatric wards in London, *Social Science and Medicine*, 63, 2105–17

Ramon, S. (1996) *Mental health in Europe*. Basingstoke, Macmillan

Rankin, J. (2005) *Mental health and social inclusion*. London, Institute for Public Policy Research

Rapaport, J. *et al.* (2006) Carers and confidentiality in mental health care: considering the role of the carer's assessment: a study of service users', carers' and practitioners' views, *Health and Social Care in the Community*, 14(4), 357–65

Rassool, G.H. (ed.) (2002) *Dual diagnosis: substance misuse and psychiatric disorders*. Oxford, Blackwell Science

Read, J. and Baker, S. (1996) *Not just sticks and stones: a survey of the discrimination experienced by people with mental health problems*. London, Mind

Read, J. and Reynolds, J. (eds) (2000) *Speaking our minds: an anthology*. Basingstoke, Palgrave

Reed, J.L. and Lyne, M. (2000) Inpatient care of mentally ill people in prison: results of a year's programme of semistructured inspections, *British Medical Journal*, 320, 1031–4

Rees, G. *et al.* (2004) Joint working in community mental health teams: implementation of an integrated care pathway, *Health and Social Care in the Community*, 16(3), 271–81

Regen, E., Smith, J. and Shapiro, J. (1999) *First off the starting blocks: lessons from GP commissioning pilots for PCGs*. Birmingham, HSMC, University of Birmingham

Regier, D.A. *et al.* (1988) The NIMH depression awareness, recognition, and treatment program: structure, aims, and scientific basis, *American Journal of Psychiatry*, 145, 1351–7

Reilly, S. *et al.* (2007) Care management in mental health services in England and Northern Ireland: do integrated organizations promote integrated practice?, *Journal of Health Services Research and Policy*, 12(4), 236–41

Repper, J. and Breeze, J. (2006) User and carer involvement in the training and education of health professionals: a review of the literature, *International Journal of Nursing Studies*, 44(3), 511–19

Rethink (2003a) *Reaching people early: a status report on the early support received by people with severe mental illness and their informal carers*. London, Rethink

Rethink (2003b) *Who cares? The experiences of mental health carers accessing services and information*. London, Rethink

Rethink (2003c) *Under pressure*. London, Rethink

Rethink (2005) *Future perfect*. London, Rethink

Rethink (2007) *Our voice: the Pakistani community's view of mental health services in Birmingham*. London, Rethink

Rethink/CSIP (2007) *Involving carers in out of area treatments: a good practice guide*. London, Rethink/CSIP

Rethink/Sane/Zito Trust/NAPICU (2006) *Behind closed doors: acute mental health care in the UK*. London, Rethink

Ridley, J. and Jones, L. (2002) *'Direct what?' A study of direct payments to mental health service users*. Edinburgh, Scottish Executive Central Research Unit

Rimington, L.D., Davies, D.H. and Pearson, M.G. (2001) Relationship between anxiety, depression and morbidity in adult asthma patients, *Thorax*, 56, 266–71

Ritchie Report (1994) *Report of the inquiry into the care and treatment of Christopher Clunis*. London, HMSO

Robert, G. *et al.* (2003) Redesigning mental health services: lessons on user involvement from the Mental Health Collaborative, *Health Expectations*, 6, 60–71

Roberts, P. and Priest, H. (1997) Achieving interprofessional working in mental health, *Nursing Standard*, 12(2), 39–41

Robinson, G., Beaton, S. and White, P. (1993) Attitudes towards practice nurses, *British Journal of General Practice*, 43, 25–9

Rogers, A. and Pilgrim, D. (2001) *Mental health policy in Britain* (2nd edn) Basingstoke, Palgrave

Rogers, A. and Pilgrim, D. (2003) *Mental health and inequalities*. Basingstoke, Palgrave Macmillan

Rogers, A. *et al.* (2002) Some national service frameworks are more equal than others: implementing clinical governance for mental health in primary care groups and trusts, *Journal of Mental Health*, 11, 199–212

Rogers, H. (2000) Breaking the ice: developing strategies for collaborative working with carers of older people with mental health problems, in H. Kemshall and R. Littlechild (eds) *User involvement and participation in social care: research informing practice*. London, Jessica Kingsley

Romme, M. and Escher, A. (1989) Hearing voices, *Schizophrenia Bulletin*, 15, 209–16

Rooney, P. (2002) *Mental health policy implementation guide: adult acute inpatient care provision*. London, Department of Health

Rose, D. (2001) *Users' voices: the perspectives of mental health service users on community and hospital care*. London, Sainsbury Centre for Mental Health

Rosenhan, D.L. (1973) On being sane in insane places, *Science*, 179, 250–8

Royal College of General Practitioners (RCGP) (2001) *The primary care workforce.* London, RCGP

Royal College of General Practitioners (2002) *RCGP information sheet number 4: general practice in the UK.* London, RCGP

Royal College of General Practitioners (2003a) *RCGP information sheet number 21: the primary health care team.* London, RCGP

Royal College of General Practitioners (2003b) *RCGP information sheet number 1: profile of UK general practitioners.* London, RCGP

Royal College of General Practitioners (2006) *RCGP information sheet: general practitioners with special interests.* London, RCGP

Royal College of Nursing (RCN)/CSIP/NIMHE (2008) *Informed gender practice: mental health acute care that works for women.* London, CSIP/Department of Health

Royal College of Psychiatrists (1997) *Community psychiatric nursing* (Occasional paper OP40). London, Royal College of Psychiatrists

Royal College of Psychiatrists (2002) *Acute hospitals should be at the forefront of psychiatric services* (press release, 1st March). London, Royal College of Psychiatrists

Royal College of Psychiatrists (2009) *Standards for safe and appropriate care for young people on adult mental health wards.* London, Royal College of Psychiatrists

Royal College of Psychiatrists/Healthcare Commission (2007) *Healthcare Commission National Audit of Violence 2006–7.* London, Royal College of Psychiatrists

Rutherford, M. (2008) Imprisonment for public protection: genesis and mental health implementation, *Mental Health Review,* 13(2), 47–55

Rutherford, M. and Duggan, S. (2007) *Forensic mental health services: facts and figures on current provision.* London, Sainsbury Centre for Mental Health

Ryan, T. (2002) Exploring the risk management strategies of informal carers of mental health service users, *Journal of Mental Health,* 11(1), 17–25

Ryan, T. and Bamber, C. (2002) A survey of policy and practice on expenses and other payments to mental health service users and carers participating in service development, *Journal of Mental Health,* 11(6), 635–44

Sainsbury Centre for Mental Health (1998a) *Keys to engagement: review of care for people with severe mental illness who are hard to engage with services.* London, Sainsbury Centre for Mental Health

Sainsbury Centre for Mental Health (1998b) *Acute problems: a survey of the quality of care in acute psychiatric wards.* London, Sainsbury Centre for Mental Health

Sainsbury Centre for Mental Health (1999) *The national service framework for mental health: an executive briefing.* London, Sainsbury Centre for Mental Health

Sainsbury Centre for Mental Health (2000) *Taking your partners: using opportunities for inter-agency partnership in mental health.* London, Sainsbury Centre for Mental Health

Sainsbury Centre for Mental Health (2001) *Setting the standard: the new agenda for primary care organisations commissioning mental health services.* London, Sainsbury Centre for Mental Health

Sainsbury Centre for Mental Health (2002a) *Being there in a crisis.* London, Mental Health Foundation/Sainsbury Centre for Mental Health

Sainsbury Centre for Mental Health (2002b) *An executive briefing on adult acute inpatient care for people with mental health problems* (briefing 16). London, Sainsbury Centre for Mental Health

Sainsbury Centre for Mental Health (2002c) *The search for acute solutions: a project to improve and evaluate acute mental health inpatient care.* London, Sainsbury Centre for Mental Health

Sainsbury Centre for Mental Health (2002d) *Acute inpatient care (mental health topics)*. London, Sainsbury Centre for Mental Health

Sainsbury Centre for Mental Health (2002e) *Breaking the circles of fear*. London, Sainsbury Centre for Mental Health

Sainsbury Centre For Mental Health (2003) *Policy paper 3: the economic and social costs of mental illness*. London, Sainsbury Centre for Mental Health

Sainsbury Centre for Mental Health (2004a) *Practice based commissioning in the NHS: the implications for mental health*. London, Sainsbury Centre for Mental Health

Sainsbury Centre for Mental Health (2004b) *Acute care 2004: a national survey of adult psychiatric wards in England* (briefing 28). London, Sainsbury Centre for Mental Health

Sainsbury Centre for Mental Health (2005) *Beyond the water towers: the unfinished revolution in mental health services 1985–2005*. London, Sainsbury Centre for Mental Health

Sainsbury Centre for Mental Health (2006a) *The search for acute solutions: improving the quality of care in acute psychiatric wards*. London, Sainsbury Centre for Mental Health

Sainsbury Centre for Mental Health (2006b) *London's prison mental health services: a review*. London, Sainsbury Centre for Mental Health

Sainsbury Centre for Mental Health (2006c) *First steps to work – a study at Broadmoor hospital*. London, Sainsbury Centre for Mental Health

Sainsbury Centre for Mental Health (2006d) *The costs of race inequality*. London, Sainsbury Centre for Mental Health

Sainsbury Centre for Mental Health (2007a) *Mental health at work: developing the business case* (policy paper 8). London, Sainsbury Centre for Mental Health

Sainsbury Centre for Mental Health (2007b) *Work and wellbeing: developing primary mental health care services*. London, Sainsbury Centre for Mental Health

Sainsbury Centre for Mental Health (2007c) *Mental health care in prisons*. London, Sainsbury Centre for Mental Health

Sainsbury Centre for Mental Health (2007d) *Getting the basics right: developing a primary care mental health service in prisons*. London, Sainsbury Centre for Mental Health

Sainsbury Centre for Mental Health (2008) *Short-changed: spending on prison mental health care*. London, Sainsbury Centre for Mental Health

Sainsbury Centre for Mental Health (2009a) *Securing employment for offenders with mental health problems: towards a better way*. London, Sainsbury Centre for Mental Health

Sainsbury Centre for Mental Health (2009b) *The Bradley Report and the government's response*. London, Sainsbury Centre for Mental Health

Sainsbury Centre for Mental Health (2009c) *Mental health care and the criminal justice system*. London, Sainsbury Centre for Mental Health

Sainsbury Centre for Mental Health (n.d.) *Commissioning mental health care in the criminal justice system: 10 top tips for PCT boards*. London, Sainsbury Centre for Mental Health

Salisbury, C. *et al.* (2005) Evaluation of a general practitioner with special interest service for dermatology: randomised controlled trial, *British Medical Journal*, 331, 1441–6

Salmon, G. and Rapport, F. (2005) Multi-agency voices: a thematic analysis of multi-agency working practices within the setting of a Child and Adolescent Mental Health Service, *Journal of Interprofessional Care*, 19(5), 429–43

Sashidharan, S.P. (1999) Alternatives to institutional psychiatry, in D. Bhugra and V. Bahl (eds) *Ethnicity: an agenda for mental health*. London, Gaskell

Sashidharan, S., Smythe, M. and Owen, A. (1999) PRiSM psychosis study : thro' a glass darkly: a distorted appraisal of community care, *British Journal of Psychiatry*, 175, 504–7

Saultz, J.W. (2003) Defining and measuring interpersonal care, *Annals of Family Medicine*, 3, 134–44

Sayce, L. (1997) Stigma and social exclusion: top priorities for mental health professionals, *Eurohealth*, 3(3), 5–7

Sayce, L. (1999) High time for justice, *Nursing Times*, 95(9), 64–6

Sayce, L. (2000) *From psychiatric patient to citizen: overcoming discrimination and social exclusion*. Basingstoke, Palgrave

Sayce, L. (2001) Social inclusion and mental health, *Psychiatric Bulletin*, 25, 121–3

Sayce, L. and Morris, D. (1999) *Outsiders coming in? Achieving social inclusion for people with mental health problems*. London, Mind

Sayce, L., Craig, T.K.J. and Boardman, A.P. (1991) The development of community mental health centres in the UK, *Social Psychiatry and Psychiatric Epidemiology*, 26, 14–20

Schon, D. (1983) *The reflective practitioner: how professionals think in action*. London, Temple Smith

Scull, A. (1977) *De-carceration: community treatment and the deviant – a radical view*. Englewood-Cliffs (NJ), Prentice-Hall

Scull, A. (1979) *Museums of madness*. Harmondsworth, Penguin

Scull, A. (1993) *The most solitary of afflictions: madness in society in Britain, 1700–1900*. New Haven, Connecticut, Yale University Press

Secker, J. *et al.* (2000) Mental health in the community: roles, responsibilities and organisation of primary care and specialist services, *Journal of Interprofessional Care*, 14 (1), 49–58

Selbie, D. (2006) *Local delivery plans – mental health early intervention services: letter to SHA Chief Executives, SHA Directors of Performance and Directors of Social Services*. London, Department of Health

SDO (2006) *Sharing mental health information with carers: pointers to good practice for service providers* (SDO briefing paper). London, SDO

Sharpley, M. *et al.* (2001) Understanding the excess of psychosis among the African-Caribbean population in England: review of current hypotheses, *British Journal of Psychiatry*, 178(Supplement 40), 60–8

Shaw, J., Appleby, L. and Baker, D. (2003) *Safer prisons: a national study of prison suicides, 1999–2000 by the National Confidential Inquiry into Suicides and Homicides by People with Services Mental Illness*. London, Department of Health

Shekelle, P. (2003) New contract for general practitioners, *British Medical Journal*, 326, 457–8

Shelter (2003) *House keeping: preventing homelessness through tackling rent arrears in social housing*. London, Shelter

Shepherd, G. (1998) Models of community care, *Journal of Mental Health*, 7(2), 165–77

Shepherd, G. *et al.* (1997) Relation between bed use, social deprivation, and overall bed availability in acute adult psychiatric units, and alternative residential options: a cross sectional survey, one day census data, and staff interviews, *British Medical Journal*, 314, 262–6

Shepherd, M. (1966) *Psychiatric illness in general practice*. London, Oxford University Press

Sign (n.d.) *Mental health services for deaf people: are they appropriate?* Beaconsfield, Sign

Sims, J. (2004) Sam's Bill, *Care and Health*, 4–18th February, 25

Singh, S.P. and Burns, T. (2006) Race and mental health: there is more to race than racism, *British Medical Journal*, 333, 648–51

Singleton, N., Meltzer, H. and Gatward, R. (1998) *Psychiatric morbidity among prisoners in England and Wales*. London, Office for National Statistics

Singleton, N. *et al.* (2001) *Psychiatric morbidity among adults living in private households, 2000*. London, TSO

Singleton, N. *et al.* (2002) *Mental health of carers*. London, TSO

6, P. (2002) Can policy making be evidence based?, *Managing Community* Care, 10(1), 3–8

6, P., Glasby, J. and Lester, H. (2007) Incremental change without policy learning: explaining information rejection in English mental health services, *Journal of Comparative Policy Analysis*, 9(1), 21–46

6, P. *et al.* (2002) *Towards holistic governance: the new reform agenda*. Basingstoke, Palgrave

Smyth, M. and Hoult, J. (2000) The home treatment enigma, *British Medical Journal*, 320, 305–9

Social Care Institute for Excellence (SCIE) (2003) *Users at the heart: user participation in the governance and operations of social care regulatory bodies*. London, SCIE

Sorohan, H. *et al.* (2002) The role of the practice nurses in primary care mental health: challenges and opportunities, *Primary Care Psychiatry*, 8, 41–6

Spandler, H. (2007) From social exclusion to inclusion? A critique of the inclusion imperative in mental health, *Medical Sociology Online* V2, 2, November, 3–16

Spandler, H. and Vick, N. (2004) *Direct payments, independent living and mental health: an evaluation*. London, Health and Social Care Advisory Service

Spiers, S., Harney, K. and Chilvers, C. (2005) Service user involvement in forensic mental health: can it work?, *Journal of Forensic Psychiatry and Psychology*, 16(2), 211–20

Sproston, K. and Nazroo, J. (2002) *The ethnic minority psychiatric morbidity survey*. London, TSO

Stalker, K. (ed.) (2003) *Reconceptualising work with 'carers': new directions for policy and practice*. London, Jessica Kingsley

Steadman, H.J. *et al.* (1998) Violence by people discharged from acute psychiatric inpatient facilities and by others in the same neighbourhoods, *Archives of General Psychiatry*, 55, 1–9

Stein, L.I. and Test, M.A. (1980) An alternative to mental hospital treatment, *Archives of General Psychiatry*, 37, 392–9

Stone, M. (1985) Shellshock and the psychologists, in W.F. Bynum, R. Porter and M. Shepherd (eds) *The anatomy of madness: volume 2*. London, Taverstock

Stott, N.C.H. and Davis, R.H. (1979) The exceptional potential in each primary care consultation, *Journal of the Royal College of General Practice*, 29, 201–5

Styron, W. (2001) *Darkness visible*. London, Vintage

Sullivan, H. and Skelcher, C. (2002) *Working across boundaries: collaboration in public services*. Basingstoke, Palgrave

Summers, A. (2003) Involving users in the development of mental health services: a study of psychiatrists' views, *Journal of Mental Health*, 12(2), 161–74

Swain, J. *et al.* (eds) (2004) *Disabling barriers – enabling environments* (2nd edn). London, Sage

Swanson, J. *et al.* (1990) Violence and psychiatric disorder in the community: evidence from the epidemiological catchment area surveys, *Hospital and Community Psychiatry*, 41, 761–70

Symons, L., Tylee, A., and Mann, A. (2002) *Nurse facilitated open access depression clinic in primary care – London pilot*. London, Institute of Psychiatry. Kings College London (unpublished)

Szasz, T. (1960) The myth of mental illness, *American Psychologist*, 15, 564–80

Szasz, T. (1970) *Ideology and insanity: essays on the psychiatric dehumanisation of man*. Garden City, Double Day

Szasz, T. (2003) The psychiatric protection order for the 'battered mental patient', *British Medical Journal*, 327, 1449–51

Tabassum, R., Macaskill, A. and Ahmad, I. (2000) Attitudes towards mental health in an urban Pakistani community in the United Kingdom, *International Journal of Social Psychiatry*, 46(3), 170–81

Taylor, P.J. and Gunn, J. (1999) Homicides by people with mental illness: myth and reality, *British Journal of Psychiatry*, 174, 9–14

Telfer, J. (2000) Balancing care and control: introducing the care programme approach in a prison setting, *Mental Health Care*, 4(3), 93–6

Telford, R. and Faulkner, A. (2004) Learning about service user involvement in mental health research, *Journal of Mental Health*, 13(6), 549–59

Tew, J. (ed.) (2005) *Social perspectives in mental health*. London, Jessica Kingsley

The Stationery Office (2002) *Draft Mental Health Bill, Cm 5538-I*. London, TSO

Thomas, R. and Corney, R. (1993) The role of the practice nurse in mental health: a survey, *Journal of Mental Health*, 2, 65–72

Thompson, N. (2006) *Anti-discriminatory practice* (4th edn). Basingstoke, Palgrave Macmillan

Thomson, L., Galt, V. and Darjee, R. (2004) *An evaluation of appropriate adult schemes in Scotland* (Scottish Executive Research Findings 78/2004). Edinburgh, University of Edinburgh

Thorne, A. (2001) Blood-letting politics over Health Concern, *Birmingham Post*, 2nd February

Thornicroft, G. (2006) *Shunned: discrimination against people with mental illness*. Oxford, Oxford University Press

Thornicroft, G., Parkman, S. and Ruggeri, M. (1999) Satisfaction with mental health services: issues for ethnic minorities, in D. Bhugra and V. Bahl (eds) *Ethnicity: an agenda for mental health*. London, Gaskell

Thornicroft, G. *et al.* (2002) What are the research priorities of mental health service users?, *Journal of Mental Health*, 11 (1), 1–5

Thornicroft, G. *et al.* (1998a) Rationale and design: PRiSM psychosis study 1, *British Journal of Psychiatry*, 173, 363–70

Thornicroft, G. *et al.* (1998b) From efficacy to effectiveness in community mental health services. PRiSM psychosis study 10, *British Journal of Psychiatry*, 173, 423–7

Tiemans, B., Ormel, J. and Simon, G. (1996) Occurrence, recognition and outcome of psychological disorders in primary care, *Psychological Medicine*, 153, 636–44

Tien, A.Y. (1991) The distribution of hallucinations in the population, *Social Psychiatry and Psychiatric Epidemiology*, 26, 287–92

Tierney, A.J. *et al.* (1994) Discharge of patients from hospital – current practice and perceptions of hospital and community staff in Scotland, *Health Bulletin*, 52(6), 479–91

Timmins, N. (2001) Anger over local hospital gives real bite to underdog doctor's campaign, *Financial Times*, 28 May

Titmuss, R.M. (1968) *Commitment to welfare*. London, George Allen and Unwin

Todd, Lord A.R. (1968) *The Todd Report: Royal Commission on Medical Education*. London, HMSO

Took, M. (2002) Mental breakdown and recovery in the UK, *Journal of Psychiatric and Mental Health Nursing*, 935–7

Twigg, J., Atkin, K. and Perring, C. (1990) *Carers and services: a review of research*. London, HMSO

Tudor Hart, J. (1988) *A new kind of doctor.* London, Merlin Press

Tyrer, P. and Steinberg, D. (2003) *Models for mental disorders: conceptual models in psychiatry.* Chichester, John Wiley and Sons

Tyrer, P. *et al.* (2006) The Bed Requirement Inventory: a simple measure to estimate the need for a psychiatric bed, *International Journal of Social Psychiatry,* 52(3), 267–77

Ungerson, C. (1987) *Policy is personal: sex, gender and informal care.* London, Tavistock

Union of Physically Impaired Against Segregation (UPIAS) (1976) *Fundamental principles of disability.* London, UPIAS

Ustun, T.B. *et al.* (1999) Multiple-informant ranking of the disabling effects of different health conditions in 14 countries: WHO/NIH Joint Project CAR Study Group, *Lancet,* 354, 111–15

Valios, N. (2000) Appeal court broadens definition of disability, *Community Care,* 22nd–28th June, 11

Valuing People Support Team (2004) *Green light for mental health* (parts A and B). London, Valuing People Support Team/Department of Health

Vanderwall, C. (1997) The role of the community forensic mental health nurse: initiatives for across agency working, *Psychiatric Care,* 4(6), 283–6

Vaughan, P.J. (1999) A consortium approach to commissioning services for mentally disordered offenders, *Journal of Forensic Psychiatry,* 10(3), 553–66

Vaughan, P.J. and Stevenson, S. (2003) An opinion survey of mentally disordered service users, *Prison Service Journal,* 147, 11–17

Vaughan, P., Kelly, M. and Pullen, N. (2000) Services for mentally disordered offenders in community psychiatry teams, *Journal of Forensic Psychiatry,* 11(3), 571–86

Vaughan, P.J., Kelly, M. and Pullen, N. (2001) The working practices of the police in relation to mentally disordered offenders and diversion schemes, *Medicine, Science and the Law,* 41(1), 13–20

Victor, C. (1991) *Health and health care in later life.* Milton Keynes, Open University Press

Waddell, G. and Burton, A.K. (2006) *Is work good for your health and well-being?* Norwich, TSO

Wade, D. and Halligan, P. (2004) Do biomedical models of illness make for good healthcare systems?, *British Medical Journal,* 329, 1398–401

Wahl, O.F. (1995) *Media madness: public images of mental illness.* New Jersey, Rutgers University Press

Wallcraft, J. and Bryant, M. (2003) *The mental health service users movement in England.* London, Sainsbury Centre for Mental Health

Walsh, E. and Fahy, T. (2002) Violence in society, *British Medical Journal,* 325, 507–8

Walsh, E., Buchanan, A. and Fahy, T. (2002) Violence and schizophrenia: examining the evidence, *British Journal of Psychiatry,* 188, 490–5

Walshe, K. *et al.* (2004) Primary care trusts: premature reorganisation with mergers, may be harmful, *British Medical Journal,* 329, 871–2

Walton, P. (2000) Psychiatric hospital care: a case of the more things change, the more they remain the same, *Journal of Mental Health,* 9(1), 77–88

Wanless, D. (2002) *Securing our future health: taking a long term view.* London, Department of Health

Warner, L. and Ford, R. (1998) Conditions for women in in-patient psychiatric units: the Mental Health Act Commission 1996 national visit, *Mental Health Care,* 1(7), 225–8

Warner, L. *et al.* (2000a) Could this be you? Evaluating quality and standards of care in the inpatient psychiatric setting, *Mental Health and Learning Disabilities Care,* 4(3), 89–92

Warner, L. *et al.* (2000b) *National visit 2: a visit by the Mental Health Act Commission to 104 mental health and learning disability units in England and Wales – improving care for detained patients from black and minority ethnic communities (preliminary report).* London, Sainsbury Centre for Mental Health

Warner, R. (1985) *Recovery from schizophrenia: psychiatry and political economy.* London, Routledge

Warner, R. *et al.* (1993) The effects of a new mental health service based in primary care on the work of general practitioners, *British Journal of General Practice*, 43, 507–11

Watson, A. (1997) *Services for mentally disordered offenders in the community: an inspection report.* London, Department of Health

Watson, A. (2001) *Detained: inspection of compulsory mental health admissions.* London, Department of Health

Waxman, R., Tennant, A., Halliwell, P. (1999) Community survey of factors associated with consultation for low back pain, *British Medical Journal*, 317, 1564–7

Weaver, T. *et al.* (1997a) The Bentham Unit: a pilot remand and assessment service for male mentally disordered remand prisoners, *British Journal of Psychiatry*, 170, 462–6

Weaver, T. *et al.* (1997b) Impact of a dedicated service for male mentally disordered remand prisoners in north west London: retrospective study, *British Medical Journal*, 314, 1244–5

Webb, Y. *et al.* (2000) Comparing patients' experience of mental health services in England: a five-Trust survey, *International Journal of Health Care Quality Assurance*, 13(6/7), 273–81

Webbe, A. (1998) Ethnicity and mental health, *Psychiatric Care*, 5(1), 12–16

Webster, C. (2002) *The National Health Service: a political history.* Oxford, Oxford University Press

Weinberg, A. and Huxley, P. (2000) An evaluation of the impact of voluntary sector family support workers on the quality of life of carers of schizophrenia sufferers, *Journal of Mental Health*, 9(5), 495–503

White, E. (1990) The work of the Community Psychiatric Nurses Association: a survey of the membership, *Community Psychiatric Nursing Journal*, 10, 30–5

White, E. (1993) Community psychiatric nursing, 1980–1990: a review of organisation, education and practice, in C. Brooker and E. White (eds) *Community psychiatric nursing: a research perspective* (volume II). London, Chappleman and Hall

White, E. and Brooker, C. (2001) The fourth quinquennial national community mental health nursing census of England and Wales, *International Journal of Nursing Studies*, 38(1), 61–70

Whittle, M.C. and Scally, M.D. (1998) Model of forensic psychiatric community care, *Psychiatric Bulletin*, 22(12), 748–50

Widgery, D. (1991) GP mourns the dying East End, *GP Magazine*, July, 32

Wilkinson, R.G. (1996) *Unhealthy societies: the afflictions of inequality.* London, Routledge

Williams, B. and Pow, J. (2007) Gender differences and mental health: an exploratory study of knowledge and attitudes to mental health among Scottish teenagers, *Child and Adolescent Mental Health*, 12(1), 8–12

Williams, R. (1976) *Keywords.* London, Croomhelm

Willis, J. (1995) *The paradox of progress.* Abingdon, Radcliffe Medical Press

Wilson, M. and Francis, J. (1997) *Raised voices: African-Caribbean and African users' views and experiences of mental health services in England and Wales.* London, Mind

Wilson, T. and Holt, T. (2001) Complexity science: complexity and clinical care, *British Medical Journal*, 323, 685–688

Winchester, R. (2001) Pushed to breaking point, *Community Care*, 7–13 June, 18–20

Wistow, G. and Fuller, S. (1982) *Joint planning in perspective*. Birmingham, Centre for Research in Social Policy and National Association of Health Authorities

Witcher, S. *et al.* (2000) *Direct payments: the impact on choice and control for disabled people*. Edinburgh, Scottish Executive Central Research Unit

World Health Organization (WHO) (1978) *Alma Ata, Global Strategy for Health for All by the Year 2000*. Geneva, World Health Organization

World Health Organization (1999) *The world health report: making a difference*. Geneva, World Health Organization

World Health Organization (2001) *World health report 2001: mental health, new understanding, new hope*. Geneva, World Health Organization

World Health Organization (2004) *WHO guide to mental and neurological health in primary care*. London, Royal Society of Medicine Press

World Health Organization Europe (2008) *Policies and practices for mental health in Europe*. Geneva, World Health Organization

WHO/WONCA (2008) *Integrating mental health into primary care: a global perspective*. Geneva, World Health Organization

Wright, A.F. (1995) Continuing to defeat depression, *British Journal of General Practice*, 45, 170–1

Wright, S. *et al.* (2000) *Thematic review of NHS R&D funded mental health research in relation to the National Service Framework for Mental Health*. London, Institute of Psychiatry

Yates, M. and Deakes, C. (1998) Introducing multidisciplinary record keeping in a forensic setting, *Psychiatric Care*, 5(6), 204–7

Yuen, P. (2003) *Compendium of health statistics* (15th edn). London, Office of Health Economics

Index